Sober Secure

Also By Nina Pick

The Mind-Body Guide to the Twelve Steps: Finding Joy, Sensuality, and Pleasure in Recovery

Tall Oak and Small Owl

The Gardener Says: Quotes, Quips, and Words of Wisdom

At the Edge of the Dirac Sea

Sober Secure

An Attachment-Based Guide to Dating, Sex, and Love in Recovery

Nina Pick

North Atlantic Books
Huichin, unceded Ohlone land
Berkeley, California

North Atlantic Books
Huichin, unceded Ohlone land
2526 Martin Luther King Jr Way
Berkeley, CA 94704 USA
www.northatlanticbooks.com

Cover art © ma_rish via Getty Images
Cover design by Jess Morphew
Book design by Happenstance Type-O-Rama

Printed in Canada

Sober Secure: An Attachment-Based Guide to Dating, Sex, and Love in Recovery is sponsored and published by North Atlantic Books, an educational nonprofit that collaborates with partners to develop cross-cultural perspectives; nurture holistic views of art, science, the humanities, and healing; and seed personal and global transformation by publishing work on the relationship of body, spirit, and nature.

North Atlantic Books's publications are distributed to the US trade and internationally by Penguin Random House Publisher Services. For further information, visit our website at www.northatlanticbooks.com.

The authorized representative in the EU for product safety and compliance is Eucomply OÜ, Pärnu mnt 139b-14, 11317 Tallinn, Estonia, hello@eucompliancepartner.com, +33757690241.

DISCLAIMER: The following information is intended for general information purposes only. Any application of the material set forth in the following pages is at the reader's discretion and is their sole responsibility. This book does not intend to be diagnostic in any way and is not a substitute for a thorough clinical assessment and professional treatment. If you are at medical risk of withdrawal or in a serious psychiatric emergency, you are encouraged to present for medical attention immediately.

Library of Congress Cataloging-in-Publication Data

Names: Pick, Nina author
Title: Sober secure : an attachment-based guide to dating, sex, and love in recovery / Nina Pick.
Description: Berkeley, CA : North Atlantic Books, 2026. | Includes bibliographical references and index. | Summary: "An attachment-first path to lasting recovery: build the love, safety, and belonging that keep you sober—and help your relationships thrive. Practical, body-based tools for dating, intimacy, and partnership in sobriety."— Provided by publisher.
Identifiers: LCCN 2025048380 (print) | LCCN 2025048381 (ebook) | ISBN 9798889843740 trade paperback | ISBN 9798889843757 ebook
Subjects: LCSH: Addicts—Rehabilitation | Substance abuse—Treatment | Attachment behavior
Classification: LCC HV4998 .P53 2026 (print) | LCC HV4998 (ebook)
LC record available at https://lccn.loc.gov/2025048380
LC ebook record available at https://lccn.loc.gov/2025048381

1 2 3 4 5 6 7 8 9 FRIESENS 31 30 29 28 27 26

Contents

The distance from your pain, your grief, your unattended wounds, is the distance from your partner. And the distance from your partner is your distance from your living truth, your own great nature. Whatever maintains that distance, that separation from ourselves and our beloveds, must be investigated with mercy and awareness. This distance is not overcome by one "giving up their space to another," but by both partners entering together the unknown between them. The mind creates the abyss but the heart crosses it.

—STEPHEN AND ONDREA LEVINE

Introduction

All beings are flowers
blossoming
in a blossoming universe.

—SOEN NAKAGAWA

Individuation is the process, simple or complex as the case may be, by which every living organism becomes what it was destined to become from the beginning.

—CARL JUNG

Recovery is an act of love. This love moves on many levels—between us and those who support our recovery, those whom we support, and those whom our recovery benefits. This book is about these interconnected threads of love and how we deepen the potential of the relational field to be a space of healing. It explores what can happen if we place love at the center of our recovery. It is also meant to serve as a corrective to the destructive messages about addiction and relationship propagated in mainstream culture and at times even in Alcoholics Anonymous and other Twelve Step fellowships. I wrote this book for people in recovery, for their partners, for clinicians and practitioners working in addiction treatment, and, more generally, for anyone wishing to cultivate strong and vibrant relationships through the principles of secure attachment.

As I look around at my friends and fellows in recovery, I often feel sad and frustrated that, even as we grow and our lives change, so many of us seem lost when it comes to dating and partnership; the Twelve Step wisdom that has served us so well in other areas doesn't quite meet our need for a contemporary, psychologically attuned roadmap to the realm of relationships. With deep respect, appreciation, and reverence for the program and how it has saved my life and the lives of so many others, I want to suggest ways that we can weave in attachment theory to make Twelve Step fellowships more responsive to the needs of their members. An attachment-based approach to recovery opens the doors for a more trauma-sensitive, welcoming space, one that is attuned to the deep needs of people in recovery and human beings in general.

People in recovery come into the rooms of AA and other Twelve Step fellowships with the unmet early development needs that feed addiction. When the messages in the room reiterate these core wounds, recovery can be a space not of healing but of fear, shame, and self-abnegation. Rather than the healing we seek, we find recapitulations of the shame-based messages that fed our addiction, isolation, anxiety, and depression in the first place.

Now, with the widespread popularization of attachment theory, the contributions of somatic therapy, and the development of polyvagal theory, we can bring to recovery what the early AA founders could not: a holistic body-mind approach based in neurobiology and developmental psychology that can evolve the program beyond its original framework and provide better, more attuned support for the journey of healing from addiction. With this book, I aim to bring together these wise perspectives on relationship and shine their light through the prism of recovery to make a one-stop resource for you to navigate the journey of relationship in recovery, including everything from dipping your feet in the shallow end of the dating pool to the long-term, in-depth psychospiritual work involved in sharing your life with another human being.

It is impossible to talk about addiction without talking about love. We might mourn the loss of love, numb our hearts to it, or compulsively seek it in sex or substances. The more conscious we are, however, of love's lack as the core wound of which addiction is but a symptom, the more we can turn to love as addiction's mitigating force. For addiction stems from a wound to the heart, and the deepest remedy for addiction is love. Rather than seeing addiction as a disease or a chemical imbalance in the brain, from an attachment-based perspective located in developmental psychology, we can see that early relational wounds are the underlying cause of addiction, and that healthy, reparative attachment experiences are the medicine.

If you attend Recovery Dharma meetings or engage in other forms of Buddhist practice, you will have heard the term *attachment* in a very different context than the one in which I use it here. In Buddhism, *attachment* refers to our clinging to things, emotional states, or experiences, and it is considered to be the root of suffering; in Buddhist practice, therefore, the focus is on renouncing our attachments. In the psychology-based world of attachment theory, however, which is the context I refer to in this book, *attachment* simply refers to the bonds that exist between individuals. Attachment is part of our most fundamental human blueprint and is an essential need that runs throughout our lifespan. Secure attachment is interwoven with experiences of love, safety, attuned touch, healthy boundaries, and belonging, and it should be nurtured and prioritized in both our childhood and our adult relationships. As couples therapist Sue Johnson emphasizes, "This drive to emotionally attach—to find someone to whom we can turn and say 'Hold me tight'—is wired into our genes and our bodies. It is as basic to life, health, and happiness as the drives for food, shelter, or sex."[1] Unfortunately, in a culture that prioritizes individualism and technology at the expense of real connection, where people are more and more cut off from the extended intergenerational village that our ancestors once knew, conditions are ripe for addiction as a response to attachment loss.

As a practitioner of relational somatics with a master's degree in marriage and family therapy, I work with clients primarily on relationship issues. In relational somatics we focus on present-time, embodied experiences in the relational field: the relationship between the therapist and client, between the client and the people in their life, between the client's adult self and their inner child, and between the mind and body. We focus on repairing attachment wounds oriented in early childhood and shifting the deep-rooted imprints and identities that developed in response to failures in that primary environment. Many of my clients are drawn to relational somatics hoping to meet the pain of loneliness and disconnection in a new way, with love and nurturance. Some clients feel isolated, alternately frightened of and longing for connection, while others are stuck in a wash-and-repeat cycle of distress with their partners. Many others experience in their friendships or workplaces the relational dynamics that painfully replicate their earliest wounds.

In this work, I've seen the suffering that comes with repeating old patterns and the joy and healing that comes with connecting to others in new ways. Similarly, as a group facilitator for men in transitional living, I've had the heart-opening opportunity to witness men grapple with new conceptions of relationships, masculinity, and intimacy as they explore these areas sober for the first time. The great capacity for love and the depth of pain that these young men bring to their recovery has inspired me, humbled me, and taught me so much about men's experience and inner life.

At the same time, as I've supported others in moving into healthier relationships, my own journey into conscious relationship has not been an easy one. A painful relationship I experienced at the age of twenty-five, with a woman I can now see was struggling with extreme symptoms of disorganized attachment, highlighted for me my own difficulties in sustaining intimacy. After disentangling myself from that relationship several months after attending my first Twelve Step meeting, I spent the next three years in a state of freeze, feeling as if the flow of my life-force and sexuality was simply shut off, until an encounter with an old high-school crush propelled a dramatic reawakening of my sexuality and an equally dramatic move across the country.

Though over the years I had a lot of experiences of dating and sex, I didn't have my first serious relationship until I was nine years sober, at the age of thirty-four. My partner was ten years sober at the time, and together we navigated the ins and outs of relationship in recovery as we dated, moved in together, and negotiated questions of long-term commitment. Three years in, just as I was starting to think about marriage, the relationship unexpectedly imploded, shattered by the stressors of the COVID crisis and the pressures of deepening intimacy. My next relationship was healthy and loving, but I couldn't move through my immobilizing ambivalence into the depth of relationship we both desired. Over those years, dating both men and women,

I struggled to integrate these two parts of my sexuality and identity. As I navigated the dance of intimacy, I waded through chronic shame and suffocating claustrophobia. I read every dating book on the shelf, but not one of them led me to the epic love it promised. I learned a lot from recovery spaces and also heard a lot I had to toss out.

Finally, after many years, and a lot of trial and error, I can now trust myself to be the person I want to be in relationship (most of the time!). I can communicate difficult feelings with clarity and self-responsibility, tolerate greater closeness, and work with my experiences of shame as they arise. As I grew in recovery, my dating life started to look a lot healthier; relationships progressed more slowly, and I could stay more grounded through the uncertainty of the early days of getting to know someone. Developing my cognitive understanding of relationship dynamics was helpful to me, as was gradually building practical skills for self-soothing and authentic, attuned communication. My current partnership has shown me the depths of old attachment fears as it simultaneously has illuminated new pathways into secure attachment.

Love-Based Recovery

I believe strongly that cognitive understanding, in order to be impactful, must be accompanied by embodied experiences of new relational possibilities. It is this marriage of psychological frameworks and embodied practice that I aim to offer in this book.[2] Throughout the book, I'll advocate for a love-based recovery, a heart-centered recovery journey that centers the healing power of attachment. Here are the foundational principles of loved-based recovery:

Love matters: Attachment is critical to our survival. We all need love, safety, attuned touch, and a sense of belonging. As Sue Johnson notes, "Love is not the icing on the cake of life. It is a basic primary need, like oxygen or water."[3] You can learn more about attachment in Chapter 1.

Love heals: Underlying our addiction are early attachment wounds. The remedy for addiction is love. Love heals the wounds that loss of love caused. The potential for healing through reparative attachment experiences is discussed in Chapter 1 and explored throughout the book.

Love is divine: When we connect with the power of attachment, we also connect with a power greater than ourselves: the force of love. We can conceive of this force as our Higher Power, life-force, or the beauty of nature. Whatever we call it, connecting with a sense of love empowers our recovery journey. You can read more about attachment and spirituality in Chapter 1 and about sex and spirituality in Chapter 10.

Love is sacred: Through the book, I'll provide practices that bring a sense of the sacred to all aspects of relationship—including touch, sexuality, and difficult conversations. My goal is to help infuse your relationships with reverence so that you can experience all aspects of relationship, including and especially sex, as sacred ground. You can read about touch in Chapter 8 and sex in Chapter 10.

Love is embodied: Attachment isn't something that we reach through cognitive understanding alone. It needs to be felt and experienced. Many of us have trouble feeling love in an embodied way. The field of somatics offers frameworks and practices that can help develop our capacity to access the presence of love in the body. Throughout the book, I'll be providing somatic practices that encourage new pathways of body experience, helping you bridge cognitive understanding and body knowing.

Love is life-force: As our nervous system achieves greater regulation, we start to expand our capacity to be with feelings of presence, joy, and connection. We contact the life-force, the innate flow of energy that moves through our bodies and throughout the universe. We connect with the greater web of life that supports our recovery and that our recovery in turn supports. Throughout the book, I'll be offering somatic practices that open greater access to this vital energy.

Love can blossom: Throughout the book, I'll be offering practices that are designed to help you plant, water, and nurture your garden of secure attachment. No matter your background, you can develop your capacity for secure attachment by fostering reparative attachment experiences and learning new skills. In early recovery, we might not know how to create a loving relationship, but with attention and wise effort we can increase our capacity to orient from our hearts and nurture our connection with others. Chapter 1 discusses *learned secure attachment*, and Chapter 12 explores the cultivation of conscious relationship.

At a time when addiction treatment is trending toward "behavioral health," short-term cognitive-based therapy, and a reliance on psychiatric drugs, I believe it's crucially important to return to these relational principles—principles that have been articulated by pioneers in psychoanalytic and psychodynamic psychotherapy, expanded by contemporary innovators in interpersonal neurobiology and mind-body psychology, and expressed by ancestral and spiritual wisdom traditions throughout the ages.

Nested Care and Recovery

Throughout the book, I draw on psychologists Darcia Narvaez and G. A. Bradshaw's concept of the *evolved nest.*[4] Narvaez and Bradshaw use this term to describe the systems that evolve within each species to perfectly meet the developmental, physical, psychological, and social needs of the animals and their young. While an actual physical nest, den, or lodge may be part of the nexus of care, many species, such as elephants and wolves, have a social as well as a physical environment that nurtures survival and may include extended relatives and community. In close relationship with their unique habitat, each species evolved in beautifully specific ways that allow them to "optimize health and wellbeing, starting from conception through adulthood."[5]

Narvaez and Bradshaw emphasize that the ways we (modern humans) raise our young have splintered off from the environment in which we evolved, and our practices have strayed far from the evolutionary wisdom of our ancestors, much to the detriment of children's brain, body, and social-emotional development. In mainstream capitalist culture, many children are raised without the safety, security, connection, and embeddedness in nature and community that provide the developmental underpinnings for healthy growth. By the same token, caregivers are often left to raise children on their own, without the support of extended family, the teachings of wise elders, and the care that they need to be able to tend to the baby; instead they are caught up in childrearing practices that lead to developmental deficits, relational ruptures, and chronic stress for both parent and child. These widespread environmental failings inform the developmental wounds that underlie addiction.

At its best, Twelve Step recovery offers a form of nested care that is often unavailable in contemporary Western culture. Through sponsorship, friendships with fellows, and meetings, we experience meaningful relationships and find ourselves held in an expansive circle of care. When we extend the idea of the evolved nest into the space of addiction treatment, we recognize this circle of care, and the reparative attachment experiences it offers, as the key to our recovery. The ecological holism embedded in the idea of the evolved nest, however, means we can go still further in growing what Narvaez and Bradshaw call *nest consciousness*.[6] We can expand the idea of care from our immediate network to a more extensive one that includes situating ourselves in place, in nature, and in a fellowship of all beings.

In recovery, nested care can include and also extend far beyond the room of the therapy session or the Twelve Step meeting. For instance, our circle of care might include individual relationships with coaches, sponsors, fellows, therapists, or healing practitioners such as acupuncturists, bodyworkers, or nutritionists. We might look for joyful community not only at Twelve Step meetings but in dance classes, singing circles, parenting support groups, yoga, meditation, or sports. Our circle of care might include our relationship with plants and animals, and extend to our connection with the Earth itself. And we might include our ancestors; our allies from the spiritual realms; and, as we grow our capacity to sense our interbeingness, the whole universe.

In recovery we can cultivate a communal network of care, a mutually supportive and responsive evolved nest. As a person heals, they become more and more able to offer support to others, to "carry the message" by extending the blessings of their recovery to others in need of help. Nested care situates our recovery in a vast constellation of relationality and prioritizes love as the source of healing.

The Building Blocks of Addiction

This book builds on work by psychologist Philip Flores, author of *Addiction as an Attachment Disorder*, and others who explore addiction as a symptom of early attachment wounds.[7] Addiction is a symptom that arises in the absence of meaningful connection beginning in early childhood, when the environment or caregivers were unable to consistently provide the nurturance or attunement that would allow a child to develop a cohesive sense of self. These developmental deficits result in impacts to the brain, body, and autonomic nervous system (ANS), as well as to the child's developing sense of identity, which becomes characterized by fragmentation and chronic shame as a way to mitigate the pain and disappointment of unmet needs.[8]

As authors such as Flores, Jan Winhall, and Kathy Kain and Stephen Terrell have shown, substance and process addictions are the body-mind's way of trying to mitigate physiological states of *hyperarousal* (the mobilization response of fight and flight) and *hypoarousal* (the immobilization response) in an attempt to help our organism return to a state of homeostasis.[9] As ultimately harmful as addiction is, these attempts to self-regulate through substance use were essential survival strategies when other resources and recourses were absent. The trouble is that the strategies we developed early in life in order to survive in our environments and earliest relationships, strategies that were crucial to staying connected to the people our very survival depended on, often occurred at the expense of our connection with our authentic selves. These early adaptations later manifest in the painful patterns and identities, the so-called defects of character, that most of us grapple with in addiction and throughout our recovery: chronic shame, low self-esteem, isolation, dishonesty, avoidance, reactive rage, resentment, and fear.

When we learned early on that it was not safe to express core needs or emotions, we developed strategies to try to get these needs met in indirect or strategic ways, or we learned to disavow our needs and emotions, burying them deep within us until we were no longer even aware of them. When these strategies emerge in adult relationships, we find that our primary needs, desires, and emotions are hidden beneath patterns of blame, criticism, withdrawal, or anger, resulting in cycles of disconnect with those we love most. Through the process of recovery we learn to safely come in contact with those core places that we disavowed long ago, and we can learn new skills for our adult life to recognize ourselves more authentically and express ourselves more vulnerably, resulting in clearer communication and deeper connection.

About the Book

This book weaves together an understanding based in polyvagal theory—that addiction is rooted in ANS dysregulation—with a framework based in the science of attachment, which links addiction to adaptations developed in childhood that affect our adult capacities and relationships. It will discuss the impact of early developmental traumas on substance use and show how, in recovery, we can take actions and make commitments that not only heal our dependency on substances and addictive behaviors but also provide the missing pieces of contact and connection, creating new possibilities for relationship with ourselves and others. We will also look at the role of intergenerational trauma in attachment and addiction, and extend our understanding of attachment dynamics to include pre- and perinatal experience.

Drawing on the practices and frameworks elucidated by my mentor Aline LaPierre, founder of NeuroAffective Touch, we will discover how attuned touch can provide the missing pieces of belonging, safety, and connection, and how it can be incorporated into your relationships and your recovery. We'll explore imaginal exercises based in LaPierre's Body-Mind Dialogues and the Kabbalistic lineage of Colette Aboulker-Muscat and Catherine Shainberg to center ourselves in heart wisdom and body-mind wholeness.[10] We will look to Jungian psychology for a soul–spirit perspective on relationship as a path to individuation and to Buddhism for an understanding of relationship as a practice of nondualism. We will explore how early relational wounds impact our mind-body relationship, our relationship with self, and our relationship with Higher Power as much as our relationships with others, and we will draw on somatic, spiritual, and creative practices to deepen our capacities in these areas. We will expand our awareness of sexuality as a key pillar of healing, embodiment, and spiritual growth. Throughout the book we will also consider relationship as it extends to the more-than-human realm, considering relationship with animals, plants, Earth, our ancestors, and, ultimately, with Love itself. Finding the names of Higher Power that most resonate, we can approach the spiritual path with that same yearning for contact and love, exploring Spirit as the field of relational connection.

You can read this book on your own or, if you're in a romantic relationship, you might wish to read it with your partner in order to grow together. The chapters include journaling, movement, and meditation practices that you can do alone, as well as many that you can share with a partner, friend or fellow, or study buddy. Some of the partner practices can also be done in your imagination; if you're single and calling in a partnership, or if you have a partner but they don't wish to participate, doing these practices as imaginal exercises can be a great way to develop your own capacities and create the relationship you desire. I offer a wide range of practices, and it may be that not all are the right fit for you, your body, or your situation; please choose the ones that resonate most. I suggest getting a special notebook that you've reserved for working on these exercises. You can also include in it any additional journaling or artwork such as drawings, paintings, or collages that are part of your Sober Secure journey.

Some Notes on the Text

- Please note that the client profiles provided as illustration are fictionalized compilations that portray common patterns and binds experienced by people with developmental trauma and substance use disorder. All identifying characteristics have been changed.

- Throughout the book, the pronouns *they, he,* and *she* are used interchangeably to describe partners, caregivers, and children, in consideration of inclusivity and grammatical clarity.
- The word *partner* is meant to be inclusive of all genders and sexual orientations.
- My own experience is in monogamous relationships, and I don't have any lived experience of open or poly relational structures. While the principles here can apply to any configuration of relationship, I suggest the book *Polysecure* for readers looking for more specific frameworks on attachment and nonmonogamous relationships.[11]

My goal is that, as you read, you will start to make sense of confusing relationship patterns and to locate them in their proper context, bringing new meanings to old, familiar stories—and with new meanings, new beginnings. May this process help you shine a compassionate light on the mind-body responses and shame-based identifications that fuel addiction and guide you to connect with your vibrant and sensuous life-force in recovery. May you remember what your heart knows already as you reclaim your evolutionary birthright of secure attachment.

✳ Developing Relationship with Self and Others

Early attachment deficits can lead to a lack of development in our capacity to

- Foster regulation of our autonomic nervous system
- Offer ourselves nurturing care and receive it from others
- Sense our inner experience by keeping company with our sensations, emotions, needs, desires, and imaginal life (dreams, fantasies, visions) in a gentle, nonjudgmental way

- Establish healthy, mutually satisfying relationships that meet our essential attachment needs and those of our partners

These core developmental interruptions define life in addiction. In recovery, we can start to fill in these missing pieces by focusing on growth in these closely interwoven areas, understanding that growth in one area creates a positive feedback loop that facilitates development in the others. For example, practicing nervous system regulation is closely related to self-care, practicing self-care allows us to grow in our capacity to be in loving relationship with others, being in loving relationship with others allows us to more safely sense into our inner experience, while sensing our inner experience helps restore nervous system regulation.

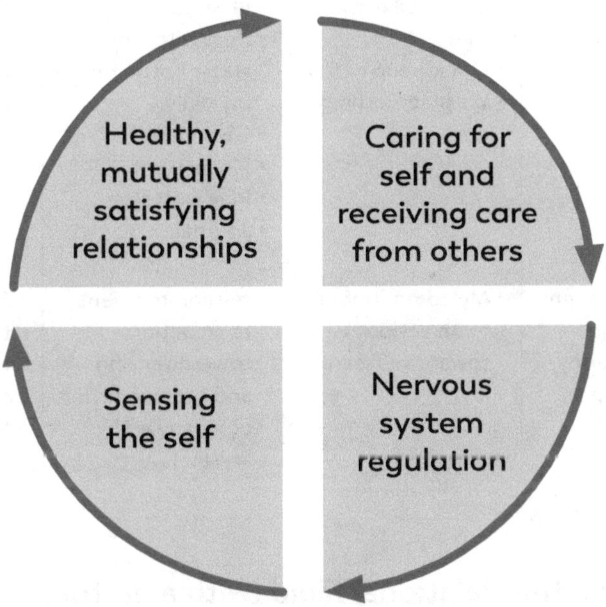

As you embark on your journey through this book, what are some commitments you can make this week for actions that support growth in each of these four areas? Choose from the following ideas or find your own.

This week I can . . .

ESTABLISH HEALTHY RELATIONSHIPS	PRACTICE CARING FOR MYSELF	PRACTICE SENSING MYSELF	REGULATE MY NERVOUS SYSTEM
• Make an out-reach call. • Drink tea with a friend or fellow. • Go on a date. • Exchange a massage with my partner. • Ask for support. • Call my sponsor. • Go to ther-apy (or find a therapist).	• Get a massage. • Go to a meeting. • Buy groceries. • Cook a meal. • Floss my teeth. • Take a dance class. • Take a bath. • Take a nap. • Give myself a facial. • Get a full night's sleep. • Drink a cup of tea. • Wear something cozy.	• Receive somatic bodywork. • Dance. • Practice meditation. • Listen to a guided imagery practice. • Give myself a foot massage. • Write down my dreams. • Rest with a hot water bottle on my belly. • Give myself a hug. • Fingerpaint. • Play with clay. • Journal.	• Take a bath. • Take several long exhalations. • Go to acupuncture. • Go for a walk. • Start the Safe and Sound Pro-tocol with a cer-tified provider. • Spend time in nature. • Spend time with an animal friend.
• My commitment to an action toward healthy relationship is ______.	• My commitment to an action toward self-care is ______.	• My commitment to an action toward sensing and keeping loving company with myself is ______.	• My commitment to an action toward nervous system regula-tion is ______.

✳ Sensing the Relational Field (with a partner)

Do this practice to grow your capacity to sense your inner environment while also sensing your partner's energy and the shared space between you.

Sit with your partner. Take a few moments to breathe together as you each bring your attention to your inner experience. You might notice the rhythms of your breath or other movements; you might also notice sensations of comfort or discomfort, pain or pleasure, texture or temperature, or sensations associated with emotions. Name to yourself what you are aware of in your inner environment; for example, "I feel my back against the chair, the movement of my breath in my chest, and a fluttery nervous feeling in my belly."

After several moments, shift your awareness to the outer environment. Take a look around the space. Notice where you are in relation to the space around you, and notice what calls your attention. For example, you might notice details about the room, the quality of the light, or objects in the space. Name to yourself what you notice in the outer environment.

Then, shift your awareness to the field of the relationship. Make eye contact with your partner, and observe the energy between you. Notice any colors or textures of the space between. Do any images come up that describe this field? Is it light or dense? Smooth or rough? Clear or cloudy? Name to yourself what you are aware of in the relational field.

After you have spent time in these three realms—inner environment, outer environment, and the relational field—take some time to share with each other what you noticed in each space.

CHAPTER 1

Addiction and Attachment

An ambience of responsiveness is as essential for psychological health as an ambience of a plentiful supply of oxygen is essential for physical health.

—ERNEST S. WOLF

Because of our culture's investment in autonomy at all costs and its accompanying fear of dependency, security has been sacrificed for independence. Our society's preoccupation with the avoidance of dependency may be one possible reason for its preoccupation with drugs.

—PHILIP FLORES

For those of us in recovery, relationship can be fraught territory. We may have grown up in homes that failed to nurture a sense of safety and consistency. In our teen years, we may have lost loved ones to addiction or suicide. In adulthood, we may have experienced betrayals, isolation, or bitter disappointment in romantic partnerships. We might look at the people around us with a sense of bewilderment, jealousy, or awe as they glide, seemingly like swans on a lake, through relationships that look, at least from the outside, healthy and secure. In recovery, we might turn to support from our fellows and sponsors only to find them to be similarly vulnerable individuals who are carrying the same unresolved wounds as we are and repeating old slogans that may not meet the questions of our hearts.

In order to understand precisely what can make relationships in recovery so difficult, it's important to go back to the beginning—our infancy and early childhood—to look at the relational imprints and survival adaptations we developed as a result of the successes and failures of our environment. As psychotherapists Anthony Bateman and Jeremy Holmes write, "The way someone responds to 'slings and arrows of outrageous fortune' is shaped by the mental [and I would add, body] structures that derive from childhood."[1] We can consider these adaptive mind-body structures from the closely interwoven perspectives of attachment theory, polyvagal theory, psychoanalytic theory, and developmental psychology.

Attachment theory teaches that our relational imprints depend on the earliest experiences of bonding in infancy and childhood. Secure bonding in adulthood, in our relationship both with ourselves and others, depends on the degree of consistency, safety, nurturance, and attunement that was available to us early in life. The attunement of the caregivers supports the child's need for closeness and security, as well as the developmentally appropriate autonomy, play, and independence that enable the child's explorations of self and the world. In this well-attuned environment, the child will experience the efficacy of her emotions, learning that her feelings will meet their purpose of getting her needs met. She experiences that her reach for connection will be met with loving care and that her cries of protest will be answered. Through these experiences of coregulation with her caregivers, she develops the brain-body capacity for self-regulation. Because her caregivers model for her how to soothe and keep company with big and uncomfortable feelings, she will develop these capacities in herself. As she grows into adulthood, she will bring these capacities with her; she will be with herself in a loving way, meeting emotions in herself and others without getting overwhelmed by their energies.

When exploring the relationship between trauma and addiction, it's important to distinguish between early developmental trauma and later shock trauma. *Developmental trauma*, also called complex post-traumatic stress disorder (C-PTSD), is trauma that occurs as the result of neglect, abuse, unrepaired relational ruptures, or chronic misattunement during key developmental phases of early childhood. These early experiences affect healthy development in both brain and body and also impact the formation of identity.[2] Though we may not recall these early experiences, we remember them—or I might say, they remember us—through procedural memory, which is nonverbal and experienced through sensation, and semantic memory, our patterns and scripts for interpersonal behavior.[3] When there are failures in this early environment, instead of developing a cohesive sense of self, the child will develop a "bad self," an identity based in shame and disappointed longings, and an outer persona, or "good self," that serves to meet the demands of the outer environment and wards off an inner sense of fragmentation. The child will also experience chronic dysregulation as she remains alert to the possibility of relational rupture or threat.

While shock traumas, such as a car crash, and later relational ruptures, such as breakups or other losses, certainly can be painful and traumatizing, they don't result in this fragmentation of self, the impairment of brain development, and the establishment of lifelong shame-based identities. In fact, the psychiatrist Henry Krystal, who worked with survivors of the Nazi concentration camps and was himself a survivor, observed that "if an individual had been raised in a loving, caring family, then even when confronted with overwhelming trauma, they had a much greater likelihood of restoring their capacity for healing and love."[4] Attuned parenting and a secure environment in childhood provide the lifelong basis for resilience and regulation, and offer the essential emotional, psychological, and neurobiological capacities that can help an individual restore from even the most devastating traumas later in life.

What can make later events so difficult and the repercussions so long-lasting is when they are a recapitulation of early experiences in which the core need for attunement, safety, and coregulation was not met, when the child was alone with overwhelming experiences in their outer world and overwhelming sensations and emotions inside. Shock trauma is impactful not merely due to the event itself but to the way it touches upon or reiterates core wounds, bringing to the surface the feelings of fragmentation, terror, rage, powerlessness, and shame based in experiences in infancy. Trauma treatment can fail if it focuses primarily on later events without also addressing any preexisting dysregulation and fragmentation.

It's important to understand addiction as fundamentally an attempt to mitigate the effects of the chronic shame, anxiety, and cognitive distortions that characterize early developmental trauma, rather than as primarily a response to the shock traumas of later life. Our actions in addiction, which cause harm to ourselves and others, stem from and in turn feed the underlying feelings of shame: We use substances in an attempt to mitigate chronic shame, and the negative effects of our use then create more shame, resulting in the feedback loop of addiction. As psychotherapist Patricia DeYoung notes, the experience of shame comes first; it is addiction's underlying cause, not its effect.

> *Although addiction adds to the load of shame, a deep pervasive shame is the cause, not the result, of the addiction. And so we are not tempted to think that if the behavior ceases, shame will disappear. In fact, shame is most dangerous when the client manages to get "clean and sober." In the absence of the addiction, the client's long-term disintegration of self becomes felt reality, along with intense feelings of worthlessness and helplessness. . . . Daily 12-step groups with personal sponsors are often a lifesaver in the early weeks and months of recovery because they meet some of this desperate need for interpersonal regulation.*[5]

As DeYoung emphasizes, for addiction treatment to be successful, it must focus, at least in part, on meeting these core shame-based identities and early relational wounds and on providing the key reparative experience—an embodied sense of safety, coregulation, and belonging.

Flores similarly emphasizes that at the root of all addiction is relational trauma in infancy and early childhood.[6] Relational trauma occurs when caregivers are not able to provide a consistent and attuned connection with the child. A child experiences attachment trauma from neglect and abuse, both physical and emotional, as well as from the less extreme but also impactful experience of inaccurate or inconsistent attunement, generally by parents who are experiencing their own overwhelm, stressors, and losses or who received detrimental parenting strategies from the culture or their own childhood experiences. This early attachment wounding leads to the child developing adaptive roles and survival strategies that, though at one time necessary, eventually lead to difficulties with relationships in adult life.[7]

At essence, substance use is an unconscious strategy for managing the overwhelming emotions and physiological states that stem from early attachment ruptures. As psychologist Ernest S. Wolf writes:

> *Frantic life styles [and] drug abuse . . . serve as desperate measures to hold on to some self-organization and avoid sliding into a fragmented state. Alcohol intoxication [is] often used to distract oneself from the unbearable aspects of fragmentation. Indeed, there are all kinds of excitements that can be used to keep away the feeling of deadness in the self. . . . Some people become compulsive gamblers, others continuously seek the excitement of daredevil activities, and still others become "workaholics" to maintain their sense of selfhood.*[8]

If our underlying attachment needs for safety and connection are not consistently met by our caregivers, and they are not available to effectively regulate or coregulate with us, we cannot develop the core capacities for self-regulation that serve us in later life. Using addictive substances and behaviors then becomes an attempt at self-regulation, self-cohesion, and self-soothing in the face of the fragmentation that threatens to overwhelm us. Although the teaching of Step One, "that our lives had become unmanageable," reflects the eventual results of our substance use, from a developmental perspective our substance use actually originated from the unmanageability of our environments, both inner and outer: Our lives were *already* unmanageable. The substance use, therefore, was an attempt at making the unmanageable manageable.

Psychotherapist Michael Barnett, speaking from an attachment-based perspective, defines addiction as "a surrogate for the care and presence of loving and dependable others in our lives when such people and circumstances were simply not an option."[9] When again and again we reached out and no one was there, we learned to dull or shut down our need for connection. Sooner or later, we found that substances and addictive behaviors could provide a semiviable simulacrum of a core attachment figure, effectively numbing or providing a substitute for our unmet attachment needs. In an ideal and healthy environment, "pleasure is a signpost to the object [the caregiver]"; the instinct for warmth, nurturance, and connection leads the child into the relational field where those needs will be met.[10] Correspondingly, the compulsive pleasure-seeking that defines addiction is a manifestation of the failure of relationship.[11]

In an oft-cited, and heartbreaking, early experiment on attachment, researcher Harry Harlow took lab-born infant monkeys and presented them with two options for surrogate mothers: one made of cloth and another built of wire mesh.[12] He discovered that, regardless of which mother had a milk bottle, the baby monkeys bonded to the cloth mother, choosing warmth and softness over the wire mother and prioritizing comfort over the availability of food. This experiment is frequently interpreted as proof for the necessity of affection, as evidenced by the fact that the monkeys opted for the comfort of the cloth mother rather than the milk provided by the wire mother—indicating, I suppose, that animals (and children) are not just hungry machines. However, there is truly no affection present. The monkeys chose the cloth mother only in the absence of what would have been a meaningful connection with the actual mother—it was a sorry and empty substitute for true contact. Choosing between a cloth mother and a wire mother is no choice at all. If anything, this study primarily proves our human capacity for cruelty to animals and the limitations of scientific frameworks for understanding the nature of love, consciousness, and the more-than-human world. Whether cloth or wire, the surrogate mother cannot offer the heart connection and love that every infant requires.

While I don't find the study to truly speak to the subject of affection, it does offer an apt metaphor for talking about addiction. In the absence of a "loving and dependable other" we, like the baby monkeys, turn toward the cloth mother, the attachment figure of the substance, to help us self-regulate and self-soothe. The false promise of the warm cloth is better than nothing. Eventually, through the work of recovery, we start to see our substance use for what it was: In spite of all its promises, and all the ways it helped us survive, beneath its familiar guise it was fundamentally a cold and empty structure whose promises to meet our deepest longings never quite materialized.

Polyvagal Theory, Trauma, and Addiction

Many readers will already be familiar with the language of polyvagal theory, developed by neuroscientist Stephen Porges, which teaches us about the three pathways of the autonomic nervous system (ANS): mobilization (fight/flight), a response of the sympathetic division of the ANS; immobilization (shutdown), a parasympathetic response; and the calm/connected state of the ventral vagal pathway (the social engagement system), also a parasympathetic response.[13] These three states are dedicated to our survival, helping us anticipate and respond to threats. In an ideal environment, we can rely on the information from our ANS, respond to an immediate threat, and return to a state of social engagement to rest and restore. Unfortunately, when we've experienced traumas or chronic stress, in a society that perpetuates existential threats such as racism, climate collapse, and food and healthcare scarcity, all in the midst of a cultural milieu of overwhelming technological and sensory input, we get stuck in our threat response of activation or collapse and rarely feel safe enough to let our guard down to return to a restorative state. Our ANS state is one of the various interrelated factors that shape our responses and tendencies in relationship.

Our fight/flight response is governed by the sympathetic nervous system; it is a state of activation and hyperarousal characterized by anxiety and designed to help us run from or fight off a potential threat. People with a tendency toward this state often receive diagnoses of generalized anxiety disorder or ADHD. An anxious attachment style, discussed in Chapter 3 in more detail, is characterized by chronic activation of the sympathetic nervous system.

The immobilization response is governed in part by the dorsal vagus nerve. A dorsal vagal state is a state of immobilization; it is meant to help us respond to an intense threat by collapsing, becoming quiet and invisible, and playing dead. A habitual dorsal vagal state is characterized by numbness, dissociation, and depressive feelings. People with a tendency toward a chronic dorsal vagal state often receive a diagnosis of depression and may have a tendency toward an avoidant attachment style. If you tend to feel overwhelmed in relationship, to shut down and withdraw, you might be feeling the workings of your dorsal vagal pathway.

In contrast, the regulated state of calm and connection stems from the social engagement system, governed in part by the ventral vagus nerve. A ventral state is a state of relaxation and presence. In ventral vagal, you'll feel available to connect with loved ones. You might feel this way with friends or fellows, when connecting with nature, or in the company of an animal friend. In a ventral vagal state you might also enjoy spending time alone, appreciating your connection with yourself and a sense of being safely held in your environment. You might feel that you can be yourself in relationship with others and feel equally at home during periods on your own, moving fluidly between social connection and connection with self. This is a state associated with secure attachment.

In addition to the three primary states, we can also experience blended states: mobilization (sympathetic) plus safety (ventral vagal), immobilization (dorsal vagal) plus safety (ventral vagal), and mobilization (sympathetic) plus immobilization (dorsal vagal).[14] Activation of the sympathetic nervous system plus ventral vagal is found in states of activity that also feel safe, such as playing a soccer game or having sex with a trusted partner. Activation of the dorsal vagal pathway plus ventral vagal is a blended state in which we experience down regulation coupled with a sense of safety; for example, resting in a cozy environment, cuddling with an animal companion, or lying on a sunny beach with a friend.

The chronic coactivation of the sympathetic nervous system and the dorsal vagal pathway occurs in response to trauma, extreme threat, or ongoing, accumulated stress. In this state, we experience the hyperarousal of sympathetic activation coupled with the immobilization response of the dorsal vagal pathway, resulting in a freeze response. This state is often described as trying to drive a car while hitting the gas pedal and the brakes at the same time.[15] You might feel anxious and restless while also feeling disconnected from your body or overcome with exhaustion, or you might

Relational Responses Through a Polyvagal Lens

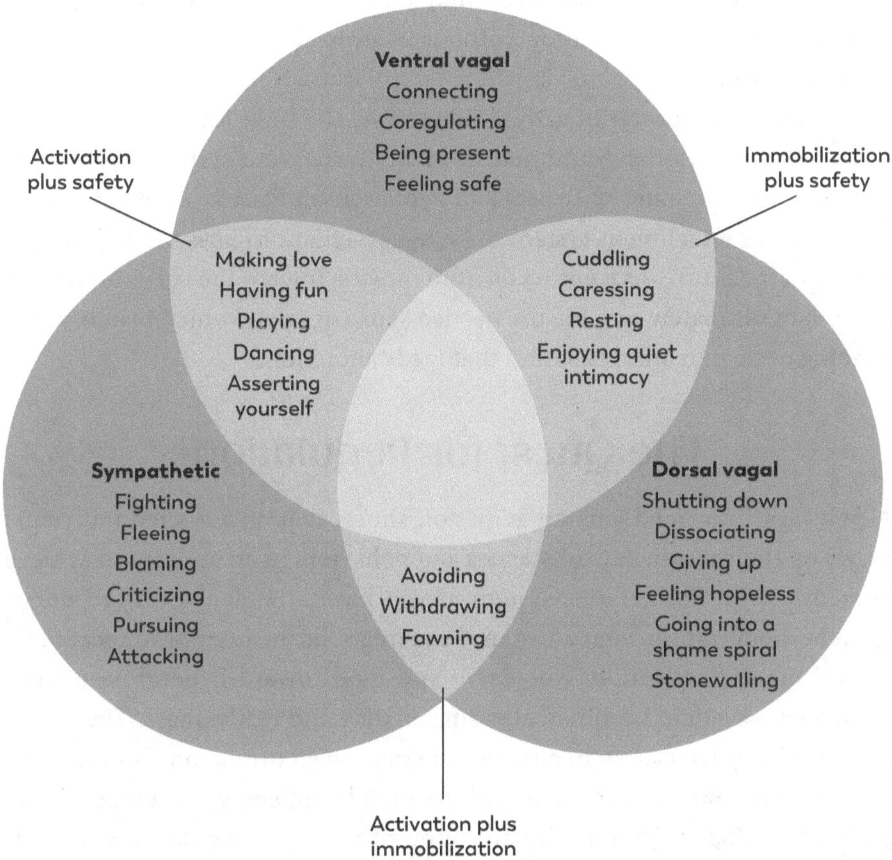

find yourself rapidly oscillating between states of activation and states of collapse. People with this nervous system tendency may receive a diagnosis of bipolar disorder.

As therapist Jan Winhall notes, addiction is characterized by this blended state: "The body constricts with a sympathetic surge, but is simultaneously immobilized with dorsal activation, creating a stopped process. . . . This stuck process is a powerful feature of addiction. From a polyvagal perspective, it makes sense that addictions act as propellers that shift the body along this continuum in a quest for safety. Sadly . . . they create an endless feedback loop that results in unsuccessful attempts to regulate."[16] In active addiction, we attempt to manage states of both hyper- and hypoarousal with substance use or addictive behaviors, which unfortunately results only in further dysregulation and state vacillation without us ever meeting our core need for secure connection.

Attachment ruptures in early childhood set the stage for chronic nervous system dysregulation in adulthood, in which the nervous system gets stuck in blended or cyclic states of hyper- and hypoarousal. Early relational ruptures also tune our attachment system to be hypervigilant to possible attachment threats in the future, preventing us from moving toward the very connection that might ultimately provide the needed sense of safety, which results in the ongoing cycle of painful isolation that feeds addiction.

The Quest for Regulation

A polyvagal-informed lens on addiction shows that an addicted individual draws on their particular substances and behaviors in an attempt to achieve homeostasis in the nervous system. If you have a tendency toward dorsal vagal immobilization, your substance use might be an attempt to recalibrate toward greater activation, whereas if you tend toward hyperarousal, your substance use might be aimed at easing anxiety and restlessness. The movement in the nervous system also has an emotional correlation. For instance, a person might turn to cocaine, with its mobilizing energy and tendency to promote feelings of grandiosity, to counter the underlying dorsal vagal collapse (physiological state) and associated feeling of powerlessness (emotional state). Another individual, overwhelmed by fear (emotion) and sympathetic activation (physiological state) might turn to cannabis for its soporific effects. For blended states, the substance use is an attempt to find regulation, to both numb anxiety and activate out of numbness—in other words, to lower the highs and heighten the lows.

Porges emphasizes two important, coexisting features of substance use, ones that will be well known to anyone who has struggled with addiction: first, that substances do indeed assist with shifting and managing autonomic states; and second, that although they may have short-term positive effects, they ultimately do not promote the baseline sense of safety and social connection that provide true regulation. Furthermore, habitual substance use often results in a heightened threat response—the same response that it is meant to mitigate—which in turn creates further cycles of disconnection and conflict. He emphasizes that the only real way of achieving a felt sense of safety is through the recruitment of the social engagement system, which is achieved through meaningful connection with others.[17]

This dilemma is the core bind faced by many of us in recovery—the relational connection that would most provide healing from addiction is the very thing that most provokes a sense of threat and terror. With this dilemma in mind, Porges emphasizes the importance of understanding the addiction experience "in terms of adaptive functions that may often be heroic."[18] The hero's journey from the isolation of addiction to the social engagement of recovery may be a long and difficult one, and one that is completely understandable from the point of view of the mind-body adaptations developed by necessity in early childhood.

Addiction and the Fragmentation of Self

Early relational ruptures and misattunements deeply impact an infant's developing sense of self. His earliest glimpses of selfhood, of interoceptive awareness, are undermined; his sensory awareness shifts to vigilance of the external environment as he learns he must scan for potential threats, reach effortfully for contact, or remain on guard against potential abandonment or boundary impingement. When a parent is unable to meet a child's needs in a sensitive and timely way, the child learns that attuning to his inner sensory experience of emotion and sensation may not result in a satisfying response. The child then begins to shut down his embodied awareness of his needs and desires, and eventually even the needs and desires themselves. He learns a series of implicit messages: His needs don't matter, it is dangerous to have needs, he is bad for having needs (i.e., his needs are shameful), and it is better to not have needs at all.

As I explore further in Chapter 7, this early fragmentation is the origin point of shame—when a child's reach for connection is rejected, he will split off from the core vulnerability of needing, sensing that this part of him must be unacceptable and that its expression will result only in more hurt. He splits into a bad self that is unacceptable and a good self that must be maintained at all costs. The role of shame (and the blessing of it, strange as it is to say!) is to protect us from the pain of disconnection ever happening again. These early ruptures feed an unconscious belief: "It must be my fault, and if I'm very good, I can prevent the pain of disconnection in the future." From these core developmental wounds grow adult relational patterns in which it is difficult to know our own needs or express them clearly to others, or we might engage in a constant cry of protest against potential abandonment, always expecting disappointment and betrayal. The underlying feeling of being bad remains with us, unconsciously motivating our actions and reactions in the world as we move through our lives with a persistent sense of fear that we'll be found out. With the unconscious aim of protecting our hearts from possible rejection, we often develop convoluted ways of expressing our feelings and desires, which in turn paradoxically create only more isolation and relational insecurity.

When young children aren't offered the safety and support they need, they shut down their reach for connection, learning to either deny their needs or meet them on their own. Later in adulthood, these early lessons in independence manifest as the kind of self-reliance that can make the task of recovery difficult. The very capacity for self-reliance that helped us survive our childhood environment becomes a liability that keeps us trapped in the isolation of addiction and makes it challenging to create our evolved nest in recovery. It is no coincidence that one of the first practices we take on in recovery is the outreach call.

Recognizing our need for others, including other people and a Higher Power, and asking for their help is a theme reiterated throughout the Steps: in Step Five, for example, we take the risk of sharing our vulnerabilities with "another human being" such as a recovery coach or sponsor; in Step Seven we ask Higher Power for help in removing our difficulties; in Step Nine we speak directly with others to make our amends; in Step Twelve we "carry the message," sharing our experience with others. These recovery actions guide us through taking the risk of making contact, helping us grow past the fantasy of omnipotence that belongs in early childhood into the healthy dependency and mutual interdependency of mature attachment in adulthood.[19] Ultimately, if we keep company with both our fear of and our longing for connection, and take small steps toward acknowledging our dependency needs, we garner a key reparative experience, one that, little by little, helps us meet the missing relational pieces that underscore addiction, ultimately providing a healing experience not only for the immediate symptom of substance use but for the foundational wounds themselves.

Early Attachment and God

Our relationships to our self and others are shaped by the implicit and explicit messages we received in childhood. If we experienced caregivers or a cultural context that was judgmental, shaming, rejecting, or abandoning, or in which love was conditional, we internalize these messages as unconscious beliefs and repeat them to ourselves. If you start to notice how your mind relates to your body, you may see a clear replication of the messages you received as a child. We may repeat these messages not only to ourselves but to others, judging them through the same lens that we turn on ourselves.

In recovery, as we seek to connect with a loving Higher Power, we may have to first wade through images of God that contain aspects of this childhood conditioning, where we may ascribe to Higher Power the elements that belong to that original context of childhood. Our Higher Power may appear judgmental, omnipotent or omniscient, rejecting, neglectful, or otherwise like a persecuting or withholding parent. It's important in recovery to start to tease out these parts so that we can connect to a presence of love that will support our recovery.

Although the literature of Alcoholics Anonymous recognizes the powerful role of attachment in healing, it is unfortunately narrowly focused on God and the power of the fellowship as the source of this attachment. While God might be a meaningful connection for some, the emphasis on Higher Power can be off-putting to others who might otherwise benefit from the Twelve Steps. As we consider our understanding of Higher Power, rather than holding God and the fellowship itself to be the only true sources of healing, we can include many sources of love and connection, including animals, trees, ancestors, and numerous allies from the spiritual realm. AA is accurate in locating the healing potency of attachment; however, we can recognize that the word *God* is only one way of describing this healing presence.

Sponsorship and Secure Attachment

In Twelve Step recovery, the practice of sponsorship can offer reparative attachment experiences for both sponsor and sponsee. A trauma-informed framework based in attachment principles honors the vulnerabilities that both parties bring to the relationship and helps sponsors understand early attachment dynamics so that they can best hold their sponsees with consistency and attunement. Possibilities for attuned engagement can include offering support, encouragement, reassurance, clarifying questions, and wider perspectives. As a sponsor, it's best if the majority of your responses focus on empathic attunement rather than confrontation or other tough-love strategies.

In addition to these types of responses, sponsoring generally includes sharing your own story—your experience, strength, and hope—and referring sponsees to the relevant Steps, program literature, or tools. Choosing the right response at the right moment is an aspect of what constitutes attunement and is part of the art (and challenge!) of sponsorship.

Here are some suggestions for sponsorship that can help you honor and prioritize the attachment relationship:

- Set clear boundaries, and stick to them, but not rigidly. If your sponsee needs extra help, consider offering additional support. However, don't sacrifice your own wellbeing for your sponsee, as this will only foster resentment.
- Let sponsees know in advance when you won't be available, for instance, on weekends or when you're going on vacation.
- Focus on rupture and repair. As in any close relationship, you will inevitably have conflicts. It's not necessary, or even useful, to avoid these. Instead, focus on the repair when ruptures do occur. Rupture and repair is a crucial part of a healing attachment experience.

- If you need to end the sponsorship relationship, do it consciously. Give your sponsee advance notice, tell them what you value about them and your time together, and support them in finding a new sponsor.
- Consciously hold the sponsee–sponsor relationship as a reparative attachment opportunity. Focus on process (attuned connection) as much as or more than content (giving words of advice, sharing experience, offering guidance).
- Follow Sue Johnson's acronym for secure attachment: Be accessible, responsive, and engaged (ARE).[20]
- Recognize that your own attachment wounds may be touched, and take the time to access your own support systems, such as therapy, meetings, self-care, and your own sponsor.
- Cultivate your own ANS regulation so that you can coregulate with your sponsee. For instance, take a moment to center yourself in your heart or exhale a few times before picking up the phone.
- Don't take on responsibility for your sponsee's successes or challenges. If you start feeling like your wellbeing depends on that of your sponsee, get your own support. Allow your sponsee their journey.

As meaningful and transformative as it can be, sponsorship is just one part of the circle of support in recovery. Encourage your sponsee to develop their evolved nest, which might include fellows, family, animal and plant friends, nature connection, friends, coaches, therapists, healing practitioners, medical professionals, and inner allies such as ancestors, angels, or other helpful guides.

The Attachment Inheritance

Early childhood wounds and relational ruptures can occur despite the best intentions of caregivers. Raising a child requires parents to chart a course through often unknown territory. Parents consciously or unconsciously draw on their own attachment inheritance, the parenting they received, so that survival adaptations are passed down between generations. Parenting choices may also be influenced by cultural norms and practices, for example, the now-discredited advice to let a child cry it out in the crib so as not to spoil them—a practice that we now know to be damaging to a child's healthy development.[21]

At the same time, caregivers may be overwhelmed and distracted by additional stressors, such as postpartum anxiety or depression, financial worries, relationship concerns, caring for other family members, or grief at the aging or death of a parent. A lack of *nestedness*—an interwoven, nature-based, intergenerational community that collectively provides care and support for parent and child—means that parents are often struggling in isolation, and baby is dependent on the care of a small number of more-or-less dependable individuals.[22]

Additionally, the intimacy of child-rearing may touch into the caregiver's attachment anxieties. Parents may fear the loss of their autonomy as their identity threatens to be subsumed into the role of parent. They may grapple with anger in response to a child's assertion of "no," or they may struggle with feelings of rejection or anxiety as the child explores the world and grows into increasing independence. Together parent and child sway in the often-delicate dance of attachment, moving in and out of closeness; depending on their background, parents may have more trouble with one end of the spectrum or the other as their own fears of engulfment or abandonment are touched.[23] A parent's own traumas—such as violence and abuse in their childhood, the imprints of poverty or racism, or the effects of war or genocide—can have a major influence on the way they respond to the stressors of parenting and the task of attuning to a child's developmental needs. These traumas can be passed down through the generations through the mind-body survival adaptations shared from parent to child; attachment styles, chronic nervous system dysregulation, physical symptoms, substance use, survival-oriented beliefs, hypervigilance, shame, and changes in genetic expression can all be passed on intergenerationally so that a caregiver's parenting is shaped by traumas experienced not only in their lifetime but in the generations prior. And indeed, the task of parenting inevitably touches into these traumas, where ideally they can be made conscious in order to be healed. As family therapist Bryana Kappadakunnel emphasizes in her excellent book *Parent Yourself First*, "It's the child's job to rattle the cage of inherited wounds and lead us to a more awakened and liberated path."[24]

Most caregivers are doing the absolute best they can with a difficult task in a society that offers little education, emotional support, or financial resources for the work of parenting. As you look at your own attachment adaptations, you might consider the ways that your parents and caregivers navigated from a place of their own immediate and inherited struggles. Absolutely, it makes sense to feel anger and grief about ways in which your needs were not met, and it is important to mourn what was lacking and what should have been present; this anger and sadness is an important part of your own healing. At the same time, it can be a relief to look at the ways your caregivers may have been parenting from a place of deficit or overwhelm, from a dysregulated nervous system resulting from trauma or chronic stress, or from their own attachment wounds, and to consider how they might have parented had their own needs been more fully met. Though certainly much may be unforgiveable, this wider perspective can help you move out of the self-armored position of blame to the tender and heartbreaking reality of shared pain, which may eventually include compassion for their own challenges.

✴ Meeting Your Parent as a Child

Close your eyes. Breathe out three times slowly.[25] Travel back in time to meet your parent when they were a young child. See and sense the child's missing needs. See the ways they were alone, frightened, or suffering.

Breathe out. See them surrounded by the attuned care, protection, or companionship they needed. How do they change when their needs are met? See them growing up from here.

Breathe out. How does having their needs met affect their capacity to be a parent? See and sense your parent in their fullest capacities for strength, love, and kindness.

Breathe out. See and sense how your parent in their fullest self could provide you with the parenting you needed as a child. What does it feel like to be parented in this way? See yourself growing up with this love and support. How does it impact the way you feel in your body? How do you feel in the world?

Breathe out, and open your eyes.

Growing Secure Attachment

If you are a parent or caregiver, you can interrupt intergenerational cycles and support yourself in the work of parenting by

- Understanding your attachment tendencies
- Developing interoceptive awareness to slow down conditioned reactive responses
- Learning attachment-based parenting practices and understanding child development and the tasks of each developmental phase[26]
- Healing shame through therapy and other reparative attachment experiences
- Being part of a supportive community, such as Twelve Step meetings or support groups for parents
- Finding support in nature connection
- Practicing asking for help
- Bringing your inner parenting into conscious awareness

Drawing on resources and tending to your own ANS regulation can interrupt family patterns of insecure attachment and support you in giving your child the love and safety you should have received yourself. This experience of support and regulation not only bolsters you in offering your child what they need but also provides a reparative experience for your own Little One, your inner child. The blessing of secure attachment in the present moment can then flow back in time to your younger self, your parents, and your ancestors, providing a healing that moves through the generations.

✳ Meeting Your Inner Parent

Explore the relationships between the entities listed in the following chart. Choose from these attributes or add your own.

Possible positive attributes:

Loving, available, curious, consistent, caring, attuned, gentle, forgiving, present, supportive, engaged, responsive

Possible negative attributes:

Judgmental, shaming, blaming, rejecting, abandoning, controlling, ignoring, cold, engulfing, suffocating, invasive, neglectful, punishing

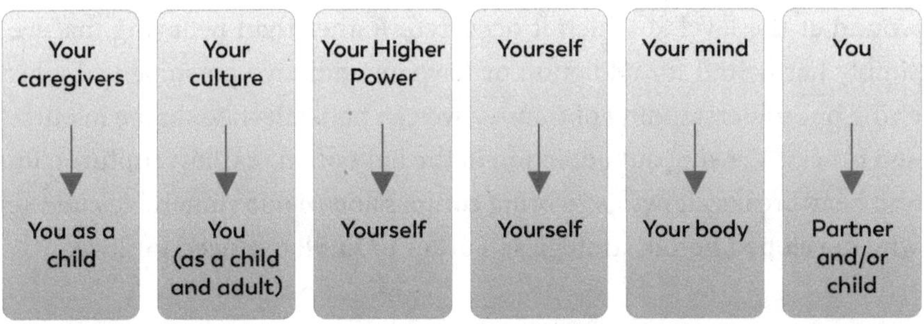

Often the critical or harsh parenting you received becomes the voice that you direct to yourself, your body, your partner, or your child. You can start to change how you parent yourself by bringing these messages into conscious awareness.

The Landscape of Trauma

The Adverse Childhood Experience (ACE) research compiled a list of the childhood traumas that can dramatically increase the likelihood of addiction later in life. Although research into ACEs has played a crucial role in raising awareness of trauma, if we singularly focus on ACE scores, we can miss the subtler levels of early relational wounding that create the shame-based identifications, attachment adaptations, and survival strategies that form the bedrock of addiction. Additionally, the ACE list leaves out pre- and perinatal trauma that occurred for the developing embryo and birthing infant, as well as systemic trauma and intergenerational trauma passed down from our ancestors. Without considering trauma through this broader lens, it's easy for individuals in recovery, as well as the therapists working with them, to miss the true roots of addiction.

While the Twelve Step program often encourages us to focus on our present-day actions and behaviors rather than seek the "why" behind our addictions, we can experience deeper healing when we contextualize and tend to addiction at its wellspring. Contextualizing our experience allows us to understand and address the developmental needs that were interrupted by attachment ruptures and environmental failures. We can then meet the wound at the level at which it occurred. Rather than believing that we are simply hardwired for addiction or have an addictive personality, by broadening our understanding of trauma, we can help alleviate shame in ourselves and others. Viewing our addiction in the light of our earliest ruptures, losses, and heartbreaks allows us to bring compassion to our vulnerable child selves who developed heroic strategies in order to fulfill our need for love.

The Landscape of Trauma Assessment

The following checklist provides an encompassing look at the roots of addiction. It considers ACEs alongside intergenerational trauma, prenatal and birth trauma, and childhood relational wounds.

Intergenerational Trauma

Ancestors experienced

- ☐ War
- ☐ Genocide
- ☐ Occupation
- ☐ Being subject to medical experimentation
- ☐ Enslavement
- ☐ Imprisonment

- ☐ Torture
- ☐ Rape
- ☐ Unmourned losses
- ☐ Murder
- ☐ Being a perpetrator of violence
- ☐ Poverty
- ☐ Loss of language, home, land connection, religion or spirituality, and/or cultural traditions
- ☐ Systemic oppression
- ☐ Prejudice
- ☐ Racism
- ☐ Chronic lack of safety
- ☐ Being denied basic human rights
- ☐ Restriction of body autonomy and freedom

Prenatal and Birth Trauma

- ☐ Being unwanted or unwelcomed at conception
- ☐ The gestating parent's stress, substance use, depression, or traumatizing experience during pregnancy
- ☐ Invasive surgeries or medical interventions experienced by the gestating parent
- ☐ Violence witnessed by the gestating parent
- ☐ Loss experienced by the gestating parent, such as the death of a family member
- ☐ The gestating parent's loss of medical control (for example, being subjected to an unwanted cesarean or epidurals during the birthing process)
- ☐ Unresolved relational ruptures or chronic distress between the parents during pregnancy

ACEs

- ☐ Sexual abuse
- ☐ Physical abuse
- ☐ Emotional abuse

- ☐ Physical neglect
- ☐ Emotional neglect
- ☐ Contentious divorce
- ☐ A family member's mental illness
- ☐ A family member's substance use disorder
- ☐ Domestic violence
- ☐ The incarceration of a family member

Childhood Relational Wounds

- ☐ Inconsistent attunement
- ☐ Chronic misattunement
- ☐ Perinatal depression
- ☐ Denial of child's sensory awareness and sensitivities
- ☐ Disallowal of child's emotional awareness and expression
- ☐ Shame used for discipline or behavior management
- ☐ Child's healthy aggression is met with the caregiver's punishment, anger, or emotional collapse
- ☐ Insufficient consistency, boundaries, and containment in environment
- ☐ Lack of nurturing touch
- ☐ Violation of child's energetic, bodily, psychological, or spatial boundaries
- ☐ Chronic distress in parents' relationship
- ☐ Caregiver's experience of loss; for example, the death of their parent
- ☐ Inaccurate or lack of mirroring of child's inner states
- ☐ Lack of support for child's autonomy, boundaries, and expression of "no"
- ☐ Parent's anxiety around child's playful explorations
- ☐ Parent's dependency on child to meet their emotional needs; parentification of child
- ☐ Impacts of intergenerational trauma
- ☐ Discrimination (racial, religious, class, gender, sexual, etc.)
- ☐ Parent's insecure attachment adaptations
- ☐ Scarcity fears and financial stress, whether or not in response to actual financial realities
- ☐ Unspoken and unacknowledged family secrets

✳ Exploring Family Roles

Children often face an impossible dilemma: To maintain connection with their caregivers, they need to sacrifice the parts of themselves they sense may not be accepted, such as assertiveness, playfulness, or dependency needs. In the family, the child unconsciously takes on the roles given to them, which can be a parent's projection of their own disavowed parts or unfulfilled desires, or roles meant to maintain homeostasis in the family. Some common roles include the Smart One, the Nice One, the Baby, the Grown-Up, the Funny One, the Rebellious One, the Sensitive One, the Peacekeeper, and the Carrier of the Family Secrets.

In your journal, explore the role you've played in your family system:

In my family, my role was _______.

My job was to _______.

This meant I had to _______.

In order to fulfill this role, I had to sacrifice _______.

✳ Exploring Your Core Needs

A child's core needs include

- Safety
- Belonging
- Attunement
- Warmth
- Comfort
- Attuned touch
- Nurturance
- Existence needs, such as food, housing, and healthcare
- Rest
- Boundaries
- Play and creativity

- Support for developing autonomy, including the expression of healthy aggression
- Support with identity formation

In a chaotic, abusive, neglectful, or inconsistent childhood environment, some or all of these core needs go unmet. In the preceding list, circle the core needs that were unmet during your childhood.

Then, in your journal, explore further with the following prompts:

How have substances or addictive behaviors served to meet my needs?

My substance use or addictive behavior has helped soothe states of hyperarousal (fight/flight) in these ways: ________

My substance use or addictive behavior has helped manage states of hypoarousal (shutdown) in these ways: ________

In what ways have I developed healthier methods to meet my needs? What resources do I have now that I didn't have before?

In what ways was I committed to the substance or addictive behavior as my primary relationship in the place of meaningful connection with others?

In what ways can I now turn to others to help meet my needs?

✳ Developing Awareness of Feelings, Needs, and Desires

Start to develop your awareness of yourself by getting to know your feelings, needs, and desires. If you are working the Twelve Steps, this can be part of a daily Tenth Step practice.

Some basic feelings are fear, longing, shame, joy, sadness, anger, and disgust. Feelings have many different tones and hues, but if you're just starting to get to know your feelings, referring to this short list can help you start to identify your experience.

Needs can include safety, love, care, attunement, touch, support, boundaries, freedom, autonomy, and physical needs such as food, water, and housing.

Desires can include the longing for certain things, activities, people, experiences, and feelings. You can think about ways you want to spend your time, people you want to be with, experiences you would like to have, or ways you want to feel. If you need a prompt, try *I want to do* _______, *to go to* _______, *to have* _______, *to be with* _______, *to be* _______, and *to feel*_______.

Right now I feel _______.

I need _______.

I want _______.

✳ Developing Awareness of Feelings, Needs, and Desires (with a partner)

You and your partner can get to know each other more deeply by completing the previous writing exercise together and sharing your responses with each other. By developing a shared vocabulary for directly discussing vulnerable feelings, needs, and desires, you can build your toolkit for honest communication, one that will serve you well in conflict. After your partner shares their writing for each category, you can use an Imago Dialogue to mirror back to them, validate their perspective, and empathize with their experience.[27]

For example:

Mirror: "I hear you saying that you need _______."

Validate: "It makes sense to me that you're needing _______."

Empathize: "It sounds really painful that your need for _______ hasn't been met."

Start with writing about your feelings, needs, and desires generally, and then, after some days of practice, expand it to specifically include the feelings, needs, and desires that come up in your relationship with your partner.

CHAPTER 2

Transforming the Attachment Inheritance

But the wild things cried, "Oh please don't go—
we'll eat you up—we love you so!"

—MAURICE SENDAK

Awareness of one's origins is like an anchor line plunged into the deep.

—CZESŁAW MIŁOSZ

When considering the landscape of addiction and attachment, it's important to travel back even further to include the experiences of our ancestors. Ancestral trauma (also called intergenerational, transgenerational, historical, or inherited trauma) is trauma that we're carrying from our ancestors' experiences. It is passed down in behaviors and beliefs, attachment wounds and patterns, stories that are told, and stories that are untold. Its impacts are carried forward in all the systems of the body, including the ANS, the brain, the heart, the gastrointestinal system, hormones, and cells.[1] These body systems collectively carry the lessons of the past in service to keeping us alive. Research in epigenetics shows that catastrophic trauma also affects gene expression so that even our DNA remembers the experiences of our forbearers. Maria Yellow Horse Brave Heart, a central figure in developing language around ancestral trauma in Indigenous communities, conceptualized a model for transgenerational trauma, finding resonances in Indigenous experience with what had been observed in Holocaust survivors and their children and grandchildren. She defined inherited trauma as the "cumulative emotional and psychological wounding over the life span and across generations, emanating from massive group trauma experiences."[2]

If you have struggled with addiction but have no conscious experiences of personal trauma, you may be sensing the impact of intergenerational trauma, which has similar effects.[3] Children and grandchildren of trauma survivors are themselves more susceptible to PTSD and anxiety.[4] Researcher Rachel Yehuda's studies of children of survivors of the Holocaust and of the World Trade Center attack on 9/11 showed that the children were born with low cortisol levels, which is associated with stress-related disorders such as PTSD, chronic pain, and chronic fatigue syndrome.[5] Ancestral trauma is deeply woven into the body, mind, and nervous system of the descendants of survivors of genocide, war, torture, enslavement and institutionalized racism, childhood sexual abuse, and systemic oppression.[6] This inherited trauma feeds a tendency toward addiction, as is evidenced by the widespread tragedy of substance use disorder on Native American reservations. In fact, in her research, Yehuda found that children who had a parent suffering from PTSD are three to four times more likely to struggle with depression, anxiety, and substance use than children in the control groups.[7] Research has shown that epigenetic changes affect not only the first generation of children of survivors but continue to influence subsequent generations of grandchildren and great-grandchildren.[8]

Psychologist Nirit Gradwohl Pisano conducted a series of psychoanalytic interviews with women who are part of the third generation of Holocaust survivors. Pisano, herself a member of the third generation, explains that unresolved trauma from the ancestors is stored in our bodies and psyches, and that it continues to escalate as it is passed down through the generations. She writes, "The unmourned suffering silently escalated in power and magnitude, seizing lead roles in their [the survivors'] lives and the lives of their children. Previous unresolved losses were thus transmitted to future generations."[9] Her research suggests that what is incomplete actually increases as it is passed down. In my work as an oral historian, I have interviewed numerous descendants of Holocaust survivors, and I have heard many similar stories. Often, when I ask the narrator how they first learned about the Holocaust, they reply that they can't recall a time before they knew, which to me is a way of saying that our bodies know already, have always known. Our bodies are, as Pisano writes, a "memory receptacle," an extensive archive of ancestral experiences.[10]

As trauma is inherited through the generations, it propagates the attachment wounds that characterize early developmental trauma, the resulting survival-based adaptations, and the incomplete survival responses of fight and flight associated with shock trauma. These ancestral and early attachment experiences merge in the tendency toward hypervigilance, anxiety, and catastrophizing commonly experienced by those who carry the legacy of intergenerational trauma. Furthermore, as psychologist Anne Ancelin Schützenberger emphasizes, "We can see, perceive or sense these complex links, although generally we do not speak about them: we experience them as part of the realm of the *unspeakable*, the *unthinkable*, the *unvoiced* or the *secret*."[11] We know these complex linkages in our bodies, and we can see them outwardly manifested in the ways we experience relationships and the world, but we cannot speak them. This unspeakability forms an intrinsic bind, wherein we know what is unknown, and see and feel what must not be seen or felt. Often what is unspoken governs the entire family dynamic.

The Land of Memory

In one of my most treasured photographs, my mother and my paternal grandmother are sitting on a beach in Manly, Australia. My mother, slightly younger than I am now, has a wide, beautiful smile and billowing curls. My grandmother, Milena, is a slim, elegant woman in a well-fitting dress, sitting daintily on the sand. What I never noticed until years later, and then could never *not* notice subsequently, was the Band-Aid on my grandmother's forearm. In the photograph it becomes what philosopher Roland Barthes calls the *punctum*, the commanding presence of a particular detail in the image from which one cannot look away. Barthes describes the punctum as the "element that rises from the scene, shoots out if it like an arrow, and pierces me. . . . This wound, this prick, this mark made by a pointed instrument . . . these marks, these wounds are so many *points* . . . punctum is also: sting, speck, cut, little hole."[12]

The punctum of the Band-Aid is made up of "so many points," precisely like the tattoo that it is covering. Though my grandmother never spoke to me directly of her concentration camp experiences, or of her family, whom I assumed had been killed in Auschwitz, or of her childhood prior, she nevertheless expressed her history in a thousand ways both large and small. From mistaking me and my mother for Nazis and locking us out of the house, to rescuing me in the middle of the night from an imagined shipwreck (and inadvertently strangling me in the process), she—and I with her—lived in a world filled with specters as magnetic as they were terrifying. Despite these struggles, she was an incredibly loving grandmother, a strong and often joyful woman whom I adored. After immigrating to Australia following the war, she experienced a breakdown in her late forties, grappled her whole life with what would now be identified as untreated PTSD, and in her later years, lost her memory to dementia. The memory loss was a deeply poignant irony for someone who had spent a lifetime alternately steeped in, grappling with, and warding off memory. During her final years, she conversed with the flowers on the front patio and with her lost family members. It seemed the veil between the world of the living and the world of the ancestors grew soft and translucent as petals.

In contrast to my grandmother, my grandfather was stoic and withdrawn. In my grandparents' house, he lived alone in the basement downstairs, and I rarely heard him speak. He, however, expressed his experience by writing a memoir, leaving our family a tremendous and courageous gift—a record of our history. In his testimonial, he writes of the horrors of Theresienstadt and Auschwitz with a brisk, understated style that would rival Hemingway's. He describes being beaten and tortured at the hands of the SS and nearly starving to death in the camps. He describes the desperate death march from Auschwitz in the final days of the war, and heartbreakingly, the death of his first wife, a young woman named Margot. In a description that is ineradicably inscribed in my memory, he describes returning alone to his hometown of Domažlice after the war and finding the Jewish community decimated. Only a few people had survived, among them, miraculously, some members of our family.

Other than his writing, his silence felt steeped in, as Emily Dickinson writes, "a pain—so utter— / It swallows substance up."[13] I remember feeling touched and surprised when, as I child, I visited his tailor shop and saw photos of me and my cousins above his desk. I understood that he loved us, and what it meant to him to have children and grandchildren. Prior to that moment, I hadn't understood that one could love without saying a word.

Ancestral Trauma and Addiction

Both ancestral trauma and developmental trauma play key roles in the development of substance use disorder. Whether it includes large-scale catastrophes such as war, starvation, or genocide, or pain in an individual family, such as loss, addiction, or poverty, ancestral experience is passed down to subsequent generations through trauma-based, survival-oriented attachment styles, explicit or implicit narratives, physiological imprints, and epigenetic adaptations. A child growing up in a home defined by intergenerational trauma may experience near-constant terror and anxiety. The child grows up waiting for the other shoe to drop, a message that is conveyed explicitly and implicitly through the words, behaviors, and nervous systems of the caregivers. The experience of love may be inextricable from the experience of pain. The child often takes on weighty roles that were placed on them even before their birth, understanding unconsciously that their life's purpose is to exist in service to the past: to rescue their parents and ancestors or to replace the children who died many years before. These unconscious expectations result in a Möbius strip of contradictory emotions—allegiance and resentment, hope and hopelessness, love and rage—in the face of this impossible task.

Given the roles they have inherited, and especially when the parents don't have a secure attachment style and cannot support a child's "no" and reach for independence, the child may experience difficulty at key stages of individuation, a process that begins in early childhood and reiterates throughout adolescence and adulthood. Parents who have experienced their own trauma,

How Intergenerational Trauma Becomes Developmental Trauma

EFFECTS IN ADULTHOOD

Individual continues to live out attachment and survival adaptations, which can include substance use disorder and challenges in relationships. If unresolved, these adaptations and identities may influence how an individual will then parent their own children, so that the effects extend into the next generation.

↑

EFFECTS IN CHILDHOOD

Child takes on parent's experiences and fear-based expectations; receives implicit and explicit messages; develops insecure attachment; lacks support for key developmental tasks; develops shame-based and compensatory identifications and survival strategies. Child has increased vulnerability toward anxiety, depression, and PTSD.

↑

ADAPTATIONS IN CHILDREN OF SURVIVORS

Due to parent's survival adaptations, child experiences parenting as neglectful, abusive, misattuned, abandoning, rejecting, confusing, inconsistent, or absent, resulting in developmental trauma and attachment wounds. Child shows epigenetic effects, including irregularities in DNA methylation and low cortisol levels.

↑

ADAPTATIONS IN SURVIVORS

Chronic ANS dysregulation, illness and physical symptoms, substance use, dissociation, survival-oriented beliefs, fear, hypervigilance, internalization of prejudice, self-blame, shame, guilt, changes in genetic expression.

↑

TRAUMATIZING EXPERIENCE

Persecution, torture, prejudice, enslavement, genocide, war, poverty, starvation, imprisonment, exile, major losses and attachment ruptures, chronic stress in response to ongoing threats.

passed on from their parents who experienced their own trauma (passed on from their parents who experienced their own trauma, and so on), can have difficulty meeting their child's developmental needs for safety, belonging, attunement, or autonomy. As Kain and Terrell note, "Children who 'inherit' parental trauma and also experience trauma themselves experience a double-whammy of sorts, and may face symptoms that arise out of two sources of trauma, and either commingle with, complicate, or contradict one another."[14] A child who grows up in a household shaped by ancestral trauma can experience both the trauma inheritance as well as profound attachment wounds and interruption of key developmental tasks and learnings throughout childhood; this constitutes the very confluence of circumstances that frequently leads to addiction.

Both ancestral and attachment trauma often present through the metaphor of a black hole. Many people, myself included, when entering deeply into body experience, soon start to access the feeling of an abyss in which all hope and meaning disappears. Clients often describe it as "a bottomless well." In my own experience, it feels like falling though the floor. In the language of AA, the "God-shaped hole" describes this primordial trauma.[15] Similar to a black hole in outer space, the black hole inside us often has a magnetic field that starts sucking us in if we get too close.

Aline LaPierre teaches that the black hole references back to a time when, as infants, ruptures in attachment meant a dire threat to our survival, when insufficient or misattuned mirroring meant we were not able to internalize a felt sense of our own existence. Not being held, physically, emotionally, or psychologically, leaves the infant in a state of fear of dissolution or annihilation; we could literally or figuratively fall into a dark well. As Freud states, "the black hole [is] connected to others"; it is a relational abyss that speaks of what is unspoken or unvoiced in the family, ancestry, or childhood experience.[16] It is the very loud silence, the tangible sensation of nothing.

A major challenge in recovery is that when we remove the substance, the medicine that was managing and masking the symptoms of ancestral and developmental trauma, we are faced with the presence of the core wound, the black hole itself. The substance use served as an attempt at self-cohesion and self-repair for the fragmented self.[17] If we remove the substance without offering a more meaningful holding environment to replace it, we run the risk of fragmentation, of falling through the floor into our primal terror, rage, and grief. This is why the task of recovery depends so heavily on the holding of a larger group and of a Higher Power that can offer reparative attachment experiences—when we start to fall, we need to feel that something will catch us. This is the paradox of admitting powerlessness in Step One: On one hand, we fear that if we stop bracing, stop controlling, stop holding ourselves up, we will fall into the abyss. On the other hand, it isn't until we take Step One, admitting our powerlessness, that we can take Step Two, which allows us to sense the loving presence of the group and a Higher Power.

Ancestral trauma can feel like a nail driven into a tree trunk; we might feel that it can't be extracted without cutting down the tree. It is intrinsic to our identity, our sense of meaning and purpose, and our view of the world. Because the love and pain are so bound together, it can be difficult to release our ancestors' experiences of suffering. We might feel that if we let go of their burdens, we are also giving up their love. It is an important part of the healing process to disentangle the love from the pain so that we have more freedom of choice about our ancestral inheritance. Ideally, a trauma-informed recovery space will hold an awareness of the role that intergenerational trauma plays in addiction and, when relevant, help members compassionately contextualize their present-day struggles, and their fear-based predictions for the future, in the light of past ancestral realities.

✳ Meeting the Abyss

Breathe out three times slowly. See yourself standing at the edge of an abyss. Know that you are able to stand here at the edge and go no further. Imagine that the hand of God, or any other kind of support you need, is protecting you from falling in. What do you notice?

Breathe out, and open your eyes.

The Unnamable

One of my early memories is of surreptitiously reading *Maus,* crouched in the dark hallway that held my father's bookshelves. I sensed that *Maus* was somehow off limits, and yet it drew me compulsively. As I grew older, other books followed: *The Diary of Anne Frank*, followed by *Generations of the Holocaust*, the imposing tome of *The Rise and Fall of the Third Reich*. In various YA novels, I learned about the *Muselmänner*, the Auschwitz prisoners who were so starved and haunted they were like the walking dead. I felt guilty for reading—ashamed of my fascination, the pull of the darkness—but I couldn't resist.

It wasn't until years later that I understood what I had been looking for. I had been trying to name and organize the impossibly unnamable and chaotic experience of growing up in the shadow of the Holocaust. I had internalized an overwhelming and amorphous cloud of fear, shame, and anxiety, which grew and compounded throughout my childhood, eventually manifesting in an eating disorder, addiction, and annihilating depression in my early twenties. I felt there was something rotten inside of me. Or rather, I sensed that my insides were rotten, that if someone came close, they would realize that inside the body of a petite, smiling, outwardly functional young woman were piles of corpses. This fear was coupled with a seemingly paradoxical desire to be loved and touched, which I couldn't allow unless I was drunk. I felt like a fraud. There was a pulse from the underworld, a sense of belonging more to the past than to the present, more to the dead than to the living.

My parents were very loving and did their best to explain this background to me, showing me the family archive: a postcard, the memoir, my father's little fur coat that he had worn when, at the age of three, he was smuggled out of Communist-controlled Czechoslovakia. But how can a parent explain to a child what is beyond language, what they themself don't fully understand? To explain that your perceptions, beliefs, relationships, and gene expression are intrinsically altered by the horrors your ancestors experienced. To explain that you will shape your life around the terror of losing the places and people you love. When I was growing up, the research on intergenerational trauma hadn't yet come into the cultural consciousness. Few words existed to describe the experience. I had to make it up as I went along, looking for language in those novels and memoirs.

When I think of my childhood, I think of that dark hallway, lined with books.

Our Ancestors Can Help Heal Our Ancestral Trauma

A few times, as a child, when I was quietly absorbed in painting a picture, I heard the voices of my deceased relatives—my mother's father, and other ancestors further back. It was entirely unalarming, and I just listened in a quiet kind of way. It wasn't until many years later that I realized that the ancestors themselves could be a source of healing for ancestral trauma.

Intact cultures have ancestral reverence practices that serve to honor our predecessors and awaken us to receive their wisdom. Indigenous traditions such as storytelling, song, and Earth stewardship are all crucial aspects of intergenerational connection, maintaining the bridge between ancestors and subsequent generations.[18] Rituals, such as the observance of the Yahrzeit in Jewish tradition or the Día de los Muertos in Mexican culture, keep us in relationship with our ancestors and interweave their continuing presence into the cycles of our days and years. There are many similar rituals across religions and cultures, and no matter your lineage, you will likely have numerous meaningful ancestralization practices that were once a deeply embedded part of your own ancestors' worldview. I believe that one of the reasons ancestral trauma is so pervasive in our society is that, unfortunately, so many of us have lost contact with these healing traditions, and therefore with our ancestors. Our pain, and our continuing living-forward of their wounds, thus serves as our primary bond, and our bind.

When we don't have practices that honor our ancestors and help them, and us, resolve the unhealed wounds, a process that would free us both, we remain in a knot of entangled love and pain. We may believe that if we let go of the pain, we will lose the love as well. Many of us feel we might be betraying our ancestors if we release their belief systems and survival strategies, even the ones that are rooted in their suffering and that continue to harm us, keeping us small and scared and disconnected. Our attachment to them is based on unconscious contracts we have made—to stay safe in the ways they learned to stay safe, to protect our hearts in the ways they needed to protect their hearts.

By rooting into ancestral reverence practices and connecting with our ancestors through imagery, embodiment, ritual, art, poetry, and dreaming, we can restore the health of our ancestral relationship. We can cultivate a relationship with them as we would with a living friend or relative; we pick up an imaginal phone, write a letter, light a candle for them, offer gifts, or ask for help. We let them know we are available to them and that we welcome their support. As we help our ancestors complete what was unfinished from their lifetimes, they can finally rest in their own connection to infinite wisdom. We open our hearts to receive their guidance, and they move into their rightful role as loving allies in the spirit world.

Learning Secure Attachment

Regardless of our ancestral inheritance or early childhood experiences, we all have the capacity to develop secure attachment. *Earned secure attachment* is a phrase often used to describe our capacity to develop secure attachment in adulthood. No matter our history, our brains are changeable and have the tremendous capacity to develop new neural pathways. As we release our trauma imprints, the dominance of the fear-based midbrain and brainstem lessens and we can access more readily the more linear thinking of the cortex. From this place, we have more capacity to develop a skillset for relationship building, skills that in turn help us feel safer in the world and more connected with others, creating a positive feedback loop that continues to rewrite brain and body mappings in the direction of secure attachment. When we feel safe on an unconscious, embodied level, we can create more safety by making self-nurturing choices, establishing healthy boundaries, and communicating skillfully; when we can create more safety, we in turn feel safer.

I like to call this process *learned secure attachment* to indicate that secure attachment isn't a privilege we have to earn but rather a skill, like a language or a craft, that we can all develop with practice. In recovery, regardless of our backgrounds, we can all take steps to grow into secure attachment. We can do this by getting to know both our fear of relationship and our longing for connection; by holding our need–fear dilemma with care and compassion; by aligning ourselves with reparative attachment experiences, such as those found with a skilled therapist or an attuned sponsor; by seeking out partners and friends who can offer consistent, mutual care and emotional accessibility; and, little by little, by prioritizing relational connection in our lives as the crucial key to healing in recovery.

Children who grew up in families impacted by ancestral traumas carry what can feel like an impossible tangle. In our mind, heart, ANS, and genetic expression, we carry the grief, terror, rage, and dreams of our ancestors, given to us even before we were born. It can feel like our very bones are carrying their memories. We are given roles and tasks that place on us the responsibility of saving those who died many years before our birth, or of redeeming their death. We can feel a complex knot of responsibility, guilt, allegiance, and anger at being placed in these roles, all of which provide a cover for the much deeper experience—the abyssal grief that comes with the realization that truly there was nothing we could have done, the acceptance of the loss itself.

Those of us with intergenerational trauma may have never had an experience of feeling held in a benevolent universe. Learning from our ancestors' experiences, we understood we needed to be on guard against always-imminent catastrophe; the world and the people around us could not be trusted to keep us safe. As we experience healing of our attachment wounds, we gain a felt sense that mutual love, not merely shared pain, is what binds us to them. Through meeting early developmental needs and gaining reparative attachment experiences, we repair the threads that weave one generation to the next, providing new possibilities for loving connection.

✳ Connecting with Your Ancestors (solo or with a partner)

Using the following questions, invite your partner to share the story of their ancestral lineage. Or, if doing this exercise by yourself, you can explore these questions in your journal. (Note: If you were adopted, you can do this exercise with a focus on either your adoptive family or your birth family, as preferred.)

This practice can also be done as an imaginal exercise: Invite your imagination to travel back in time to connect with your ancestors as if you are revisiting a dream or writing a story. Your ancestors' stories are present inside you, regardless of whether you know them consciously. Let yourself be guided by your body and your dreaming.

- Where was your family from?
- What stories were passed down in your family?
- Is there an ancestor you feel particularly connected to?
- What were your ancestors' religious or spiritual practices?
- What healing practices or plant allies did they draw on?[19]
- What professions were in your family?
- What languages did they speak?
- What was their relationship to the place they lived?
- What foods were important to them?
- What do you imagine they believed about the world? What were some important values and ethics for them?
- What helped them survive during difficult times?
- Where has your family lineage experienced healing? What wounds still need tending?
- Where are there gaps in your ancestral connection? How can they be mended?

Then, if doing this practice with a partner, switch roles, telling your story in response to your partner's questions.

After you have explored your ancestral lineage, take a few moments to notice how you feel in your body and any images or emotions that are present. Then conclude by reflecting: What is one thing I would like to do to nourish my connection with my ancestral lineage? For example, you could cook an ancestral food, make an ancestor altar, put up a photograph, plant an herb that was important to them, write a poem, or create some art. Make a commitment to one action that can help cultivate ongoing connection with your ancestors.

CHAPTER 3

Early Attachment and Adult Relationships

People are only as needy as their unmet needs.

—AMIR LEVINE AND RACHEL HELLER

Romantic love offers not just the excitement of the moment but the possibility for dramatic change in the self. It is, in fact, an agent of change.

—ETHEL PERSON

Our attachment inheritance and experiences in early life inform the development of our adult attachment style. Popularized by books such as *Attached, The Power of Attachment,* and *A General Theory of Love,* the framework describing adult attachment originated with psychologists John Bowlby and Mary Ainsworth's renowned research into young children's attachment behavior in relationship to their mothers.[1] These early relational patterns form what Bowlby called the *internal working model,* the set of inner representations and expectations that go on to shape relationships in adulthood with one's self and others.[2]

Adult attachment styles stem from the survival adaptations that developed in relation to the successes, limitations, and failures of the child's environment.[3] As explored in Chapter 1, children's basic needs include physical and emotional safety, love and connection, play, healthy boundaries, and support for their developing autonomy, all provided by dependable caregivers. In relation to how well and how consistently these needs are met, children will develop the beliefs and behaviors that allow them to best adapt to their environment. Often, to preserve the attachment with caregivers, the child must sacrifice her authenticity; if, for example, the parents are not able to hold the child's healthy aggression—the vital energy that supports selfhood, empowerment, and boundaries—the child will cut herself off from her anger in an attempt to maintain the loving connection that her survival depends upon.

In the midst of these early relational ruptures and misattunements, we develop a set of core binds that continue to define our journey through relationship in adulthood: our longing for connection versus our fear of connection; our need for authenticity versus our need to preserve the relationship at any cost; our impulse toward symbiotic union versus our reach for autonomy. These are the dilemmas that must be acknowledged and honored as the keystones of our behaviors in addiction and beyond. A critical part of the recovery journey is coming into contact with both sides of our dilemmas and holding the full picture: both our desire to isolate *and* our longing to connect; both our wish to express ourselves authentically *and* our fear of what might happen if we do so.

We can see our early attachment adaptations reflected in our adult relationships. If, for example, as a child you needed to protect yourself from boundary violations, your default mode in adulthood might be to retreat when feeling stressed. If as a child you experienced physical or emotional abandonment, in your adult relationship you may frantically pursue connection. Partners tend to have parallel wounds and complementary (i.e., opposing) attachment styles.

Adult attachment styles are generally categorized into secure attachment and three types of insecure attachment: anxious, avoidant, and disorganized. Insecure attachment goes hand in hand with addiction as we turn toward substances and addictive behaviors to navigate our core dilemmas and to mitigate feelings of anxiety, loneliness, rage, grief, and shame. So understanding your attachment tendencies can give you insight into your challenges and gifts as well as those of your partner. You can work with this understanding to develop more awareness of your underlying attachment needs and grow the skills to address these needs more directly.

If you are someone who has struggled with addiction, you will likely see yourself reflected in one of the descriptions of insecure attachment. The good news is, you're in great company! The tools of recovery, such as meetings, sponsorship, outreach calls, and meditation, are all ways we practice coming into contact with ourselves and others as we navigate the challenges of relationship and practice developing secure attachment skills together.

It's important to remember that our attachment tendencies are just that—tendencies. We all have a mix of the various styles, and certain ones may be triggered more than others, depending on the situation and relationship. Our attachment tendencies are malleable, and when our attachment needs are consistently met and our anxieties soothed, we all have the capacity to grow toward more secure attachment.

Secure Attachment

When Melissa met Jenny at a friend's dinner party, she immediately felt at ease. They started dating, and two years later they got married. Melissa experiences secure attachment in her partnership with Jenny; she and Jenny enjoy spending time together and can also spend time apart; when Jenny travels for work, they stay in contact with daily phone calls, and Melissa enjoys the time alone to focus on her music. She and Jenny navigate differences easily and come back together quickly after arguments. She can communicate her feelings in a calm way without blaming others, and she tolerates the ebb and flow of closeness without distress. In addition to Jenny, Melissa has a rich community of friends whom she looks to for support. While her professional life can be stressful, instead of turning to substances or technology to numb out, she draws on somatic practices, meditation, and daily walks to help diffuse feelings of anxiety.

Despite some substantial challenges in her childhood environment, Melissa's early relationships gave her what she needed to grow into an adult who navigates the realm of relationship with relative ease—in other words,

Melissa demonstrates secure attachment. Her tendency toward secure attachment was further developed by her journey in somatic therapy, which helped her gain awareness of the impact of early family dynamics, including the impact of intergenerational trauma, and allowed her to build a more connected relationship between her body and mind.

People with secure attachment tendencies generally feel loved in a loving universe. Their childhood environment provided the attunement, safety, and consistency that they needed to physically and emotionally thrive, to feel connected to others, and to develop confidence in themselves. They generally relate to others easily and with few preoccupations, and they can transition from time alone to time together with relative ease. Secure attachment is associated with the ventral vagal state; securely attached individuals can locate themselves more easily in their social engagement system and navigate the world anchored in a state of regulation. They can offer themselves love and encouragement, having internalized these qualities from their caregivers, and their mind will be able to attune to body experience with a sense of gentle curiosity.

Luckily, regardless of your childhood experiences, you can learn secure attachment in adulthood by seeking out reparative attachment experiences, healing the underlying traumas, and developing a new skill set for navigating your relationship with yourself and others. If you are a securely attached individual, you will likely attract and be comfortable in relationship with securely attached partners or will be able to help a more insecurely attached partner grow toward secure attachment.[4]

Anxious Attachment

Now in her early fifties, Anya has a core abandonment wound. As one of three siblings raised by a mother whom Anya describes as cold and emotionally absent, Anya's early needs for connection were rarely met. Her parents separated when she was young, and Anya and her siblings were caught in a difficult custody battle. While they were financially well-off, the overall feeling in her family was of emotional poverty. I notice how her childlike demeanor and endearing smile give me the feeling of wanting to take care of her; she never had what she needed to grow up fully.

Understandably, Anya moves through life with an underlying fear of abandonment. Her mother's emotional distance left Anya with a pervasive sense that her reach for connection will be rejected. Anya replicates this abandonment in herself as she focuses her energy on saving others, while remaining cut off from her own feelings and sensations. She approaches her husband, David, as a project to fix. Her distrust of him is discernable as she constantly urges him to dress better and work harder. He responds with big expressions of rage, which only serve to deepen her fear of abandonment and her expectation that her needs cannot be met.

Because her mother wasn't able to offer soothing coregulation, Anya didn't develop the skills for self-soothing and self-regulation, and she is easily overwhelmed by relational stressors. Her nervous system tends toward a constant state of high activation as she remains on the alert for potential abandonment, protesting any ruptures in connection. She attempts to manage this activation through the regular use of cannabis; the drug use also serves as a shared bond between her and David.

As a result of the emotional deficits of her early environment, Anya developed a strong tendency toward anxious attachment. Anxious attachment is an insecure attachment adaptation characterized by underlying fears of abandonment. Although it is also called ambivalent or preoccupied attachment, I like the term *anxious* because that's exactly what it feels like—intense worry triggered by the pain of real or perceived relational ruptures and the ever present possibility of loss.

The anxious attachment adaptation results from inconsistent, unreliable, or abandoning caregiving in childhood, stemming from the caregivers' own attachment wounds and anxieties. Children in this environment learn to be closely attuned to their caregivers, to scan for and predict possible shifts in the relational connection. They learn that moments of connection may be closely followed by abandonment, so it's hard for them to rely on and trust in the goodness of connection. As they start to explore the world, they may take on the parent's anxiety about possible threats, and they may not receive the support they need to develop autonomy and healthy boundaries.

In adulthood, people with this attachment adaptation tend to be vigilant to potential ruptures in relationship and require a lot of reassurance of the continued connection. For those of us with this attachment style, our core need is for love and nourishment, and we will often feel preoccupied until we receive the reassurance that we are cared for. In our intense focus on others, however, we also repeat our early abandonment by again and again abandoning ourselves.[5] Having learned that we needed to be vigilant to threats or sudden changes in our environment, it can be difficult to turn our awareness inward to track our sensations and emotions. Because our caregiver's mirroring was often insufficient or inconsistent, we may lack a basic vocabulary to describe our inner experience and may feel alone in the face of big feelings.

Anxious attachment can feed into addiction, as we reach to the substance or addictive behavior in an attempt to manage states of sympathetic activation, soothe our worries, and meet the attachment need that we feel cannot be met by another person.[6] As Diane Poole Heller writes, "If your self-regulatory functions aren't well developed, you will constantly look to others to down regulate, or calm, your overactive nervous system and oversensitive attachment system."[7] Inside our addicted adult self is a young child reaching for a nurturing presence. Underlying our anxiety are the fears that we are unlovable and that love is scarce, a limited resource, and that as much as we work for connection, our needs can never be met. While we will continually look for reassurance, for the missing pieces of coregulation, we're so hopeless of our needs ever being satisfied that when they are, we might not be able to really take it in. Laurence Heller and Aline LaPierre describe the core bind of those of us with this attachment style, saying, "There is a conflict between, on one hand, the expression of the need for physical or emotional nourishment, and the expectation of disappointment on the other."[8] Although we're comfortably familiar with the discomfort of hopeless yearning, we're not as adept at noticing and receiving love.

When our need for nourishment isn't met, we engage in the adult version of a child's protest cry. Unfortunately if you didn't experience the safety or learn the skills to express your needs directly, this distress can often come out as blame, jealousy, or criticism, unfortunately resulting in the opposite effect than intended as partners feel shamed, pressured, or rejected, and in turn protect themselves by withdrawing or defending themselves with anger. As Thich Nhat Hanh wrote, "You must love in such a way that the person you love feels free."[9] For those of us with an anxious attachment style, this is easier said than done, as we often default to controlling behavior in an attempt to get our needs met.

Because we are navigating so much of our own pain, it is difficult for us to see our part in conflicts. The less we feel heard, the louder we will cry out in an attempt to communicate our pain to the other person. Furthermore, when our partners do offer care, it can be hard to receive their nurturance since we tend to distrust it or dismiss it, fearing it will soon be taken away. We might also project our own fears of intimacy onto our partners, believing they are the ones blocking the closeness we are longing for; however, while they may be the one most explicitly asserting the need for space, our own fears of intimacy are an equivalent part of this dynamic. If they were to turn and meet us fully in the intimacy we are craving, we may soon start to encounter our own disavowed fear of closeness and need for autonomy.

Those of us with this attachment style have a tendency to see the relationship through a negative lens or as a problem to be solved, whereas our partners may prefer to leave well enough alone. We may be more inclined to discuss our concerns and seek out help, though our tendency may be to blame our partner and see them as the source of the problem, rather than to view the field of the relationship as a shared and cocreated space. A big learning for anxiously attached individuals comes when we fully realize that we are equal partners in the dance of disconnection.

Each attachment style also comes with many gifts. People with a tendency toward anxious attachment are often caring and attentive to others, empathically attuned, and intuitive. Recognizing the way we abandon ourselves, we can benefit from learning to compassionately turn our caring capacities toward our own inner experience, to track sensation and emotions, and identify and honor our needs and desires. If you have a friend, fellow, sponsee, or partner with this relational style, you can help them achieve more secure attachment by offering consistency and reassurance, saying "I'm right here with you" or "I'm not going anywhere" and being curious with them about their inner experience, helping them find words to describe their internal world.

If you have this attachment adaptation, you may also wish to learn some skills to express your needs in ways that won't feed into cycles of disconnect in your relationship; you can learn to ask for help in getting your connection needs met, to make a direct request instead of waiting for your partner to guess your needs, and to speak from your underlying vulnerability instead of the self-protective stance of blame and criticism. Nonviolent Communication, Imago, and Emotionally Focused Therapy all offer helpful frameworks for creating heart-connected conversations and looking at our part in the shared dynamic. For people like Anya, and for all of us with this attachment tendency, growth occurs through developing our capacity to soothe our fearful Little One, building our awareness of our needs and emotions, repairing abandonment wounds by lovingly tending to our inner experience, and learning new skills for communication.

At its best, Twelve Step recovery can support this attachment style by helping members develop skills for self-soothing and self-nurturance. Program practices such as prayer and meditation, self-care, and reaching out for support from the fellowship can help those of us with anxious attachment develop more capacity for self-regulation and help meet our need for nurturing relationship. At its worst, the program can keep members stuck in the loop of insecure relationship dynamics: Sponsors and fellows may give uninformed advice, label our anxieties as codependent, or urge us to detach from our partners instead of teaching us how to ask for the connection and reassurance we need. For anxiously attached members, meetings may become a space to complain about their partnerships, which they do in place of learning the skills to express their vulnerable feelings directly to their partners. These common program pitfalls can reiterate the disavowal or suppression of our core needs and recapitulate old narratives based in shame and self-judgment. Similarly, many program adages speak from and reiterate this shame: "I don't have relationships, I take hostages" or "my picker is broken." These adages add shame to shame, failing to recognize with compassion that our choice of partners and our anxious actions in relationships are a reflection of the profound abandonment pain that we carry from childhood when our reach for loving connection was not met.

If you tend toward anxious attachment, it is likely your partner will have avoidant attachment tendencies, so it can be useful to learn more about those tendencies in order to best understand and meet your partner, and to interrupt cycles of disconnection when they occur.

Skill-Building for People with an Anxious Attachment Style

✳ Creating a Vocabulary of Experience

As a way of getting to know your inner experience, you can start by getting to know your sensations. Start by closing your eyes and inviting the muscles behind your eyes to soften. Notice your breathing without needing to change it. Then bring your awareness to meet the sensations around the exterior of the body: Notice the sensations where your hands are meeting each other or resting on your legs; feel your back where it meets the chair behind you; sense your buttocks and thighs where they meet the seat beneath you. You can also notice the sensation of your clothing touching your skin, or your glasses resting on the bridge of your nose. Start by doing this practice for five minutes a day or until it feels complete. After completing the meditation, take a moment to make a list in your journal of the sensations you noticed. Sensations may include words of texture, temperature, or pressure, such as *itchy*, *soft*, *heavy*, *warm*, and *cool*; the sensations of emotions or impulses, such as *safe*, *tearful*, *restless*, *comfortable*, and *irritated*; and colors or images, such as *blue*, *round*, *metallic*, *tangled*, and *sunshine*.

After practicing this for some time, for several weeks or until you feel like you're establishing a sensation vocabulary, expand the practice to include sensations in the interior of the body. You can add on to the prior meditation, bringing your awareness to notice sensations in your pelvic bowl. Then notice any awareness in your belly. Expand your awareness to include your solar plexus and the respiratory diaphragm traversing the body inside the ribcage. Then expand your attention to include your heart, and then include an awareness of your throat, mouth, and face. If you can't sense the interior of the body, it can be helpful to find a little movement rocking your body side to side, or offer yourself some touch, resting your hand on the place on your body where you are bringing your attention. Then add this sensation vocabulary to your journal, including sensation words such as *light*, *dense*, *spacious*, *pain*, *ease*; emotions or impulses, such as *sadness*, *anger*, *frustration*, *joy*; and any colors or images that come to mind.

✳ Practicing Direct Communication

In our best attempt to communicate our feelings to our partners, sometimes we can express ourselves in ways that may land as criticism, which in turn triggers our partners' self-protective strategies. For example, we might say, "Where were you last night? You said you'd be home at ten." Unfortunately, rather than empathizing with our unmet need for connection, our partner will likely sense the implicit criticism in this statement, which touches their shame. They will then likely reply defensively with anger or withdrawal. We will then feel even more abandoned and will escalate our protest cries, which emerge as more anger and blame. This in turn only further touches our partners' shame and self-protection. At this point we might have lost sight entirely of the original issue and are now caught in a painful cycle of disconnection, wherein both partners feel hurt and misunderstood.

In order to interrupt this cycle, or prevent it from starting in the first place, you can use the following template for more direct communication. If it feels vulnerable to express your needs directly, it can be helpful to imagine that you are advocating for your child self, who did not have the support or safety they needed in order to learn to express themself and their needs authentically at the time.

[*Factual description of the event*] + [*core feelings*] + [*core need*] + [*direct request*]

For instance:

"When you arrived home at eleven instead of ten [*factual description of event*], I felt angry and fearful [core feelings]. I'm needing some reassurance that you love me and that you're not going to disappear on me [*core need*]. Next time you're going to be out late, would you be willing to let me know [*direct request*]?"

In addition to practicing new conversation skills, it's helpful to develop the capacity for a *meta-conversation*, that is, having a conversation about the conversation. The practice of meta-conversation can help you and your partner learn more about what happens when you get caught in cycles of disconnect and what works best to repair connection. So after trying out this conversation skill, ask your partner how it was to hear you express yourself in this way. You can share with them as well how it was for you to try out this skill.

✱ Finding the Need-Noun

Because we carry the implicit belief that our needs cannot be met, we often express them in forceful but indirect ways that can be confusing or triggering for the other person. One way that we can clarify our expression and ease communication with our partner is to frame the need with a *need-noun* instead of a pronoun: I need + [*need-noun*] (*love, reassurance, touch, space, support, commitment*) instead of I need + [*pronoun*] (*you to commit, you to give me space, you to respect me*). Unfortunately, though common in American English, the communication tendency of "I need you to . . ." can land for the other person as an attempt to control them, especially if they have any childhood wounding in the area of autonomy; they will then react from their own triggers rather than hearing your need. Instead, if you want to ask someone to do something or change their behavior, try framing it as a request: "I need some support right now. Could you please take care of dinner?"

It is easy to replace this old habit with more skillful communication. Simply notice if you are going to say, "I need you to . . .," omit the "you to . . .," and replace it with an expression of the core need. It can be helpful to write out your statements before a conversation while you're getting the hang of it.

Try it out with these various need-nouns or find your own:

- Love
- Support
- Nurturance
- Touch (what kind would feel best right now?)
- Time
- Space
- I need _______.
- I need _______.
- I need _______.

Follow this with a specific request for your partner to meet your need:

"Could you please _______ [feed the cat / give me a hug / rub my feet / give me a few days to think about it]?"

✳ What Are You Fighting For?

When you and your partner are in a conflict, ask for a pause to explore the question "What am I fighting for?" Journal or meditate to inquire: What is the need that I am advocating for? For instance, you might be fighting for connection or to feel heard, understood, and acknowledged. If you feel the need to be right, what would "being right" offer you or help you feel at the deepest level?

Then return to the conversation and express this need to your partner, inviting them to share their need as well. It's helpful to reassure your partner that you are upset precisely because they mean so much to you. This reassurance will help assuage their worry about "not getting it right" and remind them that your anger is a cry that protests a breach in connection. Remind your partner that your feelings are arising precisely because of your yearning for loving connection with them.

✱ From "Why" to Core Feelings

For those of us with an anxious attachment style, we can have the tendency to ask "why" or express confusion when actually we're feeling angry. "Why" questions can be an oblique expression of disappointment, anger, and our underlying needs, and they tend to land for our partners as implicit criticism. For instance, "Why didn't you do the dishes?" can express two things:

First (and this is generally what it means): "I'm angry at you for not doing the dishes."

Second, an actual question: "I don't understand what happened."

Regardless, your partner will likely hear: "You are such a jerk for not doing the dishes."

So instead of "Why didn't you do the dishes?" try expressing the core feeling underneath: "When you didn't do the dishes, I felt angry." If your question is an expression of genuine curiosity, you can use the phrase "Help me understand"; for example, "Help me understand what was going on for you when you didn't do the dishes."

Expressing anger is challenging because early on we learned that doing so could threaten relational connection. We had to choose between our authenticity and the relationship. However, the fact is that if we name our anger, in a direct and calm way, it actually increases connection, whereas the strategies that attempt to avoid expressing anger generally result in further escalation and disconnect. Naming our anger is a risk we can start to take in recovery, and one that may result in greater closeness as you find that the dance is different now than the one you learned in childhood.

✳ Recognizing Your Partner's Need for Space

As your partner is practicing their own assertion of needs, you can support them by proactively offering them time and space. If they seem like they're starting to get overwhelmed, as indicated by their irritation, anger, or withdrawal, you can offer them some time to regroup: "I wonder if this might be a good time to pause for a little bit, and then reconvene in twenty minutes to finish the conversation. How does that sound to you?" This can be challenging to do in the middle of a conflict, when both people's nervous systems are responding to a perceived threat, and when your own tendency might be to fight for a restoration of the connection as quickly as possible. It can be helpful to practice this skill in less intense moments—for instance, at the end of a long day when you sense your partner might just be needing some time to recharge—so that you have the skill in your toolkit for more challenging situations.

✳ Self-Regulating in the Pause

During the pause, take the time to offer your child self some love. Your Little One is scared of abandonment and worried their needs for connection can't be met. So you can help soothe your child self by bringing in some practices for regulation through connection with yourself or others, such as breathing with long exhalations, making a phone call to a friend or fellow, practicing prayer or meditation, going for a walk, or any other practice that is part of your toolkit of resources.

Avoidant Attachment

Marcus grew up in a chaotic family as the oldest of four siblings. His parents worked hard to meet his material needs and provide him with a top education. Neither parent, however, could offer warmth or consistent emotional connection; his father, a distant masculine presence, was consumed by a high-stress job and eventually moved away, and his mother, while more available, was unpredictable and would often explode in anger. After his father left, she was completely dependent on Marcus for emotional connection. Marcus struggled to meet his parents' high expectations of him, including that he become a lawyer like his father.

In adulthood Marcus tends to get stuck in long-term relationships with women whom he describes as needy and dependent. He finds himself unable to leave them when he wants to, relying on a move to another city or an affair to exit the relationship. He has no trouble meeting women; indeed, many find him irresistible, as his withdrawn energy comes across as mysterious and seductive. In each relationship, he devotes himself to meeting his girlfriend's needs, and when she expresses discontent in any form, he blows up in anger or shuts down. Of his current relationship, he explains, "No matter what I do, it's never good enough for her." When I ask him to stay with what's going on inside, he describes feeling cold, numb, and alone. His nervous system is speaking in the language of dorsal vagal collapse. Marcus, who has been in recovery from cocaine for several years, now recognizes that he had been using the drug's activating qualities to mitigate this immobilization response.

Marcus has a strong tendency toward avoidant attachment, a tendency that is further provoked by his partner's anxious attachment style. The avoidant attachment adaptation results from a child's experience of inconsistent, rejecting, or engulfing parenting. The child might have learned that love was conditional, that it depended on meeting the caregivers' spoken or unspoken needs and expectations. Children in this environment will learn not to rely on others to meet their needs, developing a false identity of self-sufficiency. They will shut down their needs and authentic expression of emotions, cutting off body awareness and desires, and withdraw into themselves when others' energies or emotions threaten their boundaries. In order to ensure love, they will often develop an outer persona meant to appeal to others, a nice, successful, or entertaining self that hides the parts of the self that are deemed unacceptable—the underlying shame and rage.

Because their needs were not sufficiently attuned to as children, people with this attachment tendency are split off from their dependency needs, which they experience as shameful. In adulthood, those of us with this attachment adaptation will often view others as needy and emotional, as we project the seemingly unacceptable parts of ourselves onto the other person.

Our sense of safety can heavily depend on our partner's happiness; if we can "make" our partner happy, we feel a tenuous sense of security and self-coherence; if our partner's mood fluctuates or they express disappointment in us or the relationship, touching our underlying shame and fragmentation, we can respond with controlling, angry, or distancing behavior in an attempt to bring our self back into coherence. In Marcus's case, his sense of selfhood depended on fulfilling his role as his mother's protector, a job he replicated in his romantic relationships.

This attachment style can present as self-sufficiency and avoidance of intimacy. Cut off from our own emotions, we are easily overwhelmed by the emotions of others. We may avoid connection, need lots of space, and shut down or suddenly blow up in conflict. Fearful of being annihilated, we may withdraw in an attempt to shore up a fragile sense of selfhood. Due to a lack of attunement and mirroring in childhood, we didn't develop capacities for self-regulation, so we may get flooded by emotion, both our own and others, and we will withdraw in order to protect ourselves, or we will show an outburst of rage to set boundaries we don't know how to assert in other ways. Because our wellbeing depends on our partner's happiness, and our own feelings are disavowed, we will implicitly or explicitly communicate the message to our partners that their feelings are crazy, unacceptable, or "too much."

The core fears here are "If I'm truly seen, I'll be rejected," "love is conditional," and "I'm never enough." Of the two attachment styles, those of us with avoidant attachment may seem as if we are cool and collected, independent, and self-reliant. However, our avoidance is a strategy we use to manage the fear of connection, and when we start to move toward greater intimacy, we often experience hyperarousal and become flooded with anxiety. When we do, we may shut down as a way of managing this overwhelm. Accordingly, we are often less inclined than our partners to seek out support such as individual or couples therapy for issues in the relationship, and we will often minimize problems or prefer to let sleeping dogs lie.

For Marcus, growth will occur when he can reclaim the missing pieces of autonomy, healthy dependency, and authenticity. Instead of shutting down or blowing up when overwhelmed, he can recognize his need for space and communicate this need to his girlfriend. As he finds the boundaries that weren't supported in childhood, he can make a more conscious decision about staying in relationships and feel less stuck in a morass of what feels like external circumstances. As he grows in his capacity to come into relationship with himself and his Little One, he can start to unwind his chronic shame, recognizing the shame response as not merely a present-day reaction to his partner's complaints but as the cry of a young child whose needs went unmet. When feeling rejected, he can practice asking for reassurance that he is loved, desired, and good enough for his partner.

For those of us with this attachment adaptation, the key skills are to develop the capacity to track internal sensation and emotion, to notice when we're starting to get flooded, and to ask for time and space to self-regulate. Learning to set limits is an essential capacity. Then, once we return to the relational field in a more regulated way, having been able to successfully assert our needs for time and space, we can offer our partners the connection they need. We can practice self-regulation while also learning to ask for and accept love and coregulation from our partners. As we learn to trust in our capacity to assert our boundaries in more direct ways, we start to feel safer in relationship. Having clear boundaries facilitates loving connection; in turn, loving connection facilitates a more solid sense of self, allowing us to renegotiate old narratives and core fears through the healing power of being seen, cherished, and accepted.

At its best, Twelve Step recovery can support people with avoidant attachment tendencies by encouraging them to lean into relationship, to reach out for help, and to start to develop healthy dependency on a sponsor and the group. At its worst, the program can reiterate avoidant patterns of self-reliance by discouraging members from pursuing dating relationships, deemphasizing current partnerships and the attachment needs of partners in order to "prioritize recovery," and encouraging a reliance on Step work and program slogans instead of promoting trauma-informed therapies.[10]

If your tendency is toward avoidant attachment, it is highly likely that your partner will have anxious attachment tendencies. It can be useful to learn more about their tendencies as well as your own in order to better understand and meet your partner and to interrupt cycles of conflict when they occur.

Skill-Building for People with an Avoidant Attachment Style

✳ Tracking Sensations of Overwhelm

As soon as you and your partner are starting to get into an argument, ask for a pause, and check in with your body sensations and the related impulse. Do you feel hot? Cold? Agitated? Numb? How do these sensations relate to your movement impulse? Do you feel like you want to fight? Run away? Hide? Getting to know your inner experience will help you start to recognize when you are starting to feel flooded and interrupt the cycle before you default to old strategies.

✳ Asking for Time and Space

Let your partner know that the next time you feel overwhelmed you are going to ask for some time out but that you will be back soon. Discuss with your partner how much time would feel right for you for a reset while also not leaving them in the lurch. I would suggest twenty minutes, but you can decide on another time period if something different would feel better to you both.

Next time you notice you are starting to feel flooded, consciously take this time out. Communicate your request directly to your partner while also meeting their need for reassurance so as not to trigger their fears of abandonment. You can try saying: "I'm feeling pretty overwhelmed right now. I'd like to take twenty minutes to reset, and then let's check in. How does that sound to you?"

Remember that your partner's core fear may be abandonment. So if you take time to pause, let them know when you'll be back, and then stick to your promise. This will help soothe their fear, and when you do come back together, you'll both be more able to have a connecting conversation.

✳ Self-Regulating in the Pause

During the break, take the time to offer your overwhelmed inner child some love. Your Little One is scared of rejection, or worried that their fragile, developing self might be swallowed up. You can help soothe your Little One by bringing in your favorite practices for self-regulation, such as breathing with long exhalations, practicing prayer or meditation, taking a walk, making some art, journaling, writing a list of your needs and feelings, or any other practice that is part of your toolkit.

✳ Navigating *I* and *We*

When you integrate the word *we* into your conversations, it can help soothe your partner's anxiety and let them know that you are moving through the world in connection with them. It can also help you feel a part of the partnership as you explore being a self-in-relationship. At the same time, the word *I* can help you sense and affirm your boundaries. The word *I* can open important statements such as "I feel ________," "I want ________," and "I need ________." The words *we* and *us* can be part of phrases emphasizing a teamwork approach, such as "We'll find a solution together," "Let's explore ________," or "How might we meet this need together?" Moving between *I* and *we*, and knowing when you need to be located in each, is an important part of the growth process in recovery.

✳ Journaling 3x3

In your journal, take some time to explore your inner world. This practice can help you get in touch with parts of your inner experience that may not have had space for full expression. In your journal make three categories:

"I feel ________."

"I want ________."

"I need ________."

Each day, write a list of at least three items in each category. For example:

I feel	sad fearful lonely
I want	a vacation a garden to go for a walk
I need	space to myself rest comfort

✳ Moving with Boundaries (with a partner)

For those of us with an avoidant attachment tendency, it can be hard to assert boundaries in a healthy way because early on we learned the only way to protect our energetic space was to withdraw or disappear. Using this exercise based in Somatic Experiencing, you can practice sensing and asserting boundaries by exploring the space around you with your partner.

Start by facing your partner so that you are both holding a large pillow between you. As your partner maintains contact with the pillow and follows your movement, explore drawing the pillow toward you. When you feel like it's come close enough, explore pushing it away. Again, your partner maintains contact with the pillow as they follow your impulse. Explore these movements, of drawing it toward you and pushing it away, for several minutes. Then, when you feel complete, take a moment to check in with your emotions and sensations, and share your experience with your partner. Then switch roles, and go through the exercise again with your partner as the lead.

When they are finished with the movement practice, ask them to share their emotions and sensations with you. Then discuss: What have we learned about boundaries in our relationship? Is it easier to assert or receive them? If some aspect was challenging, what made it difficult? What does asserting and receiving boundaries bring up for us? When in the exercise did we feel most in-synch? What does the exercise highlight about ways we would each like to navigate boundaries in our relationship?

Disorganized Attachment

Josh and Elliot have been together for a year, though inconsistently since they break up every couple of weeks. Both in their early thirties, they met at an AA meeting, and this is their first sober relationship. Elliot and Josh say that when things are going well, they feel so connected; they enjoy going to the farmer's market together and walking on the beach, and the sex is fantastic. Elliot is in love with Josh's vulnerability and his warm smile. Josh appreciates Elliot's sense of humor. This sense of loving connection can quickly sour, however, as an offhand comment from Elliot will send Josh into a rage and he'll storm out. They won't speak for several days until they run into each other at a meeting and get back together. This volatile pattern goes on week after week. Josh describes Elliot as abusive and accuses him of gaslighting; meanwhile, Elliot wonders if Josh has narcissistic personality disorder, which he looked up on the internet.

Josh and Elliot display the characteristics of disorganized attachment, which results from abuse or neglect in childhood. Disorganized attachment develops when a child learns that having needs leads to pain, and that the caregiver, who is the source of love, is also a threat. The child's reach for connection is met with punishment, rejection, or violence. The child learns it's not safe to need or want love, and that having needs only results in pain. As will be discussed in Chapter 7, the caregiver's neglect of the child's needs sows the seeds for chronic shame, which then becomes the driver of addiction.

This painful cycle continues in adulthood as the person both fears and desires contact. For those of us with this attachment tendency, moments of intimacy may spark terror, and we may react with anger or by abruptly cutting off connection. When our longing for contact draws us once again into connection, our fear may once again be activated. Some core beliefs are "I don't matter," "It's not safe," and "Vulnerability will result in pain." When this fear is touched, we may react with sudden rage or abruptly shut down. Both of these strategies are meant to protect us from overwhelming feelings of fragmentation and disintegration. The nervous system of those of us with this style functions primarily in a blended state of sympathetic activation in the face of potential threat coupled with the immobilization response associated with terror and shame.

The key task for those of us with a disorganized style is to develop a core sense of safety. Self-soothing practices and the capacity to track inner states are important skills to develop. A relationship with a skilled attachment-based practitioner can be key to finding the consistency and safety that was lacking in early life. Working closely with a sponsor who can provide reassuring and stabilizing contact and lend you the regulation of their nervous system is key to navigating life in recovery. Also useful are body-centered modalities such as Somatic Experiencing or NeuroAffective Touch (see the "Resources" section on page 237) that can help you develop a felt sense of safety, resolve trauma, and restore nervous system regulation.

For couples such as Elliot and Josh, the key to interrupting cycles of disconnect is for each individual to be committed to their own healing journey. Each partner, by learning to track their inner states, can practice asking for reassurance or for space as needed. By recognizing their partner's attacks and withdrawals as cries of protest, they can take these disruptions less personally, offering phrases such as "Take all the time you need" and "I'm here when you're ready," and tending to their own self-soothing until their partner is more able to connect.[11]

Working with a couples therapist or relationship coach can help couples piece out accusations of "gaslighting," "toxicity," and "narcissism" from their overuse in pop culture and social media, and determine if a relationship is indeed abusive. If it is, the couple should draw on professional assistance to discern whether the relationship has room to grow into one that will be safe and healthy for both parties, and to get support to leave a dangerous situation or terminate the relationship if necessary. If not, the practice is for each person to more vulnerably name their own experience without using accusatory terms that will certainly trigger and confuse their partner and to instead practice the relational skill of speaking with "I" statements to share feelings, needs, and requests.

Remember that your partner is struggling as much as you are! It's not that they have it all figured out and are being intentionally obstructive. They, like you, are frightened and overwhelmed; they have trouble knowing and naming their feelings; and their ANS has the same built-in self-protective strategies as yours does. While indeed some very wounded individuals are intentionally manipulative, more often than not, people are simply struggling with fear, overwhelm, and shame and are reacting with the associated physiological responses.

If you suspect that you and/or your partner have disorganized attachment tendencies, the core practice is to work on creating a shared sense of safety, building the partnership as a sanctuary from an overwhelming world, in which you can stand side by side to meet each other's fears together. In the space of the relationship, you can each recognize your own and your partner's pain and direct your anger and sense of injustice where it belongs—at the long-ago circumstances that created the trauma in the first place—rather than toward each other. As safety is established, the relationship can become a sacred space where core wounds are renegotiated and each person moves toward secure attachment.

At their best, Twelve Step programs can support this attachment style by providing a space for connection. The fellowship can offer a circle of care to help disorganized members practice being in relationship, asserting boundaries and needs, and receiving support. Prayer, meditation, and self-care practices can help you learn to befriend inner states and learn essential skills for self-soothing. At its worst, the program can touch into early traumas if meetings and sponsors reiterate shaming messages or fail to offer trauma-sensitive care, coregulation, and reflections attuned to the profound vulnerabilities of disorganized individuals. Unless supplemented by somatic or relational therapies, the program can fail to meet the core needs of these individuals. The top-down, cognitive-behavioral approach of conventional Twelve Step recovery can mirror or even accentuate the trauma response of dissociation and immobilization that defines the experience of disorganized individuals. Instead, they need bottom-up, body-based experiences of relational safety and attunement in order to heal from trauma, negotiate new conceptions of self-identity, and establish new norms of behavior.

Skill-Building for People with a Disorganized Attachment Style

You can draw on the practices for both anxious and avoidant styles, as well as the following practices.

✳ What Does Your Little One Need?

When you are feeling upset, take some time out and imagine the upset or angry part of you as a young child. How would you approach a young child who is crying? You might imagine you are meeting your Little One with a hug and some soothing. It can be helpful to place a hand on your heart and rock your body, as if you were rocking a child. Sense what your Little One is needing—for instance, love, care, reassurance, acknowledgment, or companionship. Can you meet those needs in this moment?

✳ Meeting Your Partner's Little One (with a partner)

Sit or lie down so that you're facing each other. Cup or caress your partner's face with your hands. Soften your gaze as you take in their eyes, their expression, their mouth. Imagine that you can travel through the image of their present self back in time to see them as a child. See the sweetness of that young child in your partner's face. See their eagerness to love and be loved. See their open-hearted longing for connection. See their disappointment at the ways their longing was unmet. See the ways they were vulnerable and were hurt. Invite your heart to open to your partner's Little One. Notice what it feels like to see them in this way.

When you have completed the exercise, switch roles.

When you have both experienced each role, seeing and being seen, share with each other what it was like to do this practice. What did you perceive about the other person? How did you feel when you connected with their child self? What was it like to be seen?

✷ Being an Anchor for Your Partner

It's hard not to take your partner's reactivity personally as it can touch all of your core fears of being rejected or abandoned. Remember that your partner is responding from a young place in themself. In a moment of fragmentation, they need you to be the loving and consistent parent. A loving parent responds to a child's protest behavior by regulating their own system and being an external regulator for the frightened child.

One of the best ways you can support your partner is to stay centered in yourself when they get thrown off. Next time your partner is suddenly withdrawing or is reactively angry, take some time to anchor yourself along your midline, rocking back and forth until you feel your sit bones meeting the chair beneath you, and connecting with the movement of your breath. From this place, you can offer your partner some reassurance, such as "I'm right here with you," "I'm not going anywhere," or "Sweetie, you mean so much to me." At the same time, your practice of self-regulation can nonverbally help soothe their dysregulated nervous system and help them reorient toward connection.

Attachment Styles and the Twelve Steps

From these descriptions it's easy to see that our relational behaviors stem from a very tender place—our underlying need for safety and connection—and that the behaviors that most hurt us and others, or that inadvertently push others away, emerge from the pain and fear of abandonment, rejection, and loss. Given the profound correlation between addiction and attachment wounds, it's likely that at any given Twelve Step meeting, you will be surrounded by people who share aspects of your attachment story.

The positive side of this shared ground is that you will likely hear narratives of suffering and healing that you can relate to, that can help you feel less alone, and that, in turn, lessen shame and isolation. We're all in the same boat, sharing our pain, healing from attachment wounds, and learning secure attachment together. However, there is also a potentially detrimental side to this shared territory: When you are surrounded by others with insecure attachment tendencies, you may receive feedback and advice from fellows and sponsors who are continuing to enact insecure attachment patterns themselves, who aren't knowledgeable about the impacts of developmental trauma in themselves and others, and who haven't yet learned secure attachment skills or grown fully into their secure attachment capacities.

Many of the common slogans and narratives in the program reflect and reiterate insecure attachment dynamics; they encourage members to detach rather than practice the crucial secure attachment skill of maintaining a tether, or they urge them to "suit up and show up" instead of acknowledging the deep fear of connection and honoring this dilemma with compassion for both sides of the bind.[12] Feedback from sponsors and fellows may also inadvertently or directly shame members for their dependency needs, labeling them as codependent. These messages only serve to put salt in the wound of relational trauma, reiterating early messages that your needs cannot be met and must be shut down, messages that form the underpinnings of shame and therefore addiction itself.

In still other situations, members are sometimes encouraged not to date long past the one-year mark, shutting down the life-force of their longing for relationship, a longing that is, at essence, a sign of vitality and healing. As my friend, five years sober, said, "How am I supposed to learn how to have a relationship if I'm not allowed to have a relationship?" Being discouraged from pursuing relationship reiterates a core bind from early childhood—the hopeless longing and endless waiting that defined a reach for parental contact that never came—instead of helping members move more fluidly in the direction of their longing, which ultimately leads toward more life and a true resolution of early childhood imprints.

Bringing consciousness to attachment dynamics is one of the most important steps we can take to make recovery spaces more trauma informed and to help them grow into true spaces of healing. Instead of having to will ourselves out of our relational and dependency needs or suppress anxieties and fears, we can receive and offer attachment-informed support from the group and from sponsors who remind us that loving connection is our birthright as a human being. We can give and receive advice that can help us turn toward relationship instead of away from it, helping us meet our own deep need for connection and become more responsive allies for our partners.

Practices for All Attachment Styles

✶ The Spectrum of Attachment

Our attachment adaptations are fluid, and we cocreate with the other person the unique dance of the relationship. For example, I tend to be a bit anxious unless I'm with someone who is more anxious than I am, in which case I start becoming more avoidant. Anxious and avoidant tendencies constellate each other; one person's anxiety will bring forth the other's avoidance, and vice versa, as each person negotiates a precarious balance between the need for intimacy and the need for autonomy.

Chart out a relationship to better understand your dance of attachment. You can do this exercise for your partnership or any other significant relationship. For example:

With *my partner,* I tend to be:

Anxious ____________X________________________ Avoidant

And he tends to be:

Anxious ______________________________X__________ Avoidant

The more I . . . ***push for connection,***
the more he . . . ***shuts down.***
The more he . . . ***shuts down,***
the more I . . . ***push for connection.***

Now it's your turn!

With ______________ I tend to be:

Anxious ______________________________________ Avoidant

And they tend to be:

Anxious ______________________________________ Avoidant

The more I ______________________________________
the more they ______________________________________
The more they ______________________________________
the more I ______________________________________

✳ Accessing the Wisdom of the Heart

Our attachment adaptations are fear-based patterns, and ultimately the field of the heart is more powerful than any insecure attachment imprint. Accessing the heart's guidance can help awaken the much more potent forces of love and wisdom, allowing you and your partner to transcend any outdated protective strategies and enter into new visions for relational possibilities. Here are two practices to access heart consciousness.

Holding Your Partner in Your Heart

This practice is for reducing obsession and attachment anxiety. As you place your partner in your heart for safekeeping, you will be able to maintain the connection without relying on rumination to keep your partner "in mind." The heart is a much more spacious and capable container than the mind for keeping your partner safe and close by.

To do this practice, start by bringing an image of your partner to mind. Notice all the aspects of the image in detail. Then, imagine you are dropping the image down from your mind to your heart. Now let go of the picture and just sense that you are holding your partner in your heart. Notice how this feels inside. What shifts in your relationship to them?

Do this practice every morning. You might even let your partner know "I am holding you in my heart." You can also return to this practice anytime you find yourself anxiously ruminating about your partner or feeling suspicious, critical, or insecure. Notice how it shifts your energy.

Holding Your Partner to Your Heart (with a partner)

One person starts as the giver and the other as the receiver. As the giver, lie down on your back. Cradle your partner so that their head is resting on your heart. Hold their body, supporting the base of their skull and their back. Breathe into this connection together for several minutes, noticing your rhythms aligning as your breathing entrains with your partner's. When this feels complete, change roles.

After you have both experienced each role, take some time to share with each other about your experience.

✳ Orienting to Connection (with a partner)

When one or both partners are triggered, connection can be lost in an instant. Particularly for those of us with early trauma, the sense of loving connection can vanish the moment our shame or fear is touched. If in a moment of conflict we look at the relationship through that lens, it can feel as if all the goodness that ever existed has completely drained away, and the relationship appears doomed, rewritten entirely through the perspective of the current pain.

In order to prepare in advance for the inevitable moments of disconnection, do this exercise together at a time when you're feeling relaxed and connected. Sit down together with some paper and pens, crayons, old magazines, or other art supplies. Together, reflect on all the ways you connect, remembering the most beautiful times of contact and what you love about each other. Then, together, make a list, drawing, or collage that represents your connection, including meaningful moments you've shared, the qualities of your partner you love most, and words or pictures that describe what it feels like when you know you are loved. Put your art up somewhere where you can see it readily, and the next time your sense of relationship starts to collapse, refer to it as a reminder of the deeper truth of the relationship. This practice can serve as a relational sight line, restoring you to a wider perspective and helping you hold your current (and momentary!) rupture in the greater field of ongoing love.

✳ Building Your Secure Attachment Playlist

Those of us with a tendency toward insecure attachment often have a short playlist of available responses to relational stressors. We'll have our go-to song of withdrawal, anger, blame, or criticism, with limited access to or awareness of other possible repertoires.

In program, we are often reminded to act "as if," to practice new behaviors and take actions from a place of recovery even if we haven't yet internalized these changes or beliefs. While we are doing the slow, overarching work of healing old attachment wounds, we can practice acting "as if" in the meantime. We can respond to our partners from a place of security, creating an atmosphere of safety and responsiveness, which in turn helps them engage in a similar manner, resulting in a positive feedback loop of secure attachment. These secure attachment behaviors help us expand our playlist, giving us additional options for possible actions. You can also practice acting "as if" with friends, family members, or fellows, using many of these same skills.

Some elements of a secure attachment playlist include

- Being available: responding to calls and texts in a timely way
- Being reliable: showing up on time; keeping promises and commitments
- Staying tethered: reaching out to let your partner know you are thinking of them
- Being curious: asking questions; demonstrating you are interested in the other person's inner world; creating mutual conversation
- Inviting your partner into your world: bringing them to family, professional, or social gatherings; introducing them to the important people in your life
- Tending to the container of the relationship: not keeping other options open; closing open doors such as flirtations or other forms of energy leaks
- Making your partnership your priority and demonstrating this commitment to your partner
- Refraining from interfering: seeing the other person as complete and allowing them their own journey; not viewing them as a problem to be solved
- Growing your capacities for self-soothing and self-care
- Asking for help
- Asking for space

- Sharing your inner life: being vulnerable about feelings, thoughts, and fantasies; expressing needs and desires; sharing about what's lighting you up and sparking your curiosity
- Initiating a repair after a rupture: saying "I'm sorry" and committing to acting differently in the future

Which of these secure attachment skills would you like to practice? Choose a few to try out for a period. Once they start to feel integrated into your repertoire, try out a few more. It might feel awkward at first, but over time these new possibilities can become songs you know by heart.

CHAPTER 4

Survival Styles and the Recovery Journey

The thing I know about those days [when I was using] is that if I got just the right combination of drugs and just the right dose, I would get a moment, just a moment, where it was okay to be inside of my own skin, where I could breathe. And so, for some of the people you are sitting across from, when you ask them to let go of substances, you may be asking them to let go of the only peace that they know in the world. That's it. That longing for the moment where you can breathe, that moment of peace—they are not broken to want that. That's what we all want.

—KELLY WILSON

Developed by Laurence Heller and Aline LaPierre, the NeuroAffective Relational Model (NARM) explains with additional nuance the imprint of early childhood survival adaptations on adult relational patterns. The NARM model is based on principles from psychoanalytic theory, somatics, and developmental psychology, and it illuminates the core developmental needs of the child between the ages of zero (prenatal) to five. It shows what happens when these needs aren't met, or are met inconsistently, by the child's caregivers or environment and the survival styles the child develops in order to adapt to the limitations of her environment. It shows, as well, the core capacities—for connection, attunement, trust, autonomy, and love—that a child in a caring environment would ideally internalize at these various ages, the very capacities that we can develop or reclaim in adulthood as we move through recovery and experience healing of these early wounds.

The Connection Style

The Connection survival style develops as a result of disruptions in early life, from the prenatal period to six months old, particularly in relation to existential threats to survival, such as abuse, neglect, chronic misattunement, attachment loss (for example, a parent's death or emotional withdrawal, such as in perinatal depression), or being unwelcomed at conception or birth. Children who experience wounding at this age grow up disconnected from their bodies and live with a pervasive anxiety that relationship may result in threat.[1] The longing for the connection they never received is in constant tension with the fear that connection will lead to pain.

As a result of the missing organizing experiences in childhood—for instance, consistent mirroring and coregulation—adults may experience a chronic sense of disorganization both in mind and body. They may both long for and push away connection, which can feel confusing and hurtful for those around them. The ANS tendencies are toward a blended or cyclic state of hyper- and hypoarousal.[2] Josh and Elliot, discussed in Chapter 3, have strong tendencies toward the Connection style, which aligns with the characteristics of disorganized attachment.

The Attunement Style

The Attunement survival style is connected with early wounding around the age of six months to eighteen months. Anya, described on page 60, has a strong tendency toward the Attunement style. People with this style experienced early abandonment, cold or rejecting parenting, and a lack of nurturance.[3] They are accustomed to attuning to the needs of others but, due to a lack of coregulation in childhood, have limited capacity to self-attune. Lacking sufficient care in childhood, they often adapt by taking on caregiving roles for others, and develop keen skills for connection in order to fill in for their parents' missing capacities. They give the very love they are longing to receive, and the care they are most needing. However, they often overgive and self-sacrifice in the process, not recognizing that their compulsive care for others is not simply an expression of love but a circular attempt to get their own needs met.

Unfortunately these adaptations can create challenges in partnership as Attunement types are highly vigilant to potential ruptures and often seek to restore connection with a protest cry of blame or criticism, having learned it wasn't safe to attune to their own needs or express their feelings more directly.[4] In compulsively caregiving, they tend to self-abandon and self-neglect. The ANS state is characterized by the hyperarousal associated with vigilance to potential threats to the attachment, coupled with dorsal vagal collapse in the face of intense activation or shame. The Attunement style aligns with the characteristics of anxious attachment, discussed in Chapter 3.

The Trust Style

People with the Trust survival style experienced major interruptions to healthy development in the arena of trust and healthy dependency. The child learns that their dependency needs may result in being manipulated or used, and are therefore dangerous, so that relationship becomes associated with the potential for betrayal.[5] Parenting may be narcissistic, placing unrealistic expectations on the child to meet the parent's unmet needs or live their unlived life. Children learn that love is conditional and dependent on meeting these impossible expectations. The child learns to develop a false self, outwardly nice, attractive, or successful, while inside they are flooded with shame. In adulthood, people with this style will often be seductive, viewing sex as a form of competition or conquering, while unconsciously using it as means for shoring up the vulnerable, fragmented self. On the flip side, they may fear being used sexually or emotionally by others. They might have a tendency to dominate others to cover up the underlying feeling of powerlessness; they may unconsciously use others to avoid being used, or betray first in order to avoid being betrayed.[6] Marcus, described in Chapter 3, has a tendency toward this survival style. The ANS state is characterized by intense activation followed by dorsal vagal collapse when protective mechanisms fail. Frightened of the vulnerability that comes with true intimacy, individuals with the Trust adaptation often align with the avoidant attachment style.

The Autonomy Style

The Autonomy survival style stems from wounding in the areas of self-assertion, boundary setting, exploration, and independence. In the developmental stage often experienced by exhausted parents as the terrible twos, the child will start to differentiate herself more from her caregivers, expressing healthy aggression and asserting "no." She will start to venture out to explore the world on her own, with a sense of vibrant curiosity and playfulness. If the child's attempts at autonomy are met with the parent's anger or retaliation, anxiety, collapse, or threat of abandonment, the child will learn that her autonomy and healthy aggression pose a potential risk to the attachment bond. In order to preserve the attachment, she will learn to split off her aggression and develop a superficially "good" and "nice" persona.[7] As she internalizes her parents' anxiety, her innate infatuation with the world is suppressed, leading to dampened playfulness, creativity, and enthusiasm later in life.

In adulthood, those of us with this survival style will often be perfectionistic, self-judgmental, and outwardly compliant—good students and employees—while inwardly resentful of the demands placed on us and rebellious toward authority figures. I identify strongly with this survival style, and I can feel in my body the split that occurs (compliant smile on the outside, rebellious anger on the inside) whenever I engage with a man in a position of power. In relationship, this style can create challenges; our partners may not know where they stand with us, and we can have a bottle-up-and-explode manner of expressing anger when hidden resentments eventually become overwhelming. For many Autonomy types, our substance use serves as the vehicle of our rebellion and the embodiment of our freedom, until we come to see it in its truth—as a continuing source of confinement that replicates our childhood binds.

Driven and exacting, those of us with Autonomy style often experience hyperarousal, which may be coupled with dorsal vagal collapse stemming from unconscious or suppressed anger. We may fall into either of the categories of the anxious or avoidant attachment styles discussed in Chapter 3.

The Love and Sexuality Style

The Love and Sexuality survival style develops in response to interruptions or wounds in the area of embodiment and sexuality in early childhood, or later during the development of sexual expression in adolescence. When the child's early expressions of sensual pleasure, such as masturbation, are stifled or shamed, the child will learn to split off their sexuality. Children can also experience wounding in this area if they sense their caregiver's repulsion or discomfort with the child's body or genitals, such as during diaper changing or bath time. This survival style can also result from early heartbreak, when the child's love for the caregiver and reach for connection is met with rejection.[8]

Children with this adaptation will grow into adulthood with a split between heart feeling and genital sexuality. The adaptive patterns and shame-based identifications may start to manifest at the onset of puberty and in early dating experiences. We may view sexuality as performative rather than as an embodied, interoceptive experience of giving and receiving pleasure, and we may experience love as conditional on sexual performance.

The love–sexuality split can create challenges in relationship because those of us with this survival style may find it difficult to feel emotional intimacy and sexual excitement in the same relationship; heart connection and genital connection cannot coexist in the same sphere. Relationships will tend either toward sexual passion without heart connection or toward emotional intimacy without sexual aliveness. At its worst, this split results in affairs, in which the need for sexual vitality is met outside the primary partnership, or in settling for partnerships that are emotionally connected but devoid of the life-force of sexuality. Sex may often be associated with shame or fears about "performance." The ANS state is often a blended state of the hypoarousal of chronic shame and the hyperarousal of the anxiety associated with sexuality and relationship. You can read more about restoring heart–genital connection in Chapter 10.

Shoring Up the Self Through Substance Use

Before we had other possibilities for self-regulation and meaningful relationship, our substance use and addictive behaviors provided us with an acutely specific outlet for the challenges of each survival style, a way of managing the core binds and dilemmas, mitigating anxiety and collapsed states, and providing expression for parts of the self that could not be otherwise expressed. For each survival style, substance use and addictive behaviors offer a set of solutions for the attachment dilemmas and a way of managing ANS dysregulation:

SURVIVAL STYLE	ROLE OF SUBSTANCE USE
Connection	• Manages need–fear dilemma • Eases loneliness • Eases social anxiety and facilitates social connection • Numbs threat response • Numbs shame • Manages emotions such as fear and longing • *Manages intense activation and immobilization (blended sympathetic and dorsal vagal states)*

SURVIVAL STYLE	ROLE OF SUBSTANCE USE
Attunement	• Provides substitute for attachment figure • Numbs feelings of overwhelming need • Uninhibits expression of need • Numbs shame • Numbs feelings of anger, which are perceived as threatening to connection • *Manages the intense activation of this survival style; manages states of collapse that occur in the face of strong activation (sympathetic dominance followed by dorsal vagal collapse)*
Trust	• Feeds feelings of omnipotence in the face of underlying powerlessness • Numbs underlying desire for and fear of dependency • Numbs shame • Eases stress of maintaining an inauthentic self in a performative role • *Manages the intense activation of this survival style; manages the states of collapse that follow when survival adaptations fail (sympathetic dominance followed by dorsal vagal collapse)*[9]
Autonomy	• Offers a sense of freedom, a secret inner life that cannot be touched by others • Attempts to preserve or bolster autonomy • Eases expression of suppressed rebelliousness and assertiveness—the disavowed "no" energy • Numbs feelings such as anger that are perceived as unacceptable or threatening, or facilitates explosive expression of them • Eases stress of perfectionism, self-judgment, and impossibly high standards • Eases stress of maintaining an inauthentic self • *Manages the activation associated with perfectionism and the hypoarousal resulting from disallowed anger (sympathetic dominance coupled with dorsal vagal collapse)*

SURVIVAL STYLE	ROLE OF SUBSTANCE USE
Love-Sexuality	• Facilitates desired connection through sex • Opens momentary possibility for loving feelings • Attempts to integrate love and sexuality • Inhibits fear about sexual performance • Numbs shame • *Manages states of activation related to anxiety and shame (sympathetic dominance coupled with dorsal vagal collapse)*

Survival Adaptions and the Eighth Step

As any of us in recovery can attest to, although substance use served a necessary purpose in the absence of other resources, it ultimately results in the kind of behaviors and events that eventually end up on our Eighth Step inventory and our Ninth Step amends. We can see a direct through-line from these early survival adaptations to the actions and behaviors that cause harm to ourselves and others in our adult lives. These survival strategies, so useful in early childhood, result in the kind of body bracing and self-protective patterns that create relational disconnection in adulthood. For example, the ways that we protected ourselves in childhood by disavowing our needs and emotions can result in patterns of avoidance and withdrawal in our adult relationships. Similarly, our unconscious expectation that our needs will never be met can invoke our partner's fear of never being good enough. Underlying both pursuing and distancing behaviors in relationship is a core sense of shame that, when touched, feeds cycles of conflict and disconnect that can be difficult to interrupt.

As we look at the NARM survival adaptions in relation to the Eighth Step we can start to connect our childhood learnings to our adult behaviors, and also find a clear means of repair. We can look at the way our default tendencies in terms of mind, body, and nervous system manifest in behaviors that have harmed ourselves and others. As we explore the Eighth Step through this lens, we can consider whom we have harmed and how our fears and survival strategies have resulted in actions that have harmed them. Here is a way you can look at the Eighth Step through this lens:

CORE DEVELOPMENTAL LEARNING	CORE WOUND	FEARS	HOW HAVE I HARMED MYSELF AND OTHERS?	POTENTIAL AMENDS TO SELF	POTENTIAL AMENDS TO OTHERS
Connection: Safe and consistent connection with self and others.	Existential threat; trauma; abuse; neglect. Shame develops as early needs are not met.	Connection will result in pain; annihilation.	Withdrawing; isolating; responding reactively with family, friends, coworkers, and partners.	Learning to identify and meet needs; learning skills for self-regulation; acknowledging need for others; acknowledging ways you placed yourself in dangerous situations in adulthood; practicing embodiment skills.	Making amends for pushing others away; apologizing for reactivity; asking for and accepting offers of support.
Attunement: Awareness of and attunement to your inner environment; receiving nourishment.	Lack of nurturance; inconsistency; abandonment; cold or rejecting parenting. Child shuts down internal awareness and learns to attune to the needs of others.	Abandonment.	Engaging in protest behaviors (control, blame, criticism, rage); perpetuating self-abandonment.	Acknowledging and expressing needs; tracking internal expectation of disappointment; practicing letting in love; acknowledging self-abandonment; practicing interoceptive awareness; connecting in a loving way with your inner child.	Practicing direct communication using "I" statements; taking responsibility for your part in conflicts; making amends for blame and criticism of partner; acknowledging how rage and criticism—expressed through "you" statements—may touch partner's shame and defense; making amends for difficulty with honoring boundaries.

CORE DEVELOPMENTAL LEARNING	CORE WOUND	FEARS	HOW HAVE I HARMED MYSELF AND OTHERS?	POTENTIAL AMENDS TO SELF	POTENTIAL AMENDS TO OTHERS
Trust: Trust in self and others; healthy dependency; mutually supportive relationships.	Narcissistic parenting; violations of trust. Love is dependent on performance and meeting expectations or needs of parent.	Rejection, engulfment, being used or betrayed. Love is conditional.	Using and betraying others to protect self from being used and betrayed; avoiding connection; exaggerating self-reliance at the expense of letting in support from others; perpetuating self-betrayal.	Acknowledging dependency needs; recognizing how you have shut out others and their offers of support; practicing accepting love and support; acknowledging self-betrayal.	Making amends for using others (emotionally, sexually, physically, financially) and for betraying others' trust; apologizing for pushing others away and rejecting offers of support and connection.
Autonomy: Healthy aggression and assertiveness; exploration, playfulness, and independence.	Anxious parenting; lack of support for play and exploration. Exploration is met with anxiety or undue restrictions. Parenting is reactive or collapsing, rather than receptive, to child's "no."	Rejection, annihilation. Setting boundaries or asserting autonomy will result in loss of connection.	Experiencing difficulties with boundary-setting; acting compliant while inwardly feeling resentment toward partners and authority figures such as employers; feeling ambivalent in relationship; engaging in self-judgement and perfectionism; suppressing creativity and play.	Practicing setting healthy boundaries; expressing "no"; honoring both sides of ambivalence without forcing solutions; practicing letting go of "nice" persona; relaxing forced smiles; honoring the anger inside of resentment and listening to its message; making amends to self for perfectionism and harsh inner critic; engaging in play and creative practice.	Setting limits; making amends for how ambivalence may have harmed partners; making amends for how your false persona has impacted others; making amends for long-held resentment that has led to explosive expressions of anger.

CORE DEVELOPMENTAL LEARNING	CORE WOUND	FEARS	HOW HAVE I HARMED MYSELF AND OTHERS?	POTENTIAL AMENDS TO SELF	POTENTIAL AMENDS TO OTHERS
Love and sexuality: Integration of heart and genital sexuality; integration of emotional vulnerability and sexual passion.	Shaming around early expressions and explorations of sexuality. Love is conditional on performance or looks.	Rejection. Love is conditional on outer performance; emotional connection and passion cannot coexist in the same partnership.	Splitting between love and sexuality in relationship; harming self and others by having a closed heart; engaging in affairs; being emotionally absent in sexual relationships; feeling conditional self-acceptance that depends on acceptance from others.	Practicing heart–sexuality connection; embodying connection between heart and genitals; practicing somatic healing in relation to sexuality; acknowledging the pain of having sex without love, and vice versa; making amends to self for conditional self-acceptance.	Acknowledging how unintegrated love and sexuality may have impacted others; acknowledging how a closed heart has kept others out; making amends for using others sexually; making amends for lack of emotional connection with sexual partners.

With the Eighth and Ninth Step work, we can see the ways we can not only make amends for our reliance on these old patterns but also make living amends, a commitment to act differently going forward. We can offer living amends to ourselves and others as well as to our child self by offering the repair and providing the missing pieces of connection, love, belonging, and safety that were missing in early life. Instead of continuing to act out old patterns, we can see the specific ways to nurture relational connection and draw on more life-giving resources in the future. Recognizing that we now have many more ways of keeping ourselves safe than we had in early childhood (see the Step Six exercise on page 116), we can start to engage in more life-giving behaviors, taking the risk to connect with others, share ourselves more authentically, and receive support.

✳ Exploring Your Survival Style

In your journal, explore your survival style with the following prompts:

I identify most strongly with the following survival style(s):

- ☐ Connection
- ☐ Attunement
- ☐ Trust
- ☐ Autonomy
- ☐ Love–Sexuality

I relate to the following characteristics of the survival style: ________

How were these characteristics necessary in response to my childhood environment?

How have these characteristics protected me?

How have they harmed me in the past?

How do they continue to harm me in the present?

How have they harmed others?

How do they continue to harm others?

What do I need to mourn in relation to this pattern?

What are the living amends I can make to myself with an intention to behave differently in the future?

What are the living amends I can make to others?

CHAPTER 5

Unprogramming the Program

It doesn't matter who you are or what you've experienced; your richness, fullness, and capacity for connection and relationship are all right there. And as soon as you encounter the right situation and open to it, your inclination for authentic love and intimacy will flower. Your core is intact! Your essence is alive!

—DIANE POOLE HELLER

Dependency [is] integral to the human condition, and autonomy the false goal of a consumerist society.

—ANTHONY BATEMAN AND JEREMY HOLMES

In Twelve Step programs, as well as in the culture at large, we often hear messages that, well-intentioned as they may be, fail to speak from an attachment-informed perspective and only reinforce the shame, constriction, and denial of healthy dependency needs that underscore addiction.[1] While it is a wise guideline not to date during the first year of recovery (or to date someone in their first year of recovery, also called *Thirteen Stepping*), I believe that the overarching work of recovery is about coming more fully into relationship, including romantic relationships if desired. After that first year, the guidance of fellows, sponsors, and program literature should support any budding interest in relationship that relative newcomers might show, seeing and reflecting this as an expression of the person's movement into life. If you need additional support exploring sex and/or dating in recovery, or if you have struggled with compulsive behaviors in these areas, seeing a therapist who specializes in sex addiction can be helpful, as can attending programs such as Sex Addicts Anonymous that can offer literature, tools, and group support for integrating sexuality and Twelve Step recovery.

From the perspective of attachment theory, the program mantra and pop culture adage that "you have to love yourself first" before you seek out a relationship is simply not true. We learn to love ourselves through affirming and attuned relationships that have the effect of consolidating and reifying our sense of self; receiving loving and accurate reflection from another person *comes before* our capacity to affirm and maintain a sense of our own selfhood.[2] In early childhood, attuned mirroring by a loving caregiver is what allows us to grow our capacities to sense ourselves from the inside out and develop a perception of ourselves as good and loveable. If our need for attunement went unmet in childhood, we'll have difficulties in adulthood offering ourselves the attuned responses that constitute love. And regardless of our childhood experiences, we all need affirming reflection throughout adulthood if we wish to maintain a cohesive sense of self.

If we wait until we love ourselves before seeking out meaningful relationship, we will wait forever. Our longing for relationship—that is, the pain of the lack of relationship—should instead be honored as the fuel for finding the relationships we desire. Additionally, many of us are very skillful at attuning to others, and therefore we are more than capable of offering love to another person long before we are capable of receiving this kindness from ourselves or others. In fact, the most difficult part, and the most distant point, of the relationship journey may be expanding our capacity for receiving love.

When, through the work of recovery and other healing modalities, we have more fully developed our sense of a cohesive self and greater nervous system regulation, a sense of love flows naturally. We don't have to work at it. Paradoxically we no longer need to "love ourselves" since there is no longer a split between parts of the self—in this case, between the part that loves and the part that is loved (and generally a third part, which does not believe, for all the repetitions in the world of the mandate to "love yourself first," that the self is loveable). When we sense our own wholeness, we return to our true nature, which is love itself. We are love in a universe of love.

So rather than talking about self-love, we can see love as a creative, co-arising phenomenon. It is through the practice of finding safety in the world and healthy, loving attachment with others that love arises in the field, the way it arises in a parent–child bond. Coregulation is a core need that often cries out to be met. Those of us with very early childhood trauma, from the prenatal period to eighteen months, may need to go all the way back to face that broken symbiosis between parent and child and find ways to provide the missing pieces of love and connection in the present moment. It is by meeting and mending these core wounds through reparative attachment experiences that we grow toward healing, becoming a cohesive self that knows itself as love. We can then sense love flowing through us in the currents of energy, in the movement of our breath and bodies, in the energetic field of the heart, and perhaps only then in the messages that our mind directs inwardly toward ourselves. This state of love does not take effort; rather, it is a healing of the familiar efforting toward love that is the lingering imprint of childhood relational wounds. As we heal, we can start to simply rest back into the love that is the universe, trusting that we are held, that we are safe, and that our needs are easefully met. It is from this place of safety that we come to know ourselves, healing the fragmentation that was a result of early traumas. To be whole and cohesive is synonymous with love.

"Codependent" No More

Codependency is a term that we hear frequently in Twelve Step programs and in the culture at large. It is important to remember that this term was created in a specific context and with a specific meaning: a co-addictive process that occurs in relationship with a person who is struggling with addiction.[3] Texts on codependency, such as Melody Beattie's books and the Co-Dependents Anonymous (CoDA) literature, encourage partners and family members of addicted individuals to look at their own participation, projections, and behaviors in relationship with the addicted partner. Naming the phenomenon of codependency was an important step in the field of recovery and played an important role in destigmatizing addiction; it freed the addicted individual from the role of the "identified patient" and encouraged partners to look more closely at their own experience, to practice self-care, and to tend to their own healing. The language of codependency helped take the brunt of blame and pathology off the shoulders of the addicted individual and demonstrated that addiction is a shared dance between partners, with both individuals bringing their own patterns and learned behaviors.

While the term may be useful in this context, it can also touch into a lot of shame as partners and family members take on the stigma associated with it and attempt to shut down their love and care, and their own needs for connection, lest these needs be deemed enabling or codependent.[4] The stigma recapitulates the shame rooted in early relational wounding, when needs for connection were unmet, and reiterates narratives learned in childhood that "there's something wrong with me, my needs, and my longing for love." In fact, it's completely natural to care about your loved one's sobriety and to feel invested in their recovery process. It is not enabling or codependent to offer them support or to continue to offer care through the ups and downs of their recovery journey, to long for their love, and to feel preoccupied with reestablishing connection when contact is broken—it's a neurobiological inevitability and part of our innate human blueprint for attachment.[5] There may simply be something to discover about patterns in your own history, ones that might have set you up for feelings of hopeless longing or loyal waiting, that can invite you more deeply into your own healing and bring in more options for response in relation to your loved one.[6]

Codependency is often defined by the following characteristics:

- Lack of self-worth
- People-pleasing or caretaking behaviors

- Difficulty with setting boundaries
- Excessive reliance on another person
- Tendency to enable others
- Impaired autonomy
- Fear of abandonment
- Tendency to neglect one's own needs in order to tend to others
- Submissive, clingy, or controlling behavior in relationship[7]

When we look at these characteristics from the perspective of early attachment, we can see that these qualities are adaptations that allow the child to do their best to survive in a difficult environment. A child growing up in an unsafe or inconsistent environment will learn to carefully track subtle shifts in the emotions, facial expressions, body language, and psychological states of their caregivers in order to predict and hopefully ward off any potential volatility or relational ruptures. Sacrificing their own self-awareness for an outward focus helps the child carefully track the external environment. They learn to self-abandon and self-neglect in order to tend to the relational connection with their caregivers. In adulthood they compulsively give to others the care and nurturance they are longing to receive.

Generally the child will have experienced wounds in the area of autonomy. Early boundary violations, a lack of boundary modeling, or a lack of support for the child's developing self-assertion results in understandable difficulties in setting boundaries in adulthood. Additionally, in order to meet the parents' expectations and attempt to maintain a sense of safety and connection, the child will develop a false self, becoming a "good" and "nice" child, an adaptation often manifesting as so-called people-pleasing behaviors in adulthood.

While the term *codependency* can be useful to describe a constellation of symptoms associated with early attachment wounding, it can also be stigmatizing and shaming, which further reiterates the shame resulting from the original attachment trauma.[8] The term has traveled beyond its original usage, accumulating with it like a snowball all of the cultural misconceptions around attachment and the accruals of capitalism—the assumption of separateness that is necessary to keep capitalism afloat at the expense of our interbeing with each other and the more-than-human world. Its current usage has traveled far from the original intent, and to my mind, it doesn't serve a useful purpose in the recovery field for either the partner or the addicted individual. Instead, it is important for us to work somatically with the hypervigilance, fear of abandonment, unsupported boundaries, and self-neglect, and little by little, build up pathways that allow us to turn gently and lovingly toward our own experience at the right time and with the right support.

I still remember when, a few days after a heartbreaking breakup, I made a program call to a fellow who is active in Al-Anon, and she brusquely told me to "keep the focus on myself." This was a massive miss in terms of empathy, and it still stings a little when I think about it. It is normal to become obsessed with our attachment figure in the face of a rupture as we frantically seek to repair the breach in connection.[9] Looking to others serves a function; when you are feeling fragmented in yourself, it is not possible to love yourself first or keep the focus on yourself. We attune intimately to others in an attempt to tend to or repair the connection. All of us do this in a crisis such as a breakup, and many of us do it throughout a relationship to ward off the possibility of impending rupture. Although paradoxically this heightened focus on others can end up intensifying anxiety and self-abandonment, reiterating childhood abandonment wounds, it is, at essence, an understandable and courageous effort to restore loving connection in the face of potential heartbreak.[10]

Little bothers me more in recovery spaces and the culture at large than the term *codependency* used outside of its original context. Much of what we call codependency should be redefined as a courageous attempt at interdependence and interbeing. Sometimes we go about it in ways that harm ourselves and others, but the fundamental yearning is sacred and should be treated with reverence. Like horses each stabled in a separate stall, human beings are similarly cut off from the herd and confined—confined within our roles in our culture, confined within our small selves that believe ourselves to be separate from each other—when in fact we are animals whose bodies, minds, and souls are meant to be intrinsically interwoven with the beingness of all beings. Our work in recovery is to clear away the shame and to reclaim and hold as sacred our longing for connection.

I find the term *codependent* offensive especially as it has gained stigma in our culture. It implies that if you can't, as Al-Anon says, "keep the focus on yourself," then something is wrong with you. However, in truth, outward focus is a necessary survival strategy. It takes time and practice to experience a felt sense of safety, of being at ease in the world, so that we can learn, little by little, to bring our focus inward to attune to our own experience. This repatterning is a bottom-up process that involves establishing a felt sense of safety in the body, mind, and brain and, therefore, the other-focused patterns are not something to be willed through or overcome. If we could, we would. Overall, I prefer the term *anxious attachment*, which, to my mind and body, is free of much of the stigma and more clearly emphasizes that the constellation of characteristics results from early childhood attachment experiences.

As Amir Levine and Rachel Heller note, the characteristics generally categorized as codependent are actually *activating strategies*, meant to generate closeness with your partner, and *protest behaviors*, which protest breaches in connection in an attempt to restore contact.[11] For example, if I ruminate about my partner after an argument, the obsessive thoughts are my attachment system's way of asking, again and again, "Are you still there?" as I attempt to reassure myself of his continued presence. Thinking of him feels like clinging to a mast in a stormy ocean. Keeping him in my mind is an attempt to keep him in my heart.

Likewise, if he threatens to leave in the midst of an argument, that's his attachment system protesting in hurt and pain, calling out to get my attention and be brought back into loving connection, asking to be reassured that he is still wanted. When these early signs of protest are unheard, we cry out louder and louder to try and get our partner's attention; these cries can easily escalate to rage, blaming, criticizing, or withdrawal behavior directed toward our partner. Although these actions often produce the opposite of what we were longing for, their underlying intent is a beautiful and sacred one: the restoration of love. Activating strategies and protest behaviors are soothed when we learn to communicate clearly their underlying attachment message and our partner in turn learns to meet us with presence, reassurance, and care.

Growing Toward Dependency

In the rooms, I find a substantial amount of confusion between codependency, dependency, and interdependency. In the process of trying to will ourselves out of what we fear may be deemed codependency, we deny our intrinsic dependency needs. This denial reiterates early trauma, when these needs were not met by our environment. In fact, the denial of these needs, and the shame about having needs, is a *symptom* of the pain of those needs not being met.

As Flores astutely notes, the fantasy of omnipotence, of self-sufficiency, belongs to a very early developmental phase in which the infant experiences herself at the center of a world that seamlessly meets her needs (to be fed, changed, picked up, etc.). She cries and the breast magically appears; she cannot yet see that she is reliant on the help of others outside herself for her survival. If our needs are sufficiently met at this early stage, we can grow into later phases of our development in which we come to understand that our survival depends on mutual relationship, support, and connection with others who exist independently of ourselves. Flores explains that the work of Step One is to move from the infant's fantasy of omnipotence that characterizes addiction ("I don't have a problem and I don't need anyone") into the later developmental phase of relational dependency that is based in reality ("I have a problem and I need help").[12] The learning in recovery is to meet, get to know, and accept the actuality of our dependency needs.

It is emblematic of a capitalist-based culture that we have two poles, a simplistic and false dichotomy between independence and dependency. Although we all have very real and important needs for autonomy and selfhood, complete independence is a fantasy. No one survives without the help of others; no person alive has truly pulled themself up by the bootstraps. Whether or not we can see it, our lives are interwoven with a vast tapestry of support—the ancestors and parents who gave us life, the invisible labor of thousands of people who create the homes we live in and the clothes we wear, the Earth that gives us nutrients and oxygen. As my friend Katie Eberle wrote, after a long period of convalescence following a brutal concussion: "When I was reduced to a very basic, plant-like sort of existence, I began to see help everywhere. Help was the sun, and then it was the relief of the shade. Help was the scent of a flowering bush on the street, and then the exciting mess of the fuchsia petals on the ground two weeks later."[13] I have her letter taped to my fridge to remind me of the power of seeing support in its true nature.

All around us are the destructive effects of the myth of independence. This myth is a pride-based identification built on the disavowal of our vulnerability and is simply the flipside of shame. The journey in recovery is to recognize, accept, and honestly express our need for others while receiving their needs as well. This process is an essential aspect of moving out of shame; it offers healing to the young part of ourselves whose shame arose as a response to those needs not being met in the first place. We can then recall our innate blueprint for interconnection, a blueprint we share with the smallest atom and the largest galaxy.

Life without others is essentially the definition of addiction. Interbeing, coregulation, and the mutual meeting of each other's dependency needs is the definition of life in recovery.

Your Picker Is Just Fine

In my years of recovery, I have heard many shaming things in the rooms, words that fellows direct not only to others but, even more painfully, toward themselves. Some of the Twelve Step slogans only serve to repeat the shaming messages that we carry inside, recapitulating the disavowal of our need and our longing for connection. In *Trauma and the 12 Steps,* Jamie Marich looks at various slogans from AA and other Twelve Step programs through a trauma-informed lens.[14] In one example, Marich points out that the common slogan, "Your picker is broken," frequently heard at AA and Al-Anon meetings, is shaming and dismissive of the blessings that can emerge from challenging relationships. Marich writes that, having recently gone through a divorce, "I was avalanched with that slogan and it made me feel gross inside." Marich goes on to explain, "We cannot choose whom we love, although recovery may ask us to do a great deal of work. . . . And think of the wonderful fruits that can result from difficult situations . . . lessons that can be learned to move us forward on our journey."[15]

Our *picker* is a finely tuned instrument composed of a magical and mysterious (and yes, biological) mix of the genetic, physiological, family, and cultural influences that constitute attraction.[16] It points us perfectly toward the partners with whom we will have the possibility of forging healing attachment experiences, partners who are the same-but-different as our caregivers, with whom we can repeat the early attachment wounds—this time, with a difference: the possibility of repair. Although you can certainly learn skills for recognizing red flags and seeking out more securely attached partners (I recommend the STUDs and DUDs list in Diana Kirschner's *Love in 90 Days* and Diane Poole Heller's list on identifying secure attachment in *The Power of Attachment*[17]), these shifts will often come organically as you heal your own attachment wounds and grow your capacity for more sustained intimacy in recovery. As our own capacities grow, a partner who is inconsistent, distancing, or unavailable for conscious relationship will no longer hold the same appeal. As painful as difficult relationships can be, your picker is perfectly oriented to bringing you toward healing. There is nothing broken about it.

Honoring Resentment

In Twelve Step programs, we often talk about resentment. According to the AA Big Book, resentment is "the 'number one' offender. . . . From it stem all forms of spiritual disease, for we have been not only mentally and physically ill, we have been spiritually sick."[18] While the Big Book understands resentment to be a "spiritual malady" that must be overcome, from an attachment and developmental perspective, resentment is actually anger that we're not able to express directly.

In childhood, many of us learned that expressing anger would result in punishment, retaliation, or abandonment, threatening our attachment with caregivers, so we had to make the choice between our own authentic expression and preserving our relationships. This presented a core bind—on the one hand we could sacrifice our self and preserve the relationship with our caregivers, or on the other, we could preserve a sense of self and risk losing the relationship. Since, as children, to risk the relationship would present an existential threat, we sacrificed our authentic expression to become the person we sensed we needed to be to maintain the connection. When we couldn't express our aggression outwardly, it turned inward, into shame and self-judgement. This impaired capacity, until it is brought into consciousness and allowed to complete its development, will haunt our recovery journey.

Anger is an essential aspect of our biological life-force. It has two important roles: It lets us know when our boundaries have been violated, and it functions as a protest when our needs are unmet. As Heller and LaPierre write, "Anger is a life-supportive response intended to impact an unsupportive environment."[19] Anger is part of our psychobiological survival response; it's meant to protect us and keep us alive. I like to think of resentment as an envelope containing a letter. When we open the envelope of resentment, we find the letter of anger. When we take time to read the letter, we find an important message about our boundaries and unmet needs. Rather than try to get rid of a resentment, we can open it to learn more about the underlying message.

Once we have heard its message, we can take action to meet its requirement: Do we need to reestablish a boundary? Do we have a core need for safety, connection, support, trust, or belonging that we can take steps to meet in the ways that are available to us now? As children, we didn't have the resources to meet our own needs, the language to ask for our needs to be met, or the capacity to look outside the home when our needs weren't met by our caregivers. Now, as adults, we have access to many more resources. We have much larger bodies in which to hold our uncomfortable feelings, and we can reach out to others for support.

If you have a tendency toward feeling shame or depression, it's especially important to grow your capacity to access the energies of anger so that its life-force can flow freely in your body, which will help you mobilize out of hypoarousal. When we cannot allow ourselves to feel anger *at* something or someone who harmed us, we direct it inward, as self-judgment, self-blame, and self-annihilation. In recovery, to update our old narrative, we learn that we can allow ourselves our anger, recognizing that feeling our anger does not have to result in expressing it in a way that is damaging to ourselves or others. In fact, learning to listen to and honor our anger allows us to tend to it with love, which in turn helps us more compassionately communicate our inner experience.

Resentment is not a character defect. It is a cue from your nervous system and attachment system that needs to be listened to.[20] It might be saying that it's time to renegotiate some boundaries. It might be time to listen to what your needs are and explore the ways they can be met. It is not a sign that something is wrong with you—rather, something is very right.

There's no such thing as a negative feeling. Feelings are simply energies, neither positive nor negative, that carry an important message in service of protecting you, your body, and your connection with others.

What Feelings Are For

Joy lets us know about our feelings of connection with ourself, others, and the world.

Fear offers protection and aims to keep us safe from threats.

Longing shows us what's been missing and guides us toward greater connection and aliveness.

Sadness shows the pain of loss of connection. Our tears serve to communicate this pain to others.

Shame teaches us about our need for belonging and aims to protect us from the pain of disconnection.

Anger communicates boundaries and advocates on behalf of unmet needs.

Disgust says, "Don't put this in your body," whether toxic foods or energies.[21]

✳ Recognizing the Message of Resentment

Practice listening to the message of resentment by exploring the following prompts in your journal:

Write out your resentment: I'm resentful at ______________ because ______________.

Bring awareness to the anger: I'm angry at ______________ because ______________.

How is it to name this as anger instead of resentment?

How does anger show up in my body?

How is it to feel the anger?

In what ways does using the word *anger* not feel okay?

In what ways does it not feel safe to feel the anger? What might happen if I allow myself to feel angry?

Draw a picture of the anger: ______________

What is anger's message about boundaries?

My boundaries have been violated in these ways: ______________

What are anger's messages about my unmet needs?

I need ______________.

Put it all together: I feel angry at ______________ because they have violated my boundaries in these ways ______________ or have not met my needs in these ways ______________.

Now that I understand the underlying need, what are some ways I can meet it?

Can I have a conversation with the person or institution I'm angry with, asking them to better respect a boundary or meet a need?

If this person or institution isn't capable of meeting this request, can I meet my need in other ways?

Recovering in an Evolved Nest

The "defects of character" that we look at in Step Six are often the strategies that we developed in early life to survive in our environments. These strategies are not defects, or even "maladaptive coping skills," as they're sometimes called. Rather, they are perfectly adaptive and full of wisdom; they brilliantly evolved to meet the needs of our child selves. The word *defect* can touch a wound, as many of us are already struggling with shame-based identifications in which we see ourselves as broken, dirty, or defective.[22] As we update the language we use in recovery spaces, we can orient these spaces toward attachment, divesting them of shame and evolving them into expansive, attuned circles of care.

As we do a Sixth Step inventory, rather than turning to our resentments and character defects, we can look at the survival strategies that we developed in early childhood. We can consider how these adaptations helped us survive in our environments by preserving our safety and our relationships with caregivers. We can then look at these strategies as they appear in our adult life, exploring the ways they might no longer be necessary and may be updated with newer models for navigating the world and our place in it. I suggest this model as a Sixth Step practice that can honor the wisdom of our survival strategies and bring compassionate understanding, instead of shame, to our process of self-inquiry.

SURVIVAL STRATEGY	HOW DID THIS PROTECT ME?	HOW DOES IT CURRENTLY HARM ME OR OTHERS?	WHAT OTHER WAYS CAN I KEEP MYSELF SAFE NOW?
Example: I have trouble saying no.	I suppressed my assertiveness because I believed my anger would make people leave me.	People don't know where they stand with me. I don't say no when I need to and then I regret it later. I feel resentment because I haven't protected my boundaries.	I can set boundaries clearly. I can let people know when I'm available and when I'm not. I can listen to my body and know what "no" feels like. I can communicate my "no" by simply saying "I'm not available" or "that won't work for me."

As this exercise shows, you now have many more ways to keep yourself safe. When you were a child, you were a small and powerless creature in a very large universe. When you felt an emotion or sensation—for example, hunger, fear, sadness, or rage—you would have experienced it as a big feeling in your tiny body. If you had no one to help you make sense of this experience and to provide coregulation, you would have felt overwhelmed by discomfort and confusion. You had few sources of support, and you had no choice but to try your best to get your needs met in the only environment you had access to, no matter how imperfect it was.

Now, many years later, you have a much larger body and a fully developed mind, and you have access to many sources of care and support. You have the agency to make decisions, to place yourself in or remove yourself from environments and situations, and to seek out relationships that meet your needs. The feelings and sensations that once threatened to overwhelm your infant body can now be held in a much wider frame—the spaciousness of your adult body, the wisdom of your adult mind, and the support of your circle of care.

✳ Moving from "Small Body, Big Feelings" to "Big Body, Small Feelings"

You can remind yourself of the shift into your adult capacities by filling in the following illustrations. Refer back to these images whenever you start feeling overwhelmed by experiences in your inner or external environment. For example:

Small person, big feeling — Big person, small feeling — Big person, small feeling, held in circle of care

Now fill in your own, using shapes and colors to describe the sensations you feel inside and to illustrate the sources of support in your circle of care:

Small person, big feeling Big person, small feeling Big person, small feeling, held in circle of care

CHAPTER 6

Addiction, Attachment, and Addictive Attachments

When something's not quite enough, you can't get enough of it.

—J., AT A MEETING

Merwin finally understood the awful truth. . . .The Beautiful Mountain and the Terrible Volcano . . . they're the same place.

—BRIAN SELZNICK

Many of us in recovery are afraid to engage in relationships because sex and dating were so intricately interwoven with substance use. We might have been drunk or high every time we had sex, went on a date, or flirted, or even through the course of entire relationships. Additionally, the feeling of falling in love—with its neurobiological bubble bath of norepinephrine and dopamine—involves similar neurotransmitters and processes as substance use, and therefore it can be indistinguishable from the feelings and sensations associated with using. As one woman in recovery shared, "Dating might as well be heroin." However, these correspondences don't mean we should avoid relationship; rather, they point exactly to the work of relationship in recovery: learning to engage soberly, perhaps for the first time, in the thrills of sex and dating while also keeping our feet on the ground by regulating our nervous system and seeking partners who can meet us in the work of conscious relationship. One way that we can avoid the high "highs" of dating is to learn to recognize the signs of secure attachment and start to seek the reparative relationships that can heal, rather than replicate, addiction's underlying wounds.

For many of us, it was in early adolescence that we had our first archetypal encounters with the energies of addiction. Frequently those encounters held a numinous power, bound together with budding sexuality, a sense of belonging, mind-blowing experiences of music or movement, or an awe-inspiring connection with nature. Some of my first experiences with pot and alcohol contained a potent mix of these forces. As I look back at those teenage years, a mix of glimmering images come to mind: I'm kissing a boy under a blanket at a party; I'm in a dark field, dancing beneath a sky full of stars. We discover that not only do these early encounters with substances bring us in contact with numinous powers, they can help us manage the overwhelming emotions and psychological states that are the legacy of early trauma.

Although of course, as we see sooner or later, substance use ultimately results in a replication and exacerbation of that early relational pain, we are drawn to it for its momentary capacity to provide us with the pieces that were missing in early childhood and for its power to bring us closer to a sense of the oneness that was interrupted by early ruptures in the caregiver–child bond. The story of Adam and Eve describes the experience of being expelled from the state of early union, which forms the originary wound.[1] From the abrupt loss of the early symbiotic wholeness of life in Eden—that is, the womb, and then perinatally the caregiver's body and energy field—Adam and Eve learn shame, suddenly recognizing their nakedness, and with the fig leaf begin to cover up their vulnerability, the tender places of body and heart. In the same way that a child interprets painful losses of connection as her own fault, from the perspective of Christian theology, the story of Eve and Adam is about original sin rather than the original wound.

The differentiation from the Edenic paradise, like leaving the womb, is necessary for a child's development; indeed, in healthy development, a child organically starts moving out of symbiosis and into exploring the world as attuned caregivers support her expression of "no," her playfulness and curiosity, and her assertions of autonomy. We repeat the theme of leaving the garden multiple times throughout life as we continue the dance between desire for union and desire for separation. However, if this early symbiosis is unfulfilled or disrupted prematurely, we continue to long for it throughout our lifespan, striving again and again in our relationships to bring this developmental phase to completion, only to be repeatedly disappointed as we find we can never fully return to that merged state with another fragile human being who has dependency and autonomy needs of their own. This unconscious projection of our earliest longings and disappointments feeds much of the conflict in relationship.

In recovery, as we peel back the layers of our addictions, we start to recognize that this longing for oneness is our longing for connection with life itself. We yearn to return to a knowing of our interbeing with the universe, a longing that drives our recovery as we seek, as the Twelfth Step suggests, "through prayer and meditation to improve our conscious contact with God." This time, rather than the unconscious fusion experienced in childhood, and by Eve and Adam in the garden, we come to connection consciously. Placing our longing for union where it belongs, and seeking to find it in the arms of the universe itself, frees up our relationships from carrying the weight of that ancient longing. Seeking the fulfillment of longing in romantic relationship is a project that is defeated before it begins because embedded within the longing is the impossibility of it being fulfilled—the disappointment *already happened* long ago, and while we can experience transient, joyful states of merging, we cannot undo the past. The originary pain and the expectation of repeated loss are part and parcel of the longing itself. We can find momentary oneness in our relationships, but the ultimate wholeness that we seek is a knowing of our own life-force in its fluid dance with the infinite life-force of the universe. We find the garden where we are, in the ever-present blossoming of the present moment.

When we unconsciously embark on the project to find this primal oneness in the arms of an unavailable partner, we can get caught in what is sometimes labeled *love addiction*. When we discuss relationships in recovery, it is important to distinguish between secure love and these addictive attachments that, while certainly valuable as learning experiences, cannot result in the kind of stability that leads to developing secure attachment and healing core wounds. Experiences of addictive attachment can be so overwhelming, and feel so similar to the high of a drug or so bound together with substance use, that they can lead us to swear off relationships all together. As I mentioned earlier, I didn't date for my first three years of recovery, not because of some kind of program rule but because I didn't know how to get involved with another person without experiencing an overwhelming amount of rumination, anxiety, and an ungrounded high that felt uncomfortably familiar.

Usually in addictive attachments there is something inconsistent in the connection; for instance, the person we desire might have a very avoidant or disorganized attachment style that keeps us longing and hoping. They might be emotionally unavailable, monogamously partnered with someone else, not interested in dating, or geographically far away. I've had a few of these. One of them lives in Finland, and the other might as well live in Finland. This distance feeds anxiety and obsession and keeps our story going; we can never get to know them well enough to see their own nakedness, to see they are as wounded as we are and incapable of meeting the needs of their own child self, much less our own. We mistake them for God instead of seeing them as Adam. The insecure attachment hooks into our earliest experiences of rupture, which we repeat again and again in an attempt to heal the original pain. Unfortunately, given that the other person is unable to provide the care and stability that might finally put balm on the wound, we can end up in an endless cycle, repeating the hope and despair that we experienced long ago.

Feeling that this is the only person who can meet those needs, we are unable to look around for a more available partner. In the same way that children can't choose to opt in to another family but rather must try to get their needs met from the only providers available to them, we find ourselves similarly unable to choose another source of fulfilment. We continue "to go to the hardware store for bread," not realizing we can cross the street to the bakery.

In one of my own experiences of addictive attachment—as I mentioned earlier, I've had several—I grew preoccupied with attempting to grow a fun, sparkly, and erratic attachment into an actual, secure relationship. I felt bonded with this guy—let's call him Jeff (after my favorite singer, Jeff

Buckley)—so I kept looking to him for love, even though he had nothing to give and said so explicitly. It took a while for me to realize that when I was going to him for soothing and support, I was paradoxically going to *the source of my distress to soothe my distress.* What a tangle! After nearly a year, I finally realized on an embodied level what I had known only cognitively—that the story of "he's the only one for me" is a myth with origins long ago, and that childhood is the sole time when there are truly limited sources of love. I finally realized Jeff wasn't able to meet his needs, much less my own, which wasn't his fault or mine; it didn't matter how good, brilliant, successful, or pretty I was or wasn't, that fact wasn't going to change. My longing for him was intrinsically interwoven with his unavailability—again, part of an old and familiar storyline.

It is difficult to get out of an addictive attachment situation because of the combination of brain chemistry and early psychological imprints. The inconsistent reward of insecure attachment activates the same neurochemicals as substance use, triggering the process of craving followed by momentary fulfillment followed by craving that will be familiar to anyone who has struggled with addiction.[2] We work so hard for the little glimmers of love that when they come, we're floating on air, and when they're gone, we crash painfully to the ground. Meanwhile, our early psychological imprints inform our present-day world such that we end up in the same situation again and again; this is in part due to the psychological processes of repetition compulsion, trauma reenactment, and projective identification, wherein people unconsciously respond to our projections and act the way we expect them to, following along with the original script and often fulfilling our worst fears of abandonment or rejection. Similarly, in the language of polyvagal theory, our *neuroception,* which is our autonomic nervous system's perception of threat or safety, will work behind the scenes to ensure that we choose partners based on familiar models. As a result of trauma or chronic stress, our nervous system can develop faulty neuroception, meaning that we can perceive threats where there aren't any or perceive safety where there are actually threats. If you've experienced trauma or insecure attachment in early life, insecurely attached partners may feel safe and familiar, even if they are inconsistent, unavailable, or abusive.[3]

Here are some practices and resources for shifting an addictive attachment. You can choose the ones that feel most resonant and best meet your current situation, modifying them as needed. First and foremost, though, if you're in an abusive relationship, or you wonder if you might be, get support. Many towns have a center for domestic violence support. (See the "Resources" section at the end of this book for more information.)

- Work with a psychotherapist or somatic practitioner who can help you connect with the core story that is driving the reenactment and provide you with a reliable source of secure attachment for a reparative attachment experience.
- Locate yourself in actual, present-time secure attachment experiences, rather than seeking one that comes intermittently and is characterized by longing for what's absent. Lean into connection with reliable friends. Go to meetings and connect with fellows.
- Meet your child self. Let them know you are there for them. Offer your Little One the care, connection, and consistency that will help them grow into secure attachment.
- Watch out for red flags in dating to avoid these insecure relationships in the first place. Notice how potential partners talk about their past relationships. If they've cut off relationships abruptly, blame their exes for all the problems in the relationship, use words like *crazy* or other insults to describe an ex, or express ongoing doubts about wanting to be in a relationship again, they might not be a good bet. Are they married or partnered with someone else? Unless you're looking for a poly relationship, and everyone involved is honest, ethical, and on the same page, then this is a no-win situation that will likely involve a lot of reenactment of childhood trauma and all the accompanying heartbreak.
- Abstain. Like quitting smoking or getting sober. Don't pick up the first drink. Honor your existing relationship with this person by letting them know kindly and directly that you need to create some

distance to tend to your own needs. Ask them not to contact you until you're ready.

- Follow the fantasy. Notice your dreaming. Often our fantasies and dreams are full of important information about what we are needing and wanting. Write down, draw, or paint your daydreams or your night dreams to unfold their messages.
- What are you longing for? Move in the direction of your longing in your imagination, following it through to its endpoint. Where does it bring you? At essence our longing is a desire for closeness, union, warmth, safety, and connection. There is so much life-force here. How wonderful that your heart longs for these deeply human experiences!
- Imagine being close to the person you desire. Then let go of the image of the particular person and simply sense what you feel in your body. Any goodness, aliveness, light, or longing you sense inside belongs to you. It lives inside of you regardless of whether this person can meet you there or not, and it is a compass pointing toward what you can manifest in the outer world with an available partner.
- Enjoy it. Honor the good. The longing. The attraction and desire. Dance. Feel your pelvis. Feel your heart. You can have all this sexiness, plus the joys of secure attachment, with an available partner. In the meantime, enjoy the sparkles, and honor your body and your aliveness.

If you are in an abusive or volatile relationship, don't stick around hoping it will transform into a loving partnership. Love is consistent, stable, and life-giving; it offers a secure base from which you can venture out and live your life, knowing someone's got your back and you have a safe haven to return to at the end of the day in an often difficult world. Relationships will inevitably be hard at times, and staying with them through the rough patches can be part of growing and deepening into conscious relationship; however, a relationship with the capacity to become a mutually healing partnership is, more often than not, one in which you feel heard, seen, and held in ways that help you feel anchored and connected. Don't try to turn an abusive or energy-draining partnership into a healing force—leave that to a professional. Instead, get yourself the help you need, such as therapy, coaching, and/or support groups, to disentangle yourself from the relationship so that you are available to find actual love—healing, healthy, stable, secure, life-giving, energizing love—with an available and capable partner. As we bring consciousness both to the yearning for love and to the self-abandonment that exist side-by-side in addictive attachments, we can honor the blessings even as we create boundaries, reestablish safety, and choose healthier relationships moving forward.

✳ Going to the Bakery

When you find you're "going to the hardware store for bread," take some time for this reflection in your journal:

What needs am I trying to have met by this person?

In what ways can they meet my needs? In what ways have they met them in the past?

In what ways can they not meet my needs? In what ways have they failed to meet them in the past?

How do I feel about this person not being able to meet my needs?

Where can I go and whom can I turn to for a deeper meeting of these needs?

✳ Reclaiming Your Light

Then reclaim your light with this journal exercise:

Start by writing the person's name at the top of a piece of paper. Then make a list of everything you like about them.

Then go back to the top of the page, cross out their name, and write "I am . . ."

Acknowledge the projection of your light and bring it back home. The beauty you are drawn to in this person is your own beauty.

✱ Creating a Relationship Beyond Your Wildest Dreams

Explore the following questions in your journal to learn more about the relationship you are longing for:

Where in my recovery journey have I experienced life beyond my wildest dreams? Describe the changes you have experienced in the following areas:

- Health
- Community
- Sobriety
- Work
- Creativity
- Finances
- Friendships
- Relationships
- Family
- Other

What might a romantic relationship beyond my wildest dreams look and feel like?

Or, if you're currently in a relationship: What would be the biggest, brightest fruition of my relationship's potential?

What fears or doubts come up as I imagine experiencing a relationship beyond my wildest dreams?

What do my other experiences of living beyond my wildest dreams tell me about the possibility of a healthy relationship?

What are some next steps I can take toward this future?

CHAPTER 7

Shame

For years it lay in an iron box buried so deep inside me that I was never sure just what it was. I knew I carried slippery, combustible things more secret than sex and more dangerous than any shadow or ghost. . . . Whatever lived inside me was so potent that words crumbled before they could describe.

—HELEN EPSTEIN

Shame originates in broken relationship and can be healed by relational connection.

—PATRICIA DEYOUNG

I love talking about things that most people don't like talking about, so shame is one of my favorite topics. I don't necessarily like talking about shame-inducing experiences, but more the experience of shame itself—that combination of sensations, emotions, and thoughts that forms a morass so deep and dangerous that many of us can't even acknowledge its existence.

When we can't talk directly about shame, we often use words that gesture toward the experience without naming it directly. We might say that we feel embarrassed, awkward, bad, or guilty. We use various metaphorical descriptions: "Oh my god, I wanted to disappear!" "I wished the floor would swallow me up." We might describe it as shyness, perfectionism, or social anxiety. Or we might say "I feel fat" in an attempt to describe the body experience of shame, and then starve ourselves in an attempt to make the feeling go away.

All of these are ways of talking about shame without talking about it directly, which makes sense because even talking about shame can be a shame-inducing experience. We might believe we are the only one to feel this way, and if others knew how shameful we are, our essential badness would be revealed and we would be judged and rejected. Even at meetings, where people openly share their innermost experiences, I rarely have heard the word *shame*; instead, fellows talk around it, referring to their resentments, self-judgment, and anxiety. But everywhere shame isn't, it is. When we feel resentment, it is often an indication that our shame has been touched, and the core shame that we can't locate or name directly is interwoven with our hurt and anger.

Shame often gets a bad rap. Even the language around shame can be shaming, as if shame were something to be ashamed of. In program we are often told to disregard the experience ("feelings aren't facts"), practice affirmations, or fire the inner critic. However, shame serves an important and inevitable function: to protect us from pain. When we keep company with shame, as we would a good friend, instead of trying to ignore it or push it away, we can follow it to its essential truth—our longing for connection, and the pain of that longing not being met, that underlies the shame response. When we stay with it to its core, we hear shame's cry as a kind of keening, a howling in the wilderness as it mourns the loss of connection and calls us to remember the depth of our love.

Often called the master emotion, shame is a universal human experience associated with the dorsal vagal response in the nervous system. On a sensory level, it overrides all other sensations or emotions that might be present, such as rage or grief, and serves a numbing function while also indicating a state of urgency. As Kain and Terrell note, shame provides a functional substitute for regulation by managing and inhibiting high activation in the absence of other inner or outer resources.[1] Psychologically, shame numbs us from the pain of broken connection and unmet longing. My client describes it as a thick layer of mud over her heart. The moment she gets in touch with her longing, shame coats her heart with its familiar narrative of "I'm not deserving of love." This dense, muddy layer actually serves a protective function: It dampens down our feelings of longing and the disappointment, rage, and grief at our loving feelings not being met. As painful as shame is, it is more manageable than the pain of lost love.

Shame can have healthy and toxic functions, as well as intrapsychic, interpersonal, and societal ones. The evolutionary societal function of shame is to keep members of a community as part of the group; this can be functional, when the threat of social shaming helps members stay aligned with shared values and ethics, or toxic, when members of a community are discriminated against, ostracized, and shamed for their identities or beliefs.[2] Whether functional or toxic, with its overwhelming and unpleasant sensations, shame is, as shame educator A. J. Bond writes, "the key negative reinforcement toward our core need for belonging."[3]

On an interpersonal level, healthy shame can be mobilized to keep a young child safe; for instance, we might issue a firm "no" if a child is about to touch a hot stove, followed by a repair when the urgency is past: "Oh sweetie, I'm so sorry I scared you, I was worried you were going to get hurt." The subsequent repair allows the shame to be a learning experience rather than a relational rupture, as does emphasizing to the child that the problem lies with the behavior rather than with the child herself; for instance, we might say, "It's not okay to hit your brother" rather than "Stop being naughty" or "Nice girls don't hit." When a parent criticizes a child's being rather than their behavior, or uses shame to impose discipline or set boundaries, they inadvertently feed the development of chronic shame as the child internalizes the shaming messages that then form part of their inner landscape of self-identity.

The Landscape of Chronic Shame

The chronic shame that accompanies addiction has its roots in early experiences of rejection, abandonment, or misattunement by caregivers carrying the legacy of their own attachment injuries. In the rooms of recovery, when we do talk about shame, it's mostly in the context of feeling shame as a result of behaviors we engaged in and mistakes we made when we were using. It's important to note, however, what psychotherapist Patricia A. DeYoung emphasizes in her book *Understanding and Treating Chronic Shame*: "Although addiction adds to the load of shame, a deep, pervasive shame is the cause, not the result, of the addiction."[4]

Our substance use and addictive behaviors are an attempt to manage or numb the underlying shame; in turn, addiction results in actions and behaviors that consequently create more shame, leading to the feedback loop that defines addiction. It is difficult to stop using because the moment we do, we are left facing not only the shame-inducing events of the days, weeks, and years prior, but the foundational, permeating shame that is the legacy of early childhood trauma. In other words, what makes it so hard to stop using is that the moment we stop, we remove the very thing that was numbing the shame, and we're faced not only with the shame of our addiction but the underlying shame itself, the very thing that the substance use was meant to shield us from.

So if shame is not the result of our addictions, what does it stem from? At essence, shame is a relational experience originating in early childhood. In an ideal scenario, when a child smiles, cries, or in other ways reaches out to his caregivers, they will respond with attuned care and attention. This child will learn that his needs and feelings matter. He will have a sense of efficacy, that his self-expression leads to results in the world; for example, his cries of protest when he is hungry or tired will lead to his needs being met as his caregivers respond to his cries in attuned ways. From these early experiences of coregulation, his brain and body will eventually learn important self-regulation skills as he grows older. This child will grow into an adult who is geared toward secure attachment; he will be basically confident in expressing his needs and emotions authentically, and he will feel comfortable both with himself and with others.

Unfortunately, many children do not receive the benefits of a supportive and consistent environment. A child whose caregivers are inconsistent, neglectful, abusive, rejecting, navigating their own stressors, unable to repair after a breach in connection, or simply chronically misattuned will instead learn that an expression of her needs does not result in the longed-for care and attunement. Rather, she will experience the profound pain of disconnect as her reach for love is not reciprocated. At a time when her very life depends on the care and the relational capacities of her caregivers, she experiences these breaches in connection as an existential threat. The child believes herself to be the cause of this loss of connection, sensing the "bad feeling" as something originating from inside of her—she must be bad to be feeling this bad. From these painful experiences the child concludes that something must be wrong with her or with her needs.

In our recovery journey, it's crucially important to understand that the messages of shame, while important to explore, are not our core truth. In fact, the sensations and emotion of shame, and the pervasive thoughts of "I'm a failure" or "I'm bad," result from the pain of relational disconnect. Contrary to how you might experience it, shame is not *a result of* being bad; the shameful feeling/thought, being bad, is a result of feeling bad. The pain of relational rupture—of rejection, isolation, violation, or shaming—is the primary experience. My clients often find it helpful to learn that infants as young as fourteen months, far too young to have actually done something wrong, can experience shame[5]; even the clients most identified with their shame can see that there's no way that they were bad or responsible for bad things happening when they were a tiny child.

SHAME NARRATIVE	ACTUAL SHAME SEQUENCE
I'm bad and there's something wrong with my needs (shame) → *therefore* I'm unwelcome, rejected, or abandoned, and my needs are not met.	I reach out for connection and feel the pain of being unwelcomed, violated, rejected, or abandoned and my needs not being met → *therefore* I organize the pain of this experience as I'm bad and there's something wrong with my needs (shame).

Longing to Belong

It can be an important part of the healing process to move from the unconscious experience of shame into an awareness of the actual sequence of the shame process, which allows us to come into contact with the underlying longing to belong. This was the case with Marina, a successful stage actor in her early thirties. Marina often goes to parties with other well-known actors. Following each event she spends a lot of time ruminating on the encounters, wondering why the other actors didn't ask her about her recent performance or offer positive feedback. She wonders if she said something wrong or if her work wasn't good. Lost in a familiar shame-based narrative, she's not able to see that their responses have little to do with her, and she imagines that they are judging her and intentionally rejecting her from the community.

Because her playfulness and authentic expression were often judged harshly or shut down in her early childhood, she understandably has a lot of fears about being seen and putting her work into the world. When the actors at the events don't respond to her in the way she hopes, she goes through a painful recapitulation of these early childhood wounds from a time when she experienced love as conditional on a perfect performance. In fact, in an unconscious reenactment of her childhood trauma, she attends these events, essentially "going to the hardware store for bread," longing to heal these early wounds in the very place where they cannot be healed.

It has been helpful for her to recognize and name that she feels shame following the parties and to organize this experience to understand the actual order of events: It's not *because* she's "bad" that she is unwelcomed; rather the shame-based narrative of "being bad" *is activated by* the pain of feeling unseen and unwelcomed—at these events as in childhood. Marina's healing will begin when she can tenderly meet the pain of the lack of belonging and contextualize it in its true origins in childhood experience.

✶ Tracking a Moment of Shame

In your journal, explore a moment of shame with the following questions:

A situation in which I felt shame was _______.

When I recall the shame now, I am noticing in my body _______.

In this situation, in what ways was I reaching out for connection?

In what ways did my reach for connection go unmet?

When my reach is unmet and I feel the sensations of shame, the meaning I make (the story I tell myself) is ______.

I can see and appreciate my reach for connection right now by meeting myself in these ways: ______

Shame in Relationships

Unconscious shame plays a key role in relationships. When our shame is touched, we either act in, toward self-recrimination, or act out, blaming the other person. Both of these responses feed conflict and disconnect in relationship. Whenever there is escalating distress between partners, we can assume that both people's shame has been touched. Unconscious shame can result in criticism and blame, reactive rage, or shutdown and withdrawal. The extent to which we can't hold our partner's humanness is the extent to which we can't face our own. Paradoxically, our fearful reactions create and recapitulate the very outcomes, the rejection and abandonment, we are trying to prevent.

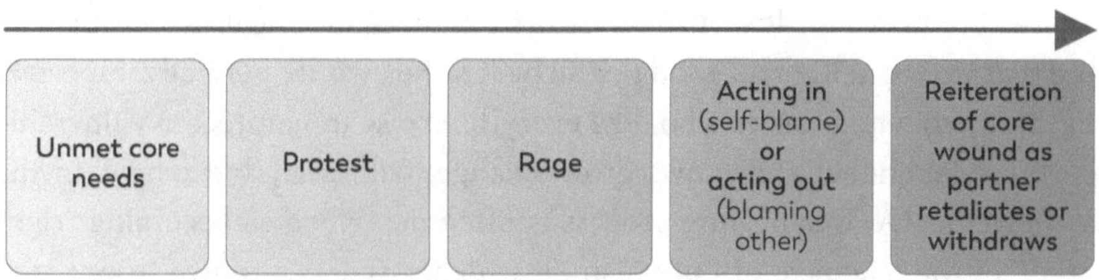

A difficult breakup taught me this painful lesson. In our relationship, my partner's deepest fear was abandonment, and mine was annihilation and rejection. He protected himself with blame, criticism, and anger (of the hair-trigger, reactive variety), and I protected myself through withdrawal and anger (of the long-term, resentful, bottle-up-and-explode variety). When, during the stress of early COVID, we got tangled in a conflict we couldn't resolve and I moved out of our shared apartment, we each reenacted an old story. Not realizing that his anger, control, and criticism had played a role in my choice to leave, he felt abandoned; he couldn't see his part in creating the scenario he most feared. In turn, as I withdrew from the relationship, I cocreated a recapitulation of my core narrative so that when he ended the relationship in a fury, abruptly cutting off all contact, I felt not only rejected but ostracized, as if I had a contagious disease, which touched into my deepest well of shame.

Another potential effect of shame on relationships and dating life is that we might be fearful about experiencing closer intimacy with our partner or having a relationship in general, afraid that we will be revealed to be unlovable if someone comes close enough to see us. They might see through our performance of perfection to the "badness" underneath. We fear they might see through the false self to a vulnerable core whose "neediness" we have learned to hide. As much as we long to be seen and known, we are simultaneously afraid that being seen and known may reveal our weakness or unworthiness.

Beneath the grandiosity or self-abnegation (which are two side of the same coin, and which people in the rooms often express as "I'm the piece of shit at the center of the universe") is a very tender, vulnerable child part whose core needs for love and care were unmet. As we heal in recovery, we find that we are neither all good nor all bad; rather, we are perfectly imperfect (i.e., human) whole selves who, like everything else in nature, are vulnerable and interdependent and move, grow, change, fall apart, and renew. In the language of AA, this healing process is often described as becoming "right sized." In the language of Buddhism, it is expressed as a return to our true nature. As Buddhist nun and poet Sister Dang Nghiem writes:

> Sometimes I think I am a mighty wave,
> Rising above all other waves.
> Sometimes I think myself a forgotten wave,
> Dying down before I am noticed.
>
> Today, I am reminded that
> My ultimate self is the water.
> Higher waves, lower waves,

Large waves, single waves,
We all return to our ultimate self,

The water.[6]

As we come to experience ourselves as more whole, we can lessen projections of our disavowed qualities onto our partners. The integration of our "good" and "bad" selves greatly benefits both our relationships and our recovery.

Situating Shame

When I was in early sobriety, I heard a woman share at a meeting that she used to feel rotten on the inside and that after a number of years in the rooms she no longer felt that way. I had never heard anyone give words to "feeling rotten on the inside," and I had never named this feeling myself because I thought I was the only one who had this experience. It felt too shameful to admit—that if I named it, surely other people would see it. It also felt like the fishbowl I was swimming in; it was hard to see and acknowledge the rottenness because it was so close to my sense of self. As you can imagine, feeling rotten inside is a major roadblock to intimacy since it feels like if someone comes close, they will uncover the secret.

Hearing the woman describe her experience was a major aha moment for me; I felt as if she was shining a small but warm beam of light into a dark corner. In retrospect, I can make sense of my experience of feeling rotten and place it in its proper context: some early developmental ruptures; intergenerational trauma (I felt like I had rotting corpses inside my body, which makes sense based on my grandparents' experiences in Auschwitz); and internalized homophobia, as I believed that my ambivalence around my sexual orientation was shameful and that my attraction to and relationships with women were illicit. The feeling was accentuated by some later life choices and circumstances: the further fragmenting of self that began when I left my hometown at eighteen and the loss of sustaining contact with my parents and friends that had kept my inner fragmentation at bay; the sacrifice of my embodiment as I abandoned activities such as dancing, singing, and time with animals and replaced them with a series of competitive academic environments in which I felt like a fraud and perpetually "less than" the other students; physical symptoms that made me feel continuously uncomfortable in my body; and the addictive substances and behaviors that resulted in harm to myself and others, further deepening my sense of shame.

Hearing this courageous woman give words to the rotten feeling was a major step in my healing. It helped me separate myself little by little from the experience of rottenness, just enough to start to bring it into awareness, which was key in starting to shift it, even though it wasn't until years later that I gained the conceptual understanding that allowed me to name the experience as chronic shame and situate it where it belonged. I say all this now so that maybe I can pass that blessing on to you, and that you too can start to find the words to bring your inner experience to light.

Shining Light on Shame

Shame thrives in the darkness. It lives in the unconscious, too painful to be acknowledged with our full awareness, a split-off part of the self that must be kept hidden. From the shadows it drives our actions and reactions, creating rifts in our relationships as we project what is deemed unacceptable in ourselves onto others, keeping the vulnerable parts of our self hidden so that we can never be fully known. Shame forms the basis of racism and prejudice, motivating widespread suffering as whole groups of people project their shadow onto other groups and these shame-based projections are internalized and passed down through the generations.[7]

We can come into a more friendly relationship with our shame by bringing it out of the shadows and into the light. We can start by recognizing our shame-based identifications; by bringing them into our awareness we can begin to lessen their power. Similarly, we can build our capacity to notice the sensations of shame, simply keeping company with the waves of sensation that move through the body. As we keep company with the sensations of shame, we can start to repair the relational wound that gave rise to shame in the first place; we let our bodies know "I am right here with you, I see you, I hear you," repairing the wound of disconnection through relational attunement with our own experience. We get to have the reparative experience of "being with," both through our relational experiences with others who can see us and be with us in our shame and through building connection with ourselves by integrating mind and body; this companionship offers a counterpoint to the aloneness of shame, meeting the most essential need that, when lacking, gave rise to shame in the first place. This bringing-to-light was the power of the #MeToo movement, which allowed women suffering from the pain of sexual violation to express their experiences, hear others' stories, and find the community and me-too-ness that are the antidote to shame.

Shame can manifest in some of the following phrases directed at the self. When we bring our awareness to our thoughts and sensations, we can gradually learn to recognize our shame-based identifications; rather than experiencing them as the pool we are swimming in, we can start to get to know them at a little distance from ourselves. Nothing is wrong with these identifications—in fact, they developed in service to our survival—so the goal is not to make them go away, but simply to notice when they arise and to situate them in their proper context as self-protective strategies that developed long ago.

Shame-based identifications can include

- "I'm bad."
- "I'm unlovable."
- "It's my fault."
- "I don't matter to other people."
- "I'm broken."
- "I'm rotten."
- "I'm ugly."
- "I'm too . . ." (Tall/short, fat/thin, smart/stupid, poor/rich, etc. It's endless. Fill in the blank!)
- "I'm not . . . enough." (Again, fill in the blank.)
- "My feelings are too much for other people."

They can also include fear-based predictions about the future:

- "If you knew me, you wouldn't love me."
- "If I share how I feel, I'll be rejected."
- "If I ask for what I want, I'll be rejected."
- "If I have needs, you'll see me as needy."
- "I'm a fraud and I'm going to be found out."

The sensations of shame—or the various hues of shame, such as shyness, embarrassment, awkwardness, or social anxiety—can include

- Tingling in the face
- Heat in the face
- Coldness along the midline, in the pelvis, belly, heart, and/or throat
- Numbness
- A movement impulse to hide or cover the face
- Curling yourself around the belly and chest and tucking the tailbone
- Shoulders rising and moving forward

As I mentioned earlier, it's important to note the dual-directional flow of thoughts and sensations. As the sensations of shame arise, the mind steps in with anxious thoughts in an attempt to make sense of the sensations and to plan for the future to avoid the bad thing happening again. At the same time, the shame-based thoughts prompt more sensations in the body as the body responds to the mind's activity. This shame-based conversation between mind and body creates a feedback loop, often recognized as a shame spiral, that can be interrupted only by bringing mindful awareness to the processes of both mind and body. It's not enough to bring awareness to and address our cognitive processes, as is done through certain kinds of step work, tools such as affirmations, and top-down therapeutic modalities such as cognitive behavioral therapy; we also need to bring awareness to the bottom-up aspect of the shame response, growing our capacity to keep company with our sensory experience.

Shame, the Guilty-Feeling Tangle, and Guilt

It's important to differentiate between chronic shame; a guilty feeling that overlays emotions such as rage and grief; and true guilt. Guilt and shame can often blur together.[8] We might use the word *guilt* to describe shame as it is more socially acceptable (i.e., less shaming). Similarly, our experience of guilt at having done something wrong might touch into shame, our sense that having *done* something wrong means we *are* wrong, triggering all-or-nothing shame thoughts such as "I always mess up," "I'll be alone forever," or "It's all my fault." I would argue that what people often refer to as Catholic or Jewish guilt is actually a pervasive experience of shame, a shame that is employed by religious, political, and other dominant institutions to wrest freedom from individuals and maintain control over populations.

Many people feel a sense of guilt even when they haven't done anything wrong, such as when setting a boundary with a family member. The guilty feeling that is often present in close family relationships is a tangle of primary emotions such as rage, fear, and grief. We might feel anger at a boundary violation or our needs not being met, sadness at a rupture in the connection, fear that our self-assertion will result in retaliation or abandonment, or disappointment that the relationship is not what we longed for. These disparate emotions are coupled together and blanketed under "feeling guilty." The guilty-feeling tangle often contains elements from early childhood, when our anger and aggression felt so powerful that we believed it could kill off our parents and, indeed, we fantasized that it might. If the development of healthy aggression was not supported by our caregivers, we might feel guilty about these destructive impulses and continue to identify with childhood fears and fantasies of our anger's annihilatory power. A child may also internalize the guilt of an abusive caregiver or ancestor, unconsciously identifying with the role of the perpetrator.

True guilt—in contrast to shame, the guilty-feeling tangle, and internalized guilt—lets us know when we've made a mistake. In recovery, we do not need to make amends for our shame; if anything, our work is to allow space for our anger, grief, and pain at our needs not being met. True guilt, however, can be a compass for the amends we need to make; it lets us know when our actions have hurt someone or when we have violated our own values or ethics. It speaks in a different language than shame or the guilty-feeling tangle, and it guides us toward a relational repair. It feels clear and meaningful, and its wisdom leads us back to ourselves and to connection with others.

True guilt speaks in phrases such as

- "I made a mistake."
- "I hurt you" (on purpose or by accident).
- "I was dishonest."
- "I was unskillful."
- "I was frightened."
- "I acted unconsciously."
- "I didn't show up in the way I said I would."
- "I betrayed my own ethics or values."
- "I let you down."
- "I wasn't acting from my highest self."
- "I expressed my anger and pain through violence, criticism, or passive-aggression."
- "I blamed you for triggering my old wounds."
- "I was emotionally cut-off."
- "I wasn't there when you needed me."
- "I used words that caused suffering."
- "I understand your point of view."
- "I'm sorry."

When we are considering making amends, it's useful to discuss our plans with a sponsor or fellow since many of us in recovery can feel a fairly continuous sense of self-judgement and self-blame. Those of us with the Autonomy survival style, for instance, may spend a lot of time ruminating on our interactions with others and all the ways we might have said something regrettable.

It's important to start to differentiate shame-based identifications such as these from the true guilt associated with an actual mistake.

Shame is healed slowly over time through reparative relational experiences. The guilty-feeling tangle can be loosened by uncoupling the underlying feelings, updating old narratives, and establishing healthy boundaries in current relationships. True guilt, on the other hand, can be rectified by making amends and acknowledging the "nature of our wrongs." We heal from shame by being loved and received by others, and by keeping loving company with our own experience. With true guilt, we often feel better after expressing our mistakes and committing to different actions in the future.

Here are some tips for healing shame in recovery:

- Track the sensations of shame (separate from the narrative and thoughts around it). You'll notice the rise and fall of sensations and might be surprised at how quickly the experience passes.
- Don't numb the shame with addictive behaviors, even more innocuous ones such as scrolling on your phone. This will just feed the cycle of disconnection. Instead, offer yourself the reparative experience of companionship by making a call to a friend or fellow.
- When you feel embarrassed or awkward, or notice the curling of your body that accompanies shame, recognize these movement impulses as shame experiences. Acknowledging these gestures as shame can help you bring your attention to the attachment rupture that may have immediately preceded it. Acknowledging the presence of shame is key to interrupting the shame cycle.
- Cultivate experiences of reparative attachment, such as with a shame-informed therapist or practitioner. If you are shopping for a practitioner, ask them if they work with shame and, if so, to describe their approach and training. Be aware that many therapists haven't learned a comprehensive mind-body framework for working with shame.
- Cultivate a loving inner parent. Your shame is connected with a young, vulnerable part of yourself. Can you offer nurturance to this part of yourself now?

- Sharing about shame in a safe-enough space brings it to light. Try taking the risk of sharing about your shame with a friend or at your favorite meeting.
- Maybe you're just lonely! Shame is deeply connected with feelings of isolation and the corresponding dorsal vagal response. Feeling shame can serve as a cue that it's time to tend to your social engagement system through a meeting or phone call, gentle movement, or time with a human or animal friend.

Cradling Your Shame

In order to interrupt shame cycles, I like to sing to my shame. I generally choose the song "Mary" by Patty Griffin because its lyrics remind me that even Mother Mary, who in my understanding is the Divine Feminine or the Earth, is covered in scars.[9] This image reminds me I'm not alone; although shame intrinsically touches on our fear of isolation and can make us feel like we're the only one who is truly *that bad*, shame is in fact a universal human experience. I am then able to turn toward my own shame with the compassion I have for others in whom it is so easy to see shame as an expression of the scared child within them. The song helps me hold my shame—at times appearing as a lonely child, at times the whole of the scarred Earth—and offer it the love that it needs. I can remember that my shame joins me to every human and to the sacredness of our shared longing for connection. Sometimes I include the person who triggered my shame, and I also sing to their Little One. You might keep an ear out for a song that you find soothing, and try the practice of singing to your shame. Singing has the additional benefit of engaging the vagus nerve, which helps the nervous system move out of the immobilization response associated with shame.

It's often so easy to look at a child, your own or others,' and see their perfection and innate lovability. You can see that their greatest longing is for love, that their playful explorations are a crucial part of their development, that their cries are attempts to communicate their needs and feelings, and whatever mistakes they make are learning experiences that are a normal part of growing up. What's harder to imagine is that this is how you would see yourself if you hadn't experienced early relational wounds that led to chronic shame.

The work of healing from shame is to clean the lens of our self-perception, turning toward ourselves to see ourselves at last in our true light. Through ANS regulation and reparative attachment experiences, we can grow our capacity for warm, heartful feelings that can cushion us from potentially shame-inducing experiences in the future, helping us land more lightly and recover more quickly. As journalist Johann Hari famously said, "The opposite of addiction is connection."[10] The opposite of shame is connection too.

✶ Understanding Your Shame Cycle

In your journal, explore these questions to better understand your shame cycle:

1. **Body sensations:** When I feel shame I feel _______ (sensation).
2. **Movement impulse:** I feel like I want to ________ (disappear, hide, run away, etc.).
3. **Narrative:** My mind interprets these sensations to mean _______ and the story I tell myself about myself is _______ .
4. **History:** I learned these messages from _________ (these people or experiences).
5. **Reaction:** When I feel and think these things, I react by _______ .
6. **Repair:** The most loving way for me to meet my shame right now is _______ .

✶ Understanding Your Shame Cycle (with a partner)

If you are doing this exercise with a partner, you can go on to explore the shame cycle in your relationship.

When you are feeling vulnerable and you fear that your "bad self" has been exposed, your partner may quickly become the "bad other," and you may react with blame, anger, or withdrawal. These reactions, in turn, rapidly trigger your partner's shame, creating the cycle of shame that characterizes relationships in distress. Our reaction is what's visible to our partner while our sensations, impulses, and narratives often remain hidden and secret. When we make these dynamics conscious, they lose their power to drive the relationship.

Start this practice with each partner doing the previous exercise on their own. Then share your answers with your partner.

Next, each fill in the following chart with your answers from the exercise on page 145.

(5) Reaction: ________________________________.
(1) Body sensations: ________________________.
(2) Movement impulse: ______________________.
(3) Narrative: _____________________________.

Using your answers from the chart above, each fill in the following sentence:

"What you see is (5), but what I'm feeling underneath is (1), (2), and (3)." Then share your sentences with each other.

Next, each explore the following:
"When I'm experiencing (1), (2), and (3), the story I tell myself about you is _______." Then share your answers with each other.

Then each fill in the cycle:
"The more shame I feel, the more I react with (5). The more I react with (5), the more I touch your shame. The more shame you feel, the more you react with (partner's 5). The more you react with (partner's 5), the more you touch my shame." Then share your answers with each other.

Finally, each complete the following sentence:
"The most loving way for you to meet my shame is _______." Then each share this with your partner.

Can you offer your partner what they're needing? If so, commit to an action or behavior:

"I commit to meeting your shame with love by _______."

✶ Having a Meta-Conversation About Shame (with a partner)

One of the most useful tools in relationship is *meta-conversation*, a conversation about having a conversation. This communication skill invites you to share your fears or shame about having the conversation, which initiates a difficult conversation from a place of tenderness, rather than guardedness. Your vulnerability invites your partner to see you and understand you, and to share with you from the same place.

In a meta-conversation, you might begin by saying how you feel about the idea of talking to your partner: "I want to talk to you about ________, but I feel ashamed at the idea of having this conversation. I'm concerned that you will _______."

By sharing your concerns as well as your desire, you can start to hold the *both/and*: the need for connection and the fear of loss of connection. You can then stand in your integrated self, which serves as loving witness to this core bind. You can invite your partner to be with you in your tenderness, and open the door for them to share with the same vulnerability and honesty.

✶ Caring for Your Shame

When you notice the sensations of shame arising or catch yourself in the midst of a shame narrative, take some time to cradle your shame. Wrap your arms around your shoulders, giving yourself a hug, or bring contact to your body in any way that feels good. Invite loving feelings into your hands, and offer yourself love through your hands. Imagine your hands are cradling a young child, and rock your body gently back and forth. You might also include a quiet song or humming sound. Do this for several minutes, staying with this practice until you note a sign of a physiological shift, such as a deeper exhalation or a feeling of ease or settling. Take the time to notice any pleasurable sensations or healing images that arise.

CHAPTER 8
Touch

It is as if the armor has become part of the skin and keeps away not only the archaic dangers, but also the always needed and longed for soft warm human touches.

—ERNEST S. WOLF

Genuine love . . . permeates every cell in the body.

—MARION WOODMAN

One learns to love not by instruction but by being loved.

—ASHLEY MONTAGU

One of the best antidotes to shame is loving, attuned touch. As we sense our body and self in relation to the people and the world around us, attuned touch lets us know that we matter and we belong. Touch is closely related to experiences of movement, and together they foster the development of *interoception* (our capacity to sense our bodies from the inside), *proprioception* (our capacity to sense our body in space), and *alteroception* (our ability to sense body-to-body connection and emotional attunement in relation to others).[1]

Our experience of touch begins in the womb. The embryo is surrounded by contact on all sides in a warm and responsive uterine environment. In a vaginal birth, the uterine contractions stimulate the baby's skin, offering the human equivalent of an animal licking her newborn young, with the same positive effects.[2] Swaddling and cradling the infant provides a sense of safety and containment, while the skin-to-skin contact of holding, rocking, and breastfeeding provides the baby with a sense of symbiotic connection and immersive wellbeing. As perinatal neuroscientist Nils Bergman emphasizes, "Skin-to-skin contact is what the newborn requires in order for the brain to be shaped in the best possible way, and breastfeeding in the fullest sense is not about eating, but about brain growth, and the development of good relationships."[3]

As the child grows, she continues to explore the world through touch, bringing objects to her mouth and reaching out for contact with the world around her. She'll seek out sensory engagement through play, enjoying the touch of stimuli such as sand, foods, animals, shapes, or water, and seeking a sense of her body in space through movement such as bouncing and swinging. These explorations aid healthy development, strengthening neural networks and fostering interoceptive and proprioceptive awareness.[4] As the child grows older, the need for play continues while some of the cuddles from caregivers may be replaced or supplemented by contact with friends. From my time teaching sixth grade, I remember how sweet it was to see the boys curl up together like puppies, as of yet unaffected by prohibitions against male touch.

Our need for loving contact continues throughout our lifespan. As time passes, the sucking and caressing of early life finds its translation in sexual relationships. We might seek to meet our need for containment through the use of a weighted blanket, or the need for caress and stimulation through a massage. We might revisit our time in the womb through a warm bath or a visit to a float tank, or enjoy sensory play through artmaking, gardening, or swinging in a hammock. At the same time, widespread touch prohibitions might start to feed into touch hunger, as some people, and many heterosexual men in particular, may find it near impossible to get their touch needs met outside of a sexual context.

Many of us in recovery have never experienced attuned touch. Touch deficits in your early childhood environment may have left you with gaps in key developmental phases. A cesarean birth, for instance, might have left you more susceptible to infections and gut imbalances, while bottle-feeding may have deprived you of the key nutrients found in breastmilk as well as the critical attachment experience informed by skin-to-skin contact.[5] Early developmental ruptures in relation to touch can include

- Birth trauma
- Early separation from parent, such as time in the NICU
- A cesarean birth[6]
- Bottle-feeding or too-early weaning
- Neglect
- Boundary violations
- Experiencing or witnessing violence
- Being subject to pain-based discipline, such as spanking
- Insufficient or inconsistent holding
- Being left in the crib to "cry it out"
- Relational losses such as parents' divorce or death
- A depressed or distracted parent whose touch is physically present but energetically uninhabited
- Cultural and family norms that prohibit or limit contact
- Restriction of movement, play, and exploration
- Illness or pain associated with touch

These early disruptions fuel disconnect from our embodied self. The chronic shame stemming from relational rupture (as discussed in Chapter 7) might mean that we feel ashamed of our needs for touch or cut off from our longing altogether. Unaware of the effects of these early disruptions, in later life we might dull our desire through substance use, or we may seek out contact primarily through sexual relationships. Split off from our need, and believing we must keep this part of ourselves hidden, we may find empty substitutes for meaningful contact in porn, food or drugs, or compulsive behaviors, keeping our desire for touch in the shadowy realm where it remains closely interwoven with shame.

Furthermore, as a result of constrictive cultural or family norms and a lack of meaningful sexual health education at school, we might never have learned about our bodies and the kind of touch we prefer. As a result of touch deficits or lack of attunement in early childhood, our interoceptive awareness might be limited, so we might not be able to sense our body's experience from the inside out to access what feels pleasurable and what does not. We might struggle to tell our partners how we like to be touched and to ask them about their touch preferences. We might not enjoy how our partners touch us but not know how to ask for the changes we want. In long-term partnership we may avoid physical contact all together, or meet the longing for contact outside the relationship, in flirtations or affairs.

Everywhere and Nowhere

Everything on Earth touches. The air touches our skin, and our skin touches back. Water flows over us, and we flow through water. A hummingbird touches a flower, and the flower touches back. A stone touches the sand, and the sand touches the stone. We pet our animal friends, and they lick and caress us in return. Touch inherently flows both ways. Even receiving touch is a form of touching. We give touch and are touched. Touch is the embodiment of mutuality in relationship.

Though touch is everywhere, in much of white American culture it is also nowhere. Touch is taboo, associated with abuses, or confined to the realm of sex. Therefore, humans, as well as many domesticated animals, are deprived of attuned and nourishing touch. Like a horse confined to a stall, many of us are similarly isolated from our herd.

If you've ever watched a herd of horses in a pasture, you'll have seen the ways they continually engage in mutually attuned relationship. When one scratches the other's withers with his lips and teeth, the other has the irresistible impulse to reciprocate. The horses will stand head to tail to keep the flies out of each other's eyes, each dependent upon and offering this gift to the other. Like horses, we evolved to be in contact with our fellow human beings and with the more-than-human world to give and receive mutual support and nurturance. This mutually attuned care is part of what keeps a community healthy.

In American culture, with its legacy of colonialism and puritanism, it can be hard to find ways to experience attuned touch. When we lost our connection to the natural world, we also lost our sense of self as embodied beings who experience ourselves and our environments through touch. When we lost the knowing of our pagan and animist ancestors, we forgot that our bodies were part of a community of fellow bodies—that we could touch and be touched by a tree, a river, or a stone as much as by another human.

With the loss of goddess worship, as much of the Western world moved toward worship of the masculine represented by the figure of Christ or a male God, the Divine Feminine was pushed into the unconscious where she splintered off into two archetypes: the virgin and the prostitute. The untouched virgin is seen as pure and clean, while her mirror image, the prostitute, who touches and is touched sexually, carries the projections of impurity and unchecked sexuality. Our culture continues to unconsciously enact the virgin/prostitute dynamic, venerating touch deprivation as "pure"—which is the pride-based counter-identification of shame, and the disavowal of the core need—while relegating touch to realm of the shadow.[7]

In dating or romantic partnerships, touch often occurs only in this shadow realm, in the context of sex. It may be coupled with sex to the extent that touch can feel like it comes with strings attached, that it serves primarily as a precursor to sex, or that it communicates a promise or expectation of sex. I've heard many men express that they cannot find other ways to experience connection outside of sexuality. They may rely on sex in order to meet the underlying needs for emotional contact or reassurance, and they may experience compulsivity in the areas of porn, masturbation, or hiring sex workers. They talk about how they feel uncomfortable hugging their father or their male friends. Some have shared about the isolation they experienced in prison when they were longing for contact with another human being, expressing the touch hunger that so many of us, whether or not we've ever been incarcerated, have painfully experienced.

Part of the cruelty of the so-called justice system that entraps so many addicted individuals is the severe touch deprivation, depriving incarcerated people of the very medicine that would most offer healing and rehabilitation. In a study of convicted adult men, researchers found that "neurobiologic dysregulation and attachment pathology (from adverse childhood experiences) explain the stark rates of criminal behavior . . . [and] that treatment interventions focusing on the crime with no attempt to heal these neurobiological wounds are 'destined to fail.'"[8] Touch deprivation repeats and reiterates the core wound—the absence of nurturance that fed the dysregulation, shame-based identities, cognitive distortions, and reactive behavior that led to drug use, violence, and other unlawful activities in the first place.

Touch in Recovery

In relationships in recovery, we can develop our connection in ways that promote the giving and receiving of attuned touch. We can have conversations with our partners about touch preferences, which can go a long way toward bringing what is unconscious into consciousness. Through somatic touch explorations, alone or with a partner, we can start to awaken our touch receptors and experience touch in new and more nuanced ways. We can also develop our toolkit of self-directed touch practices for self-regulation and self-soothing. We can use touch to deepen secure attachment in our relationships, and develop a shared vocabulary of touch with our partners. Here are some ways we can meet our core touch needs individually and with another person[9]:

TYPE OF TOUCH NEEDS	PURPOSE OF TOUCH	DEVELOPMENTAL KEYSTONE	HOW TO PROVIDE FOR SELF	HOW TO PROVIDE FOR PARTNER
Containment	Provides a sense of holding; soothes overwhelm; helps settle activation; reinforces messages of safety; says, "I'm right here and am holding you through this."	Infant is swaddled in a blanket or held in the caregiver's arms.	Wrap your body in a blanket; use a weighted blanket; self-hug; cup your knee or foot with both hands; express to your inner child, "I'm here with you, I'm helping you hold this."	Wrap them in a blanket; provide touch that offers holding, such as a hug, contact on the upper arms, or cupping a hand, foot, or shoulder with both hands; offer words such as, "I'm here with you, I'm helping you hold this."
Nurturance	Provides a sense of care, nourishment, and support.	Infant is breastfed.	Place warmth, such as a heating pad or a warm pillow, along your midline (throat to belly); gently palpate your belly; feed your skin with oil and self-massage; sip warm beverages.	Offer warmth along their midline; gently palpate their belly; gently touch their mouth and jaw; hold and cradle them; offer opportunities for kissing and sucking.
Support	Provides a sense of safety and security, the feeling that someone's got your back.	Infant is held securely with back and head supported, allowing for the crucial developmental experience of resting into reliable support.	Set up a bed or chair with pillows and a heating pad for your back and head; practice yielding into this support.	Securely hold your partner's back or head; place your hand on their back behind their heart; verbally communicate "I'm here with you, we'll figure it out together."

TYPE OF TOUCH NEEDS	PURPOSE OF TOUCH	DEVELOPMENTAL KEYSTONE	HOW TO PROVIDE FOR SELF	HOW TO PROVIDE FOR PARTNER
Protection	Provides a sense of protection, a shield for the vulnerable parts of the body.	Infant's front body is protected by contact with the body of caregiver.	Bring pillows to the front of your body; create a tent with pillows and blankets; use a weighted blanket.	Offer a shield for your partner's heart or belly with your hand or a pillow; give them a big, warm bear hug; speak words such as "I'm here to help you feel safe."
Awakening the skin	Fosters a sense of aliveness; awakens sense receptors; initiates pathway to interoceptive awareness.	Infant is washed, cleaned, caressed, massaged.	Explore texture on the skin; dry brush; wear soft fabrics; self-massage with oil; practice Havening. (See the "Resources" section.)	Offer a massage; explore different kinds of touch, pressures, and textures; caress your partner's body with your mouth, fingertips, or other parts of your body.
Rhythm	Soothing; fosters proprioceptive awareness; centers body on the midline; allows body awareness and balance to develop.	Infant is cradled and rocked; infant senses the rhythms of mother's heartbeat and breath.	Rock back and forth on your sit bones; rock your head up and down, and side to side; notice the movement of your breath; sense the rhythm of your heartbeat; swing on a hammock or swing; swim; dance.	Hold and rock your partner; place a hand over your partner's heart or on their belly; breathe together; hug and sway; dance; kiss; have sex.

TYPE OF TOUCH NEEDS	PURPOSE OF TOUCH	DEVELOPMENTAL KEYSTONE	HOW TO PROVIDE FOR SELF	HOW TO PROVIDE FOR PARTNER
Sensory engagement and stimulation (play)	Develops interoception and proprioception; develops capacity for imagination, self-regulation, and problem-solving; develops sense of self-identity and self-efficacy; develops empathy, morality, and social skills; supports brain development.[10]	Child is at play, exploring and enjoying contact with the world.	Draw, paint, sculpt; collage; garden; build; explore sand or clay; spend time in nature; play games or sports.	Play games; make art or tell stories together; grow a garden or build something together; spend time together in nature; enjoy playful, exploratory sex.

Touch needs for many people also include sexuality and eroticism, which will be discussed in more detail in the next chapter.

Practicing relationship in recovery invites in new possibilities for experiencing the power of attuned touch. Attuned touch allows for the repair of childhood attachment wounds and chronic shame as it meets the needs for safety, belonging, and connection and helps the body-mind release shame-based identifications and replace them with the core awareness of "I exist," "I belong," and "I matter."

Attuned Touch

Attuned touch is touch that emphasizes connection, care, and awareness. It is consensual and conscious. In contrast, touch that is misattuned is often touch that is primarily for one person's gain at the expense of another, rather than a gift or a mutually enjoyed encounter between two bodies. It has an energy of "giving to get." Alternately, it is self-violating and self-betraying, meeting the other person at the expense of one's own needs and desires. It may be used to maintain connection, even at the cost of one's connection with self. Misattuned touch may be a means to an end, rather than enjoyed in its own right; for instance, it is often used as a rushed precursor to sexual intimacy, as foreplay rather than *coreplay*, a patriarchal mode of sexuality that is often penis-centric and disavows the pacing and sexual response cycle of people with vulvas.[11]

Misattuned touch may be nonconsensual or consensually blurry. It hurtles through beginnings and endings, rushing in or ending abruptly. It lacks consciousness and awareness so that while the hand is physically making contact, the touch is empty and uninhabited. It is touch that is used for power, rather than to support the empowerment of the person being touched. It has unclear boundaries; it may push for energetic merging, rather than meeting and honoring the boundary of the skin and energy fields.

In attuned touch the intentions are clear and communicated verbally and nonverbally. Attuned touch honors the beginning and end, the arrival and departure, taking time to move slowly through transitions in and out of contact. The touch is fully inhabited; the person offering the touch has taken the time to locate their awareness in their hands and awaken their sensory perceptions, and is focused on listening through their hands. Attuned touch honors the intimate connection and also the boundary of the body as delineated by the skin and energy field. It says, *I am right here with you, and also I honor your body as your own.*

Exploring Touch

In our touch-deficient world we have to be creative about ways to meet our touch hunger and to ignite or reawaken our capacity for interoception. Here are some ways you can start to nurture your awareness of touch. You can do these practices by yourself or explore them with a partner.

- Dry brush your skin with a loofa or brush.
- Move your hands through clay.[12]
- Touch a tree. Cup the trunk or branch with your hand. See if you can sense the movement of its life-force. Touch grass, moss, sand, or stone.
- Make a sensory bag. Fill a bag with different objects, such as a feather, a shell, a ball, and so on. Close your eyes and choose an object. Explore getting to know each object in the bag with your hand instead of your eyes.
- Receive a massage, Reiki, or somatic bodywork.
- Try a weighted blanket.
- Next time you're at the beach, explore placing warm stones down your torso or back.
- Practice Havening. (See the "Resources" section.)
- Massage your head or feet with lavender oil.
- Wrap yourself in a soft blanket or wear something cozy.

- Make a body scrub with sea salt, sugar, or coffee grounds mixed with almond oil, and use it all over your body.
- Bring awareness into your hands. (See "Practicing Attuned Touch" at the end of this chapter.)
- Mindfully pet an animal friend. While receiving the enjoyable sensations of their hair, fur, feathers, or skin on your hand, also focus on offering pleasure by noticing what kind of touch they respond to positively and listening to cues from their body about what kinds of touch they prefer. (My cat, Mel, has let me know that just because he rolls over to show his belly doesn't mean he wants his belly touched—I've learned this the hard way! However, he'll put his chin in the air if he wants me to scratch his neck.)

As you explore touch, take the time to find the kind of touch you like, noting which sensations of texture, rhythm, temperature, and pressure you prefer. When you were a child, you might not have been supported in noticing and expressing your preferences for touch. Often children must either accept the kind of touch they are offered or receive none at all. You may also have needed to override sensory sensitivities in order to function in your home or at school, as children are often punished for expressing distaste or distress. When I was a school counselor, I often saw how a child would be distracted in class by uncomfortable smells, sounds, or textures and then reprimanded for showing signs of distress, which a teacher would misinterpret as acting out.

If you've had experiences of sensory mismatch, now is the time to offer yourself a reparative experience. You can start to meet your inner child by playfully exploring textures for clothing and furnishings and choosing the ones that feel best. Some ideas include plush, velvet, denim, satin, silk, wool, or knits. For instance, I love the feel of soft, fuzzy blankets, and I have them all over my office. Ask the same question regarding the fit of your clothes: Does your collar restrict the movement of your neck and throat? Does your bra dig into your skin or create armor over your heart? What would better support your body's ease of movement and breath? You can explore color as well: What are the colors that make your eyes and your heart sing? What colors help you feel safe and cozy? Try choosing clothing and fabrics in your environment that honor your body's preference for material, color, and fit. If your body could choose what it wanted to touch, what would it choose? Can you honor your body's desires? These kinds of tools, practices, and choices can extend into the realm of sexuality, which is the subject of the next chapter.

As you explore your touch preferences, old memories and feelings may surface. You may experience sadness at touch deficits or anger at boundary violations. You may recall a yearning to be held. Listen to the need your body is expressing, and explore further to see if you can find a way to meet that need moving forward. Where in your life might you practice asserting boundaries? What inner and outer resources do you now have to keep yourself safe that you didn't have in the past? How might you practice receiving love and support? How might you access a sense of being held?

As the authors of *Sensory Pathways to Healing from Trauma* explain, "The exploration of safe touch sensations can help the brain relearn that touch is not always dangerous and can be used to foster safe connection with others and with the world at large."[13] Attuned touch can help us reclaim boundaries, honor sensory sensitivities, and meet core relational needs. It nourishes attachment in partnership, enhances self-care, relieves chronic shame, repairs core developmental ruptures, and shifts old beliefs and identifications into more life-giving identities. We can access its power by practicing healthy and loving contact—contact that can be both attuned to others and expressive of self. We can remember ourselves as part of the more-than-human world by coming into close relationship with a tree, a body of water, or a patch of soil. We can start to take sexuality out of the shadows, allowing it its rightful place as an expression of life-force and connection in our own lives as well as advocating for crucial cultural shifts, such as equitable access to comprehensive sex education and reproductive healthcare. As we bring to conscious awareness our inner prostitute (our "bad" self with shameful needs), and ground in reality our inner virgin (our false "pure" self built on the disavowal of our needs), we integrate what had previously been split into two. We then remember our inner divinity—our essential wholeness.

✳ Exploring Touch

Explore the following prompts in your journal:

What was my experience of touch in my family of origin? What were the messages about touch that I learned?

What kind of touch experiences do I have in my life today?

What kind of touch would I like to receive? What are my deepest longings?

What would I need in order to feel safe to receive touch?

What would I need in order to feel safe to offer touch?

What kind of touch would offer a repair for any destructive or limiting messages I received in childhood?

Who can support me with this kind of touch (for example, a friend, my partner, a massage therapist, a Reiki practitioner, or a somatic bodyworker)?

What is one action I can take toward receiving the kind of touch I am longing for?

Touch and the Twelve Steps

Working with touch as a somatic practitioner has left me with no doubt that the nature of the body is love. Every cell of the body is meant for love and opens to love. When I work with clients, I can feel the way their body responds to touch under my hands; the cells starting to awaken, breathing, returning to their essential nature, which is the spaciousness of love and interbeing with all others. With attuned touch, the body reconnects to its true aliveness.

Attuned touch in a therapeutic context can address the core needs of people in recovery and allow them to embark on the journey through the Steps. A hand on the back behind the heart can give us the support we need in order to take Step One. This embodied support offers an important repair to our infant self, who may not have been given the experience of being securely held, whether physically or emotionally. You may have learned early on that you had to work hard for the nurturance of the breast or fight for emotional connection. It's difficult to admit powerlessness if we feel we'll be dropped the moment we cease trying to hold ourselves up, or that everything will fall apart if we stop fighting to keep it all together. When we can lean back and sense that we will be held, we become capable of the yield and surrender required by Step One. Whereas we once feared powerlessness as a potentially annihilatory lack of agency, we can now experience it as a gentle yield into nurturing care. This shift allows us to access our capacity to receive loving support, which empowers us to continue through the Steps cradled in the infinite hands of our Higher Power.

✶ Practicing Attuned Touch (solo or with a partner)

Bring your consciousness into your hands, filling them with your awareness. You might picture them filled with light or energy. Cup your own or your partner's hand in your hand. Sense the texture and temperature of the skin. Sense beneath the skin to the fascia and the muscles. Sense further into the hand, feeling the form of the hand, the bones. Then sense any movement of energy, such as waves or pulsations. Notice any images that come to mind. At the same time, notice the movement of your breath.

If doing this exercise with a partner, after several minutes, switch roles.

When you have finished, take a few minutes to reflect on your experience.

✶ Exploring the Texture of Sound (with a partner)

One of the most essential ways we experience touch is through sound. As it travels through space, the sound of a loved one's voice reaches the ear, vibrating and moving the body.[14] Our earliest experiences of sound are in the womb, hearing the sounds of our mother's heartbeat, which holds and regulates our body. Later in life we make connection through heartful conversation, through song, through the breath and moans of lovemaking. We are caressed by the voice, contacted through rhythm and tone.

Philosopher Roland Barthes described it beautifully: "Language is a skin: I rub my fingers against the other. It is as if I had words instead of fingers, or fingers at the tip of my words. My language trembles with desire."[15]

Through the prosody of the voice, we experience coregulation with our partner. One of the qualities I love most about my partner is the sound of his voice, which is deep and slow and resonant. Just listening to him talk about pretty much anything is a soothing experience.

We can explore what kind of auditory contact feels best. Do you prefer soft sounds, or do you need firmer contact in order to feel yourself in relation to space or another person? How does sound impact the relational field, the space between you and your partner?

Try this exercise with your partner to explore the kinds of vocal expressions that are most regulating for each of you. Start by choosing a conversation topic together, one that is fairly neutral. Then place your head on your partner's chest, and invite them to start talking. As your partner talks, expand your awareness to listen not only to their words but to the music of their voice. Listen to the timbre, rhythms, pitch, and tones of their voice. Feel the way their voice is resonating in their chest and through their body. Notice how their voice enters your ear. Feel the vibrations of the voice as it travels through your ear canal. You might notice it resonating in your chest or pelvis. Notice all the ways your body responds in relationship with the sound.

If you'd like, you can also ask your partner to explore different kinds of sounds. How would your body experience a whisper? A hum? A melody? The words you have been longing to hear?

When this feels complete, switch roles.

Afterward, take some time to share your experience with each other. What does this experience teach you about the ways you can coregulate through the voice?

CHAPTER 9

Dating in Recovery

If your heart runs
return to the place.

—FROM THE *SEFER YETZIRAH*

The intensity of the longing
Does all the work.

—KABIR

The French playwright and philosopher Jean-Paul Sartre made two opposing statements on the nature of relationship; taken together they sum up the paradox that many of us face upon considering dating in recovery. In one instance, he writes, "Hell is—other people!" and in another, "In order to exist, [we] must also consort with others."[1] As these two quotes illustrate, many of us in recovery face opposing pulls when it comes to relationships: our desire to distance ourselves from the seemingly optional hell of other people, and our desire for connection. As we dance between these two opposing poles, we will ultimately remain alone until our longing for connection grows stronger than our fear.

Dating in recovery might bring up a number of questions: When is the right time to date? How do I meet the right person? What if I repeat the mistakes of my past? When I do meet someone I like, how do I progress with dating in a sober way? In dating, for some of us the task is to move out of isolation and open our hearts, minds, and bodies more fully to the luminous tug of desire. Others of us may need to substantially slow down the process, having, in the past, moved quickly from one relationship or intrigue to the next, propelled unconsciously into unmanageable situations.

✳ Dating in Recovery

Consider what dating looked like for you in your pre-recovery life and how you can draw on the skills and principles of recovery to create new possibilities for sober dating.

Explore the following prompts in your journal:

What did dating look like for me pre-recovery?

What does dating look like now?

What are the principles and skills I have learned in recovery so far?

How can I practice these principles and skills in my dating life?

What sources of support do I have now that I didn't have in the past?

What can dating in recovery look like when I call on my support?

Should I Tell Them I'm in Recovery?

I once heard about a guy residing in a sober living home who dated a woman for a number of months without ever telling her where he lived or that he was sober. The ironic part was that the woman was a psychoanalyst! I don't know if she ever found out, or how the relationship progressed, but I can only imagine how challenging it may have been for them both to navigate a dating situation with a secret at its center.

As we date, we have the choice about how and when to tell potential partners about our recovery. Some questions may arise early on and throughout the dating relationship at key junctures: What happens if they ask me out for a drink? What do I say if they're drinking and I'm not? What happens when I meet their friends and family? How do I answer honestly when they ask me about my background in a way that touches on my addiction and recovery history?

I've tended to offer my story early on—the first or second date—because my recovery is an important part of who I am and I want to see how the person responds. However, when and how you tell potential partners about your recovery is a deeply individual choice. First and foremost, however, tend to your own safety. I would suggest waiting to tell your story until you get a sense that the person is trustworthy and your honesty won't be used against you. In the meantime, if someone asks you out for a drink or suggests a substance or situation that goes against your recovery, you can offer a simple "I don't drink (or smoke weed/eat sugar/take my clothes off on the first date, etc.)" without explaining further.

You may also want to be especially discerning if you live in a small town or if you are a well-known or public figure and are concerned about preserving your privacy and anonymity. For example, when I was a school counselor in a small, close-knit community, I was cautious about speaking about my recovery with people who might have children in the school, conscious of the continuing stigma around addiction. On the other hand, as you think about timing, you might also consider how your need for safety and the principle of anonymity are balanced with honesty, another key principle of conscious dating and recovery, and how sharing vulnerably at the right time can lay the groundwork for honesty and intimacy in the relationship as it progresses.

It is also important to consider that if you grew up with addiction or trauma in your family, you might be accustomed to guarding the "family secret," having unknowingly signed an unconscious family contract. Family systems often unconsciously arrange themselves with the unspoken imperative of keeping its histories and experiences hidden from the outside world and even from the conscious awareness of its members. You may have learned early on that some feelings and perceptions could not be spoken aloud, either within or outside of the family. For example, the family contract might have stipulated that the children had to pretend that a parent wasn't drinking and that everything was fine at home, or it might have contained agreements between the parents, in which one unconsciously agreed to overfunction in order to cover up the other's negligence, creating a home environment thick with the energies of resentment, heartbreak, and regret.

Dating may kick up fears related to the family contract as you consider when to speak about your addiction history with prospective partners. You may fear being vulnerable or visible; you might worry about being rejected or judged; or you might feel guilt or shame in speaking the *must-not-be-spoken*, in exposing to the outside world the painful secrets you learned to guard at any cost.

✳ Reading Your Family Contract

Explore these prompts in your journal:

What did my family contract say about speaking about addiction and/or trauma?

In what ways might it not feel safe to speak about my addiction, trauma, or family history?

When I consider taking steps that run counter to my family contract, what feelings come up—for example, fear, shame, or sadness?

How might my family contract affect my decision to talk to my dating partners about my addiction history and recovery?

As you consider the hesitation that comes up around sharing your recovery, you might also consider the benefits. For example, you might hear an affirming "Me too!" from a potential partner; you might have the reparative experience of speaking honestly and being received nonjudgmentally; you might experience the conversation as a scary but ultimately life-giving risk into deeper connection as you lead with the honesty and vulnerability that are the foundation stones of conscious relationship.[2] Whatever happens, sharing your story gives you the opportunity to research a potential partner as you gather important data about their capacity to receive you with acceptance, gentle curiosity, and loving presence. If they can't, that is good information as well, and learning this early will free you up to continue the quest for secure attachment elsewhere.

Dating for Secure Attachment

In recovery we practice many new skills one day at a time until a whole new way of life becomes possible. We practice showing up, present and available, for our sponsees and fellows. We learn to sit with big feelings and uncomfortable sensations without numbing or acting out. We turn our gaze inward and develop self-awareness and self-responsibility. We learn how to be of service, to set up chairs or make coffee at a meeting and share our experience, strength, and hope with others. Although we have developed these skills and can utilize them in many arenas, it can be difficult to transfer them to the realm of relationships. So how do we draw on the skills and principles we have practiced in recovery and access them in service to creating secure attachment?

It's important to have some touchpoints for what a conscious dating relationship can look like and to refer back to them to make sure you're staying grounded in dating relationships that are aligned with and support your recovery. A healthy dating relationship is not abusive, inconsistent, confusing, or spectacularly technicolor. A reliable person will be honest and upfront about themself, their expectations and hopes, and their availability. If they have other relationship commitments, they will communicate them openly. Overall, a healthy dating relationship feels clear, consistent, and grounded. While it's normal to feel anxious at the beginning as the relationship is taking shape, generally you have a good sense of where you stand, and if not, you can ask and be met with a clarifying answer. Conscious dating might not feel like past experiences of "falling in love," which are often fueled by the dopamine hits of inconsistent availability and can replicate experiences of addiction. A healthy dating relationship grows slowly and consistently over time, deepening in intimacy and commitment until it eventually offers "the secure base and safe haven" of secure attachment that allows you to go out and explore the world, knowing you have a home to return to.

The best ways to find a healthy relationship are to look for the signs of secure attachment potential in a partner—someone who either has these capacities already or is open to growing with you—and to engage in secure behaviors yourself. Diane Poole Heller suggests expressing your needs early to see how potential partners respond and keeping an eye out for how they treat others.[3] Also consider the way you navigate an early conflict together as it offers important clues to the way the relationship will unfold. To Heller's list I would add these important considerations:

- Notice how a prospective partner talks about their past relationships. You can learn a lot about someone by how they view their former partners. If all their exes are "crazy," you will likely be on that list someday. If they ended their last relationship by fleeing the country, chances are that's how they'll end their next one too.

- Notice your body and ANS responses when you're around them. While it's normal to feel excitement or anxiety on a date with someone you're just getting to know, feelings of dread, nausea, or "walking on eggshells" can be serious red flags. Do you feel activated or exhausted after spending time together? Checking in on your energy level post-date can help you access useful information from your ANS.
- Check your gut sense by tuning in to your solar plexus when you're in their space or when you bring them to mind. Learn to recognize and honor the "no" in your body. Don't override your body to try and make it work. Your body is wise, and it has information your mind might not know yet.
- Consider your recovery bottom lines. If they are in recovery, ask how long they have been sober. What kind of supports do they have? What is their relapse history? If they are not in recovery, do they drink or use drugs? How often and in what way? How about their family, friends, and community?

In active use, you might not have had an eye trained on safety. When we're in our addictions, it's all too easy to override warnings from our bodies. You might have repeatedly put yourself in dangerous situations, or had casual sex with strangers. You might have stayed with people who were abusive. You may have sacrificed your self-care in order to support your partner. You might have been overly trusting, not having learned to listen to your own discernment; alternately, you might have functioned on continuous high alert as you remained vigilant to potential threats. You might have been fearful of connection, or afraid of being used, trapped, or betrayed. You might have run from potential intimacy to protect your freedom or been overly suspicious of others, imagining the worst of intentions.

In recovery, we learn to find the balance between taking small, healthy risks toward connection and tending to our emotional and physical safety. Striking this balance between safety and risk is a key aspect of dating in recovery. At the same time, as we take the steps to learn the skills for sober dating, we can also work from the bottom up through ANS regulation and reparative attachment experiences to develop an internal sense of safety and address faulty neuroception, which gives us a stronger base within ourselves from which to evaluate dating partners for secure attachment potential.

Overall, one of the best parts of dating a person who has the capacity for secure attachment is that their attachment tendencies and ANS regulation can facilitate a feeling of safety. Practice looking for and recognizing the feeling of safety inside so that you can check to see if you feel it with a potential partner. As you coregulate, you can look for a sense of warmth, comfort, or ease, all great signs that your nervous systems are meeting in ventral vagal and that this person might feel good to be around for the long haul.

Orienting Toward Secure Attachment

While we're learning and growing toward secure attachment, it can be useful to have an external measure for healthy dating since our own relationship compass may still be a little wobbly. Diana Kirschner's "Dating Field Report" in *Love in 90 Days* is a great foundational tool for orienting toward healthy relationship, and one that I referred to frequently in early recovery.[4]

Here is a basic checklist that can help you develop your true north of secure attachment. Overall, a person with good dating potential should be showing the signs of being *available, attuned,* and *aligned.* They are available to you and to the relationship; attuned to your needs, feelings, and body, as well as to their own; and aligned with your core values and Higher-Powered vision for healthy relationship.

Is this person *available*?

- ☐ Does this person reach out to make plans? Do they show up when they say they will?
- ☐ Are they interested in me and my world? Do they ask me questions, or say "What about you?" to invite me into reciprocal conversation?
- ☐ Is this person honest? Does their story line up?

- ☐ Are they emotionally available? Are they single or in an ethically non-monogamous relationship (not in a monogamous relationship with another person)?
- ☐ Are they geographically available? Do they live in a place that I like to be and that's feasible for establishing regular, consistent contact?

Is this person *attuned*?

- ☐ Do I feel physically and emotionally safe with this person?
- ☐ Are they affectionate in the ways (physically and/or verbally) that are important to me?
- ☐ Have they had secure attachment experiences (in their family, therapy, recovery, past relationships)? If not, are they actively working to foster them?
- ☐ Do they engage in sensual, nonsexual touch, such as holding hands, hugging, caressing, or cuddling?
- ☐ Do they touch my body in a way that feels good? If not, are they open to feedback and able to align their touch with my body's desires and needs?
- ☐ If applicable: Is the sex emotionally connected? Is it embodied? Is it pleasurable? Am I attracted to them? Is the sex getting better and more connected over time?

Is this person *aligned* with my values and my vision for dating in recovery?

- ☐ Have they engaged in therapy, coaching, recovery, or other inner work?
- ☐ Do they have practices for self-care, self-soothing, and self-expression?
- ☐ Do they cultivate community and support?

- ☐ Do they engage in prayer, meditation, art-making, or other forms of spiritual practice?
- ☐ Does their long-term vision for relationship align with mine?
- ☐ Do their political perspectives and values align with mine?
- ☐ Are they on the same page as me about having or not having children?

After the first few dates, see how many of these you can check off. If you continue seeing the person, see how they grow and change as you get to know each other and start creating a secure base for each other. In a healthy relationship with good potential, these areas will continue to clarify, grow, and deepen with time.

Discerning Your Deal Breakers

In addition to finding the signs of secure attachment potential, it's also important to clarify your deal breakers, the signs that clearly spell out a hard stop. Differing from preferences—which may include physical appearance, occupation, level of education, religious or spiritual orientation, or geographical location, and which we may find to be flexible with the right person—deal breakers are the foundational roadblocks to a viable relationship. While unique to you and your values, some common deal breakers include regular drinking or drug use; rage, violence, or other signs of extreme ANS dysregulation; unfeasible financial, family, or life situations; or priorities and perspectives that are radically divergent from your own. It's important to be clear on your personal deal breakers and have them written down as a reference point, as it's all too easy to override these core values in the midst of the dopamine-fueled high of early relationship. For me, some deal breakers are habitual substance use, right-wing politics, religious dogmatism, and misogyny.

Some baseline deal breakers might include

- ☐ Habitual drug or alcohol use

- ☐ Harmful relationship behaviors in the past, such as domestic violence, infidelity, or a contentious relationship with an ex
- ☐ Currently in a monogamous relationship with another person
- ☐ Certain political perspectives, such as _______
- ☐ Certain viewpoints, such as _______
- ☐ Certain behaviors, such as _______
- ☐ Other: _______________

As you get to know a potential partner, ask yourself "Does this person check off any of my deal breakers?" If so, be realistic with yourself about the limitations of this situation, and disengage before an attachment starts growing. You can end a dating situation in these early stages by offering a sincere compliment, followed by an honest statement that you don't wish to continue to date, and concluding with your blessings or warm wishes. For example, "Thanks for a nice dinner last night. I really appreciated your kindness and sense of humor. However, I don't feel the kind of alignment I'm seeking in a partnership. I wish you all the best and hope you find just what you're looking for." Trust that your "no" here is a "yes" to a Higher-Powered partnership that is on its way in Divine timing.

The Usual Suspects

Getting to know another person also gives us the opportunity to get to know ourselves, for much of what we see of another person stems from our own personal construction of reality, a perception that is informed, in part, by the neuroceptive and psychological blueprints arising from our childhood experiences. As Lewis, Amini, and Lannon write, "Implicit memory warps our window on the world."[5] According to Imago relationship therapy, we replicate this early imprint over and over through three primary processes: We *pick* partners who fit familiar/familial patterns; we *project* our experience, our expectations, and the denied parts of ourselves onto our partner; and we *promote* replications of our expectations by drawing these qualities out of others through our own emotions and behaviors, a process called *projective identification* in which others respond in ways that meet our projections and expectations.[6]

Our perception of others is hardly an objective reality; rather we perceive them through a potent mixture of our own memories, fantasies, ANS responses, and predictions. As Lewis, Amini, and Lannon describe, "When one woman looks at an attractive man, she sees someone who wants to possess her and stifle her creativity; another sees a lonely soul who needs mothering and is crying out for her to do so; a third sees a playboy who must be seduced away from his desirable and unworthy mistress."[7] A crucial aspect of developing conscious relationship is reclaiming our projections, recognizing them as aspects of our own subjective reality, and doing the work required to see our partner more clearly.

Several months into dating my current partner, I had a potent experience of my projections falling away, one that revealed to me, in an illuminating Zen-like moment, the fiction that I had created. My story of him began on our second date. According to my memory of the conversation, I had asked him if he liked to read, and he responded by saying that he had read a book once, a John Grisham novel. Aligning this information with the fact that he is a carpenter and didn't go to college, I concluded that he didn't like to read, and perhaps might even have a learning disability that made reading difficult. This conclusion seemed to be confirmed when I went to his house for the first time and saw that while he had a truly enormous collection of records, he didn't own any books. I felt a little disappointed because, as a writer and reader myself, books are obviously important to me, and I also felt sorry for him for what must be a difficult challenge to navigate in our society. I started reading to him out loud before bed, hoping to nurture him and ease what I imagined to be his anxiety around reading.

It wasn't until several months later that my storyline unraveled, as in the final scene of *The Usual Suspects* when the whole narrative reveals itself as a construction. While we were affectionately reminiscing about our early dates, I learned that his memory of that conversation was that I had asked him if he liked novels, to which he had responded that he had read one recently, meaning he doesn't read novels often but likes many other kinds of books. He explained that he loves to read and had boxes of books stored in his attic that he hadn't unpacked yet. I realized I structured an entire view of him based on my understanding of that initial conversation and that I had made all subsequent experiences confirm that story.

I started laughing so hard I cried, and then I felt an incredible sense of relief and clarity, comparable to mind-blowing experiences I've had in meditation, realizing that my conception of reality is a subjective construction. In retrospect I can see that my view of him was a projection of an early imprint; I clearly saw the "sad man" archetype that I have chosen, created, or replicated in various relationships, in which my role is to help a man in a vulnerable position as I attempt to "heal" him so that he in turn can meet my needs. This archetype was rooted in my experience of my father who, as the son of Holocaust survivors, did indeed carry so much sadness and pain. Through my laughter and tears, my body discharged the energy of this old imprint, allowing my mind to reach a new place, a point of utter stillness from which I could see that much of what I perceive as reality is a fabrication of my own making.

Dating with the Autonomic Nervous System in Mind

In dating we can draw on somatic awareness to help us expand into greater intimacy while also staying as much as possible within our window of capacity so that we don't move into old patterns of anxiety or dissociation. You can track your ANS responses as you meet new people and get to know them, exploring how your nervous system reacts to being in their presence and in the shared field between you.

The somatic principle of *titration* allows us to touch briefly into a potentially activating experience or emotion, and then move away from it, mitigating the intensity of the experience and allowing us to integrate it a little at a time. We can draw on this principle during the overall process of dating as well in moment-by-moment exchanges. Considering titration in the overall process might lead you to think about right pacing as you get to know a new dating partner. How much time feels right to spend with this person, both in terms of hours spent on a date and the frequency of contact? When do you start to feel overwhelmed, checked out, or out of touch with yourself?

Feelings of anxiety or exhaustion can be clues that you're moving into intimacy faster than your nervous system can keep up with. After all, the job of your ANS is to be vigilant to potential threats, and from its perspective it takes a significant amount of time to get to know a person or situation and develop a felt sense of safety. Where might you be pushing through signs that intimacy is progressing too quickly? You might notice your attention wandering during emotional or physical intimacy. You might feel drained after spending time together. You might override sensations of nausea in your throat and solar plexus, or even just the more pleasant sensation of butterflies in your belly, to push yourself forward into physical contact. All these may be signs that it's time to titrate your experience, stepping momentarily back from connection with the other person in order to tend to your connection with yourself through self-care practices, such as journaling, resting, or attending a meeting.

In addition to considering titration in the overall process, you can titrate moment-by-moment exchanges by noticing the signs of ANS dysregulation, such as overwhelm and dissociation, that may be indicating that intimacy is occurring at a pace that is "too much, too soon." You can titrate by consciously lowering the intensity. You might break eye contact by looking around the room or closing your eyes; you might notice your breath or do a quick body scan to track sensations in your body. You might suggest a shift in your shared activity, moving out of face-to-face contact and into parallel play or joint attention (shared focus on a third point) by spending time in nature, playing a board game, or watching a movie. You might let your partner know you need a little time to yourself and go for a solo stroll around the block or take a few minutes for some meditation.

The principle of titration can also help you support the other person in tending to their ANS needs. Have you ever had the experience of a new partner completely disappearing after what seemed like an amazing night together filled with deep eye contact and mind-blowing sex? I certainly have, and it's terrible! One of the reasons that people disappear is that they're overwhelmed by the intensity of "too much, too soon" intimacy and lack the language to describe their experience or ask for the pacing that they're really needing. Being ghosted is a horrible experience, touching on all our core wounds of abandonment, shame, and rejection; for the other person, their feelings of overwhelm, flooding, and shutdown without ways to mitigate the intensity are also incredibly painful. You can help avoid these experiences of sudden emotional cut-off by slowing way down and drawing on the power of titration.

As a relationship develops, we can grow a shared language of coregulation. We can start to name our own signs of overwhelm and invite our partners to share their own. We can practice recognizing the somatic signs of dysregulation in our partner, through observation of their breath and bodies and through tracking our somatic resonance internally, and consciously develop shared practices for titration. In the deepening relationship, we can develop a vocabulary of touch, learning the kinds of contact that are soothing for our partner's body and that help them feel more grounded and connected. We can show them the kinds of touch we prefer, showing how a hand on our shoulder or a warm hug can help us return to a sense of love, and let them know when what we need instead is some space to breathe.

Going slowly allows your body the time it needs to get to know your new partner, who is an incredibly unique, mysterious, and miraculous creature with a nervous system just like yours. Proceeding with your shared ANS in mind from the beginning allows you to lay the groundwork for an ongoing relationship full of safety and connection.

✳ Titrating Your Dating Experience

Explore the following questions in your journal:

How do I know when a dating situation is "too much, too soon"?

What inside me lets me know I'm overwhelmed or overriding signs from my ANS?

What tools or practices can I use to titrate the experience?

What inside me lets me know if/when I feel ready to reconnect?

✳ Charting ANS Compatibility

In these charts, you'll draw the tendencies of your nervous system in relation to the people you're dating. You'll chart tendencies toward sympathetic activation (the fight/flight response), dorsal vagal collapse (the immobilization response), blended or cyclic states, and regulation in ventral vagal (social engagement). Play with different colors and shapes to illustrate your experience of each state.

Start out by charting your own ANS tendencies. Then chart the tendencies you've observed of a person you're getting to know. Then draw yours and theirs together on the same chart to see how your states impact each other through the principle of physiological entrainment, in which a shared rhythm is established between two or more neural systems.[8] Does your shared rhythm foster coregulation, or pull you toward dysregulation? You can then use this information to help you make decisions on how you'd like to proceed in the relationship.

This is not to say that you'll always entrain with your partner. Sometimes the work is to create energetic, emotional, or physical boundaries so that your partner can be having their experience "over there" and you can remain anchored in your own experience. However, it's important to be conscious of the neurobiological tendency toward entrainment and to hold the awareness that you are each likely to be affected by the other's autonomic state. Having this consciousness allows you to make more informed choices about dating and gives you various options for ways to engage in the shared relational space.

For example, here is my own baseline ANS state:

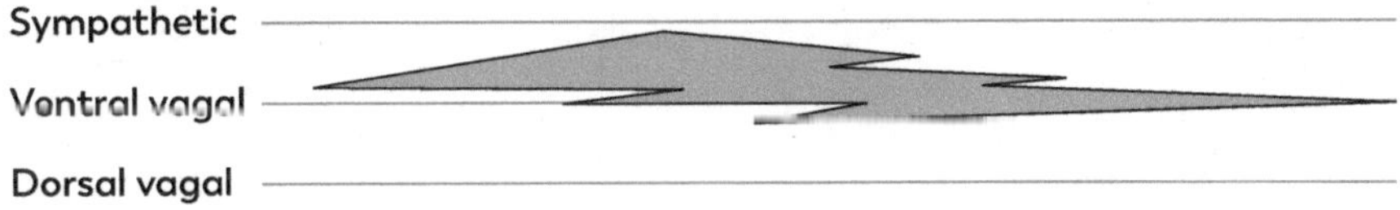

I made the following drawing after a date with a guy I'll call Noam. In recovery for cocaine addiction, Noam continues to suffer from severe PTSD. He runs a successful business, for which he works twelve-hour days, six days a week. He practices self-regulation through meditation but hasn't yet found a therapy that addresses the trauma. When he took me out for dinner, I grew anxious at the speed of his driving, and after the date I noticed I felt all jangly inside as if I held a residue of his activation. He also asked to kiss me on the first date, which felt like "too much, too soon" intimacy. The drawing illustrates how I was pulled out of my capacity for ventral vagal by our shared tendency toward activation.

Me with Noam:

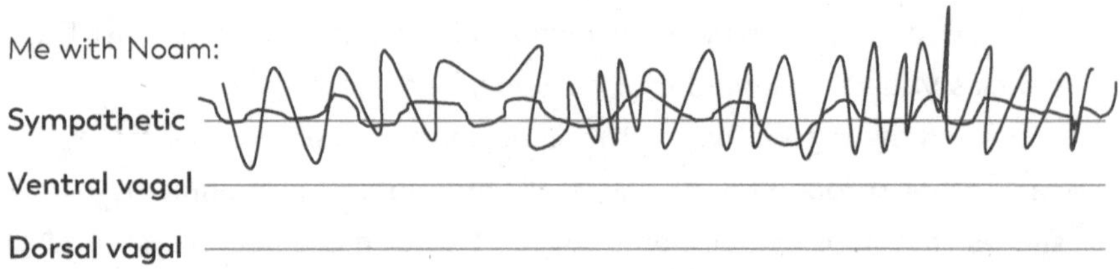

I made this next drawing after my third date with my current partner. He is quiet and shy, tending to go inward to process stress, and he moves with a slow internal rhythm, taking a lot of time to mull things over. He has a consistent life rhythm and is held by community and land connection in a place where his family has been for several generations. He self-regulates by listening to music and spending time in nature. Our physical contact proceeded slowly, allowing time for our bodies to get to know each other. As my drawing illustrates, we spent more time in ventral vagal and easily entered states of coregulation.

Me with my partner:

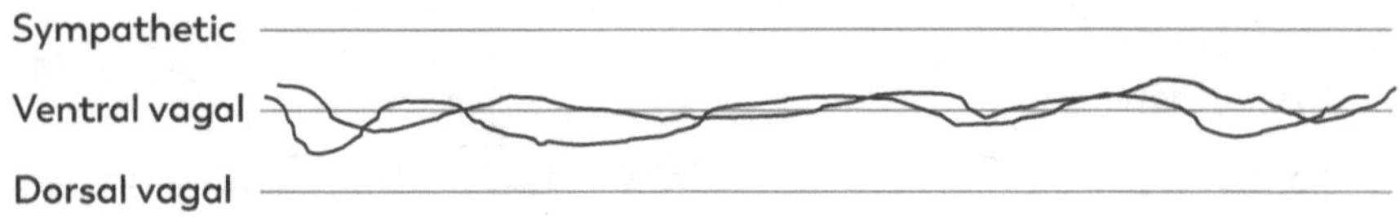

Although I liked both men, after taking the time to track my ANS responses and doing some journaling, I could see that Noam's activation fed into my tendency toward anxiety and didn't meet my vision for simplicity, spaciousness, and ease. Although we don't have as much in common culturally, I chose to pursue a relationship with my partner, whose pacing helps quiet my activation as I entrain with his slower rhythms. His embodiment and attuned touch help me feel safe, and given that touch is a primary love language for both of us, we can easefully create quiet spaces of coregulation through cuddling and listening to records. This has created an amazing repair for me, as it is exactly what my activated nervous system needed.

Now it's your turn!

My baseline ANS state is

Sympathetic ________________________________

Ventral vagal ________________________________

Dorsal vagal ________________________________

Based on my observations of _______ [potential dating partner], I hear, see, and sense that their baseline ANS state is

Sympathetic ________________________________

Ventral vagal ________________________________

Dorsal vagal ________________________________

Now put both of your states together on the same chart.

Together, our ANS states look like this:

Sympathetic ________________________________

Ventral vagal ________________________________

Dorsal vagal ________________________________

As I experience it through their words, behaviors, and touch, _______'s ANS state interacts with my ANS state so that I feel

- ☐ more "up"
- ☐ more "down"
- ☐ more regulation
- ☐ less regulation
- ☐ enjoyable and consistent coregulation

When I chart the interaction of our states, it looks like this:

Sympathetic ____

Ventral vagal ____

Dorsal vagal ____

This information from my ANS helps me see that _______.

Based on this information, I will explore these actions as next steps toward my dating vision: _______

CHAPTER 10

Sex in Recovery

How do we cleave to a God who is a consuming fire?

—FROM THE TALMUD

The erotic is the most powerful transformational force of all.

—DAVID MANN

Sexuality is one of the main arenas of relationships in recovery where we get to explore new behaviors and expressions of our authentic self. At its best, sex is a realm of creativity, vitality, embodiment, playfulness, and expansive opening to Spirit. Sexuality bridges mind and body, heart and genitals, spirit and soul, and engages us in deep connection with our physical and energetic self and the physical and energetic selves of others.

However, when we don't hold its powers consciously, sex can be a murky place full of vague or incorrect anatomical knowledge, poor self-care practices, and emotional entanglement. For many of us, when we were involved in our addictions, sexuality was a hazy territory. We may have put ourselves in dangerous sexual situations and made ourselves or others vulnerable to STIs or unwanted pregnancy. We may have woken up in bed with someone without quite knowing how we got there. Consent might have been vague at best. Sexuality and substances often went hand in hand. As one newly sober guy put it, the best way to initiate sex with a woman was to ask her, "Do you want some cocaine?"

Furthermore, the early shame resulting from childhood relational ruptures is often reiterated in sexual relationships in adulthood. Our impulse to use substances can be an attempt to numb discomfort in our body so that we can engage sexually. Our very attempts to cover up or run from our shame—through substance use, avoiding conversations about sex, compulsive sexual behavior—can result in the kinds of actions that only result in more shame as we then experience shame or guilt about our sexual engagements. This later shame builds on early shame, resulting in shame spirals related to sex and sexual embodiment.

Shame and sexual trauma remain stored in our bodies, in scar tissue and in implicit memories. We may have areas of stinging or pain in our genitals that inhibit our capacity to experience pleasure, or parts of our bodies that feel numb or absent, places that our awareness cannot inhabit. Along with our genitals, our hearts may also carry the pain of relational ruptures and betrayals of trust. Internalized shaming messages keep us from experiencing pleasure or getting to know our own bodies. We might never have learned how to bring our touch to the act of healing ourselves or how to ask for healing touch from our partners.

So what a mystery it is to have sex in recovery! How do we act without the crutch of substance use? What do we say? How do we express our desires? It can feel like we're teenagers again, exploring our body's needs and longings for the first time. Here are some of the common challenges and new experiences around sexuality that you may face in early recovery:

- Having conversations about sex, including touch preferences
- Talking about consent
- Discussing your sexual history, including any STIs
- Practicing safer sex
- Engaging sexually without substances
- Feeling anxious about having sex, including worries about sexual "performance" or fears about how to please the other person
- Navigating emotional intimacy

- Wondering what to do after sex, such as having a conversation or spending the night
- Finding the right pacing: taking the time to get to know someone instead of rushing into sex
- Navigating changes in your sexual arousal patterns
- Sensing your body and your partner's body in a new way
- Facing into realities of sexual trauma

Even after months or years of sobriety, navigating sober sexuality can feel like wading through a dense swampland of confusion and shame. The vulnerability of sexuality can touch on core attachment wounds and bring shame-based identifications to the foreground. It often represents a next level in the recovery journey when we start to navigate sexuality in a new way, attuning to embodiment, honoring the pacing and rhythms of our nervous system, and dancing consciously with the energies of fire.

Love-Based Sexuality

Love-based sexuality honors the link between physical intimacy and attachment. This correlation goes both ways: On the one hand, conscious sexual intimacy can feed secure attachment, deepening emotional connection and helping both partners feel safe and loved. On the other, secure attachment leads to better sex, as the safety and closeness of the emotional connection helps partners feel safe to deepen into the playfulness and profundity of sexual intimacy. One of the greatest tasks in recovery is to integrate heart and genital sexuality.

Before making a decision to engage sexually, it's important to consider whether you feel safe with your potential partner. Do you know them well enough to entrust them with your physical and emotional wellbeing? Have they shown themself to be honest and reliable? Rather than diving headlong into a sexual relationship, in sober sexuality we might consider the emotional, physical, and spiritual ramifications of our decision and its potential effects on ourselves and our bodies, our partners, and other people in our lives who may be affected. We might also pause at this stage to look at how sex might fit in with our recovery program. You may want to discuss it with your therapist, coach, sponsor, or fellows. Many sponsors recommend waiting to engage sexually until after you have a year of sobriety.

When you are dating and considering the timing of progressing into sexual intimacy, it's important to consider if you have gotten to know your potential partner well enough that you can both talk openly about your needs, feelings, and desires. Diana Kirshner recommends at least two months of steadily improving connection before having sex.[1] Perhaps this or a similar benchmark would make sense for you. You may want to discuss a timeframe with your sponsor based on your own history and needs, and/or write out a guideline for yourself.

In terms of timing, you might consider: Are you comfortable having honest conversations about what you want, both relationally and sexually? Can you bring both your heart and genitals into the realm of sexuality with this person, or do you feel like you need to exclude your heart to keep it safe? Are you turning toward sex when connection might be better fostered through building emotional intimacy? Conversely, are old fears and shame getting in the way of the sex that wants to happen? Do you trust that you can say a firm "no" when you need to, and a whole-hearted "yes" when it's right? Is there enough emotional intimacy that you can have upfront conversations about ways you like to be touched?

As couples therapist Sue Johnson writes, "Trying to make love without feeling safe enough to really talk is like bringing a 747 in to land without a guidebook or help from the control tower."[2] A heart-centered conversation can not only deepen emotional intimacy but also open the door to new realms of pleasure as partners express their touch preferences and show each other the kind of contact that feels most exciting or connecting. Be honest with yourself and the other person about your hopes for engaging sexually. Is this a move in the direction of long-term partnership? Is it a one-time fling in service to exploration of your self, your sexual expression, or your sexual orientation? If you are in the early stages of exploring your sexual orientation, it's especially important to be clear about this with the other person, since they may be at a very different point in their journey. It's completely okay to be in exploratory processes; the main difference in sober sexuality is that we engage in this exploration consciously, and we communicate honestly with our sexual and dating partners.

The self-care and self-valuing that we practice in recovery can extend into the realm of sexuality. Self-care can include honest communication about pleasure and touch preferences as well as logistical conversations about safer sex (including STI protection and, if applicable, pregnancy prevention) before having sex for the first time. In the midst of the dopamine high of early relationship, which can lead to passionate and impromptu decisions, you may need to remind yourself that some STIs can lead to life-threatening diseases. You have survived so much already to make it to this place, so don't risk the health you now are nurturing in sobriety—it is hard-won, miraculous, and sacred. It's a good time to bring in the rational, vigilant, future-oriented aspects of mind to collaborate with the sensuous, present-oriented qualities of body to make sure that any decisions in the moment also take into account your future wellbeing.

Some questions to consider before engaging sexually include

- ☐ Do I feel emotionally and physically safe with my potential partner?
- ☐ Have I taken the time to get to know them?
- ☐ Are we on the same page about the significance of engaging sexually?
- ☐ Are we clear about what we each want?
- ☐ Do I feel comfortable sharing my feelings, needs, and desires?
- ☐ Do I feel comfortable asking them about their feelings, needs, and desires?
- ☐ Have I given consent? Can I say no if I want to?
- ☐ Can my potential partner give informed consent? Have they given consent?
- ☐ Does sex fit in with my recovery program? Do I have more than a year of consistent sobriety?
- ☐ Do we have a plan for safer sex?

As you consider taking next steps sexually, see how many of these questions you can answer in the affirmative. Any remaining areas of vagueness can be cues for bringing in greater clarity before going forward. And whatever decisions they lead you to in terms of sex, these conversations are valuable in themselves, as they help develop deeper emotional connection and secure attachment.

✳ Exploring Sober Sexuality

Explore in your journal the sober sexuality guidelines that are most essential and meaningful for you:

What are my old patterns around sexuality that I want to shift?

How can I stay safe and healthy?

How much time do I need to get to know someone before engaging sexually?

What and whom can I turn to for support when questions or fears arise?

What guidelines that I have learned in program, from therapists and sponsors, from dating books, or from other places make the most sense for me personally?

What is my plan for STI and, if applicable, pregnancy prevention? If I don't have one, where can I get guidance and medical support? (See "Resources" at the end of this book.)

My plan for Higher-Powered sober sexuality includes ________.

Sex Ed for Grown-Ups

As we approach sexuality in recovery, we may need to revisit some of the basic guidelines for keeping ourselves and others safe. Many of us may have started using at the same time, or even before, we started having sex. Sex and substance use were so deeply intertwined that we might not have much experience of sober sex to refer back to. Any guidelines for safer sex that we might have learned have a tendency to disappear when our decision-making capacities are impaired through alcohol or drug use or when unconscious attachment anxieties are fueling our desires.

The ways that most people conceptualize and engage sexually are only scratching the surface of what's possible. As we encounter sexuality with a new level of awareness and presence, we might need to dramatically update our knowledge of sex from the version we learned in high school sex-ed, or from porn or pre-recovery sexual relationships. In conscious sexuality, we can start to center embodied pleasure, moving away from goal-oriented sex focused on orgasm to a shared intimacy that, much like the recovery journey itself, emphasizes the beauty of process rather than a specific end-point. We might discover that in heart-connected sexuality the emphasis on performance lessens as we meet each other in shared vulnerability and that, as the emotional connection deepens, so in turn does the capacity for pleasure.

> Some important recovery-based updates to our sexual learning include updating our knowledge of sexual anatomy, developing a nuanced map of our body's pleasure sensations and those of our partner, healing scar tissue and sexual trauma, becoming more aware of and releasing internalized cultural messages, and deepening into sexual practices that center the pleasure and arousal of both partners.

✳ Becoming Conscious of Sexual Messaging

Explore these questions in your journal:

What early messages did I get from my family about my body and sexuality?

Did I experience circumcision? If so, how do I imagine this experience affected my relationship with my body? What messages did I take away from it?

How do I imagine my parents might have engaged with my body when I was a child?

What messages did I receive about masturbation?

What did my parents teach me about sex?

Did I experience any touch violations?

In what ways was sexuality paired with punishment?

Did I have any shaming or embarrassing experiences when I was exploring my body or sexuality as a child?

What meaning did I make from my caregivers' responses to my developing body and sexual exploration?

What messages did I receive from religious institutions?

From school?

From peers?

From porn?

From media, such as TV, movies, or social media?

From my culture?

What do I believe now about sexuality?

Are those old messages aligned with my current beliefs?

What would I like to believe about my sexuality?

How would I like to experience my sexuality?

If exploring with your partner, take some time to share your answers with each other.

Then, alone or with your partner, explore an embodied sense of your heart–genital connection through the following imagery exercise.

✶ Blossom and Root

Close your eyes. Breathe out three times slowly. Drop your awareness into your heart. Imagine your heart as a flower. See and sense into the blossom's center.

Breathe out. Allow yourself to move down the flower's stem and into the flower's roots. Sense the roots making contact with the soil and reaching deep into the Earth.

Breathe out, and open your eyes.

Conscious Sexuality and Consent

As we engage sexuality in recovery we can start to bring a new awareness to the area of consent.[3] Depending on your age, you might have learned that sexual consent was the absence of a "no." However, as a result of a need for a clearer, more accurate definition, sexual consent is now generally defined as an "enthusiastic yes—freely given, revocable, informed, enthusiastic, and specific."[4] In addiction, sexual consent was often unspoken and hazy at best, and sadly it's not uncommon for us to have experienced boundary violations and/or to have violated the boundaries of others. As the American Health Association states, "Someone who has had too much to drink or is under the influence of drugs cannot consent to sexual activity. In addition, someone who is unconscious—whether from substances or simply sleeping—cannot consent to sexual activity."[5] Given that in active addiction, sex often occurs under these exact circumstances, we may look back now with a sense of shame, anger, grief, or regret at what we can now see was nonconsensual sex.

To explore your history around consent, start with a mini–Fourth Step sexual inventory, reflecting back on your experiences. You might then offer Ninth Step amends to former sexual partners or make living amends to your own body, promising to keep it safe and to honor its boundaries or its pleasure. As part of a living amends, it may be helpful to affirm a commitment to prioritizing consent in the future.

Having a conversation about consent can be awkward since it touches the shame response associated with making ourselves vulnerable to possible rejection. However, with practice, asking for consent can be a tender, playful, and even (believe it or not!) sexy part of lovemaking. Conversation around consent can help you understand your partner's touch preferences and communicate your own. It brings into conscious awareness your "yes" and "no," inviting you to speak your needs and desires directly instead of overriding them or enacting them nonverbally, hoping that your partner will understand. The risk of stepping into vulnerable conversation can also have huge benefits in terms of emotional intimacy.

Here are some ways to ask for consent:

"Is it okay if I _______ [sit closer, hold your hand, kiss you, take your shirt off, etc.]?"

"How does this feel to you?"

"Is there anything you need to feel comfortable?"

"Would you show me how you want me to touch you?"

"Your _______ [part of body] is so hot. Is it okay if I _______?"

When considering consent, it's important to look at the psychobiological dynamics as well. Does your partner have the psychological and physiological capacity to set the boundary they might really be needing, or is your partner's nervous system experiencing an appease or fawn response (in which they say yes in order to disarm a threat or submit in order to minimize conflict[6])? Are they afraid that if they say no they will lose the connection, or do they feel unworthy of love and therefore they take whatever affection is offered, even if it doesn't feel right? It is crucial to consider these questions for yourself as well. Do you trust yourself to be able to say no if you need or want to?

Also consider how your partner's "no" lands for you. Can you receive your partner's "no," trusting that setting boundaries is a healthy part of life and relationship, or does it touch on your shame or fear of rejection? If so, how do you respond? Do you shut down, go into a shame spiral, get angry, or pretend nothing is wrong? Do you have ways to self-soothe if your anxiety gets touched? Can you talk about your vulnerable feelings with your partner?

✶ Assessing Consent

Explore the following questions in your journal on your own or with a partner to assess capacity to give full consent:

Offering a "No"

How do I know when my body wants sex? My mind?

How do I know when my body does not want sex? My mind?

These signs from my body let me know I am sensing my "no": _______

These messages from my mind let me know I am sensing my "no": ____

When I say no, I feel _______.

If I say no, what might happen?

What's the very worst that might happen?

What is the story I tell myself about my "no"?

In what ways might it not feel safe to express anger or set a boundary? What's the worst that might happen if I feel or express anger?

What are the beliefs I carry that make it hard to ask for what I'm needing or wanting?

Do I trust myself to be able to say no when I need to? Why or why not?

Receiving a "No"

When my partner says no, I feel _______.

My mind says _______.

My body responds _______.

What is the story I tell myself about my partner's "no"? In this story, what does their "no" mean about me?

How do I react when this story gets touched?

In what ways might it not feel safe to share my feelings about my partner's "no" with my partner?

What would I need from my partner in order to feel it might be safe to share my experience with them?

In addition to speaking to my partner, what ways can I self-soothe when this story gets touched?

Do I trust my partner to be able to say no when they need to? Why or why not?

Now practice putting the cycle together:

When I say no, my partner responds with _______.

When my partner says no, I respond with _______.

The more they _______ the more I _______.

The more I _______ the more they _______.

If you are doing this exercise with your partner, take some time to share your answers with each other. What was it like to have this conversation together? How can you best support each other's boundaries moving forward?

Singing the Body Electric

Prior to recovery we might have had a limited capacity to experience embodied presence and sensation. If sensations associated with certain emotions threatened to get overwhelming, we would turn to our substance for its numbing effects. Now, in recovery, we start to come into presence in our bodies in a new way. We can explore this growing capacity in our sexuality as well, expanding our capacity to receive and offer pleasure. We can experience more nuanced sensation, making sex more vibrant and engaging. We can also start to bridge sexuality and heart-centered intimacy, connecting sex to its emotional center and bringing our emotional and somatic intelligence into our sexuality. We can move away from goal-orientation to process-orientation, prioritizing exploration, playfulness, pleasure, and connection. For deepening your journey in these areas, I recommend working with practitioners trained in sexological bodywork and somatic sex education, which offer valuable experiential practices in centering pleasure, growing somatic–sexual awareness, and healing the physical and emotional scar tissue of sexual trauma.

Emphasizing pleasure in recovery opened up entire new realms of experience for me. Because I had always experienced pain with vaginal penetration, I associated internal touch with discomfort and never felt comfortable getting to know my own body. I thought this was a normal experience and that pain was an inevitable part of sex. It wasn't until I started working with somatic sexuality practices that the pain eased, at which point my fear about getting to know my body lessened and I gained more capacity for sensation, playfulness, and pleasure. I was forty-one years old and, despite being a somatic practitioner with a highly developed capacity for sensing energy and sensation, sadly it took me this long to include sexuality in my somatic awareness. As the cervix and the heart are deeply connected, awakening intravaginal sensation, especially in the cervix, can grant new access to the somatic and energetic field of the heart.[7] I found that as I gained access to sensation internally, I also gained deeper access to my capacity to love.

✳ Waking Up the Cervix (solo or with a partner)

If you have a cervix, you can explore this practice on your own or ask your partner to support you. If you are the partner of someone with a cervix, you can guide them through the practice, supporting them with your coregulating presence, breath, or touch, as desired.

If necessary, before you begin this practice, get a clear mental picture of the cervix by looking it up online or in a book. Throughout this practice, be sure to pay careful attention to your window of capacity and take a break or stop if sensations or emotions become too intense.

Start by focusing on the natural movement of your breath, bringing your awareness to your body experience. Invite your consciousness to travel into your vaginal canal. Then meet your cervix with your awareness. Notice what you notice. How does mind feel about connecting with cervix? What is it like for cervix to come into contact with mind?

Then, starting on a gentle exhalation, bring in a low hum. Direct the sound to your cervix. Continue to hum on each exhale. Notice the connection between your throat and cervix. Sense the vibrations of the hum traveling around your cervix in a clockwise or counterclockwise direction. Imagine the sound circling your cervix as if it were traveling around a singing bowl.

As you continue to breathe and hum, notice any growing sensations, including sensations of arousal or pleasure, and any movement impulses. Continue until the practice feels complete. Then take some time to integrate by resting one hand on your pelvis and the other on your heart, noticing the movement of your breath and any sensations resonating throughout your body.

Reclaiming Our Anatomy

Unfortunately, common misrepresentations of anatomy can rob us of the embodied sensing that is our birthright. They also deprive our partners of an accurate roadmap to providing pleasure, making it more difficult for them to be in sync with us and our bodies. For example, the small structure that is commonly thought of as the clitoris is actually only the outermost part, the clitoral glans. The clitoris is in fact a multiplanar complex that has a wishbone shape with its wings extending down under the pubic bone and bulbs hugging either side of the vaginal opening.[8] With more than eight thousand nerve fibers, the clitoris is a profound source of sexual pleasure. This misrepresentation serves to cut us off from our well-spring of potency and power. Whether you have a clitoris yourself and/or are the lover of a person with a clitoris, it can be very empowering to learn the actual size, shape, and sensory capacity of this amazing organ. I firmly believe that when we fully reclaim this knowledge, the patriarchy will crumble!

Like the clitoris, the penis is subject to distorted and disempowering messages. Many people of all genders have internalized the belief that the penis is supposed to be large, hard, disconnected from emotion, and immediately responsive. However, contrary to the constant and rigid erections typically shown in porn, the penis's experience is significantly more fluid. Throughout a sexual encounter, erections may come and go; a penis may need physical stimulus to move toward an erection, and if there's a trauma history or a lack of physical or emotional safety, the penis may not feel safe to become erect. Cultural stereotypes and media representations result in intense pressure on the penis to perform, often at the expense of real pleasure, connection, and emotional intimacy.

The language around penis-oriented sex—get an erection, lose an erection, erectile unpredictability, erectile dysfunction—frames the erection as a prize to be won or lost, and any variability as a sign of dysfunction rather than part of the natural ebb and flow of the human body. As somatic sex educator Christiane Pelmas writes, "A penis that does not behave according to the culture's unrealistic (I would add, pathological and oppressive) standards can be a traumatizing experience in itself for many men (and sometimes their partners, too!), who are offered little if any diversity in the way masculine sexuality is allowed to show up."[9] Erectile unpredictability can be a symptom of trauma, and as Pelmas notes, can also be a traumatic experience in and of itself.

The penis carries the weight of fantastical and unrealistic cultural expectations as it's conflated with the archetype of the phallus, a numinous organ represented throughout history, often in magical proportions, in myth and art. In these mythological representations, the phallus as archetype is a symbol of masculine potency and the creative energies of nature.[10] This is a lot of god energy for a vulnerable human body to hold. And in truth, satisfying intimacy doesn't depend on an erection; you can explore all kinds of sexual pleasure that is less erection-focused and instead includes the whole body in giving and receiving pleasure.

When we differentiate the penis from the phallus, we allow it to be tender, vulnerable, and fluid, all qualities associated with health and healing. It can be reconnected with the rest of the body, returning to the natural ebb and flow that characterizes the movement of embodied life-force. As partners of people with penises, we can hold its movements between hard and soft, expansion and contraction, assertion and vulnerability, with gentle reverence, in the same way that we consciously engage in the dance in and out of connection that defines secure attachment.

Misrepresentations of the genitals often portray them in a binary way, which forces the expansive range of anatomical expression into an often restrictive and oppressive frame. True anatomical understanding instead honors the full spectrum of genital possibility, recognizing that genitals, like all aspects of nature, come in a multiplicity of shapes, energies, and variations.

As we expand our anatomical knowledge, we can start to safely embody our sexual center through somatic practices that prioritize ANS regulation and sensory awareness. I recommend work by Rahi Chun and other somatic sex educators, who teach practices that can help release trauma and restore aliveness. (See "Resources" at the end of this book for more information.)

Sex with the Autonomic Nervous System in Mind

In the same way that the somatic principle of titration can inform our dating life, it can also support our process around sex. The principle of titration reminds us that we dip into and move out of intimacy according to the feedback from our ANS. We can practice recognizing the signs of overwhelm, of "too much, too soon" emotional or physical intimacy, and turn down the volume on the experience to stay within our window of capacity. Sexual arousal, so often seen as the goal of physical intimacy, can push us out of our window of tolerance if sensations or emotions become overwhelming. For instance, the increased heart rate that comes with arousal can be associated with feelings of anxiety and implicit memories of traumatic events.[11] Even the entrainment that occurs during lovemaking, in which our breath and heartbeat become synchronized with our partner's rhythms, can feel like a frightening loss of control if we don't have a home base in ourselves to return to when we need it.

If you find your mind wandering during sex, whether you're dissociating to the point that you've left the building or you're simply thinking about your to-do list, it can be a sign from your nervous system that you are experiencing overwhelm. Mind is letting you know that it doesn't feel safe to stay with body. Constricted breathing or sensations of nausea can help you recognize that it's time to titrate the experience. Similarly, pain, stinging, or tension in your genitals can also be your body's way of letting you know you're outside your window of capacity. You can take these signs as a cue to titrate the experience, pausing your intimacy to talk, look around the room, make a cup of tea, or switch from sexual activities to nonsexual touch such as cuddling and caressing. You can also turn down emotional intensity by adding a point of focus such as music or a movie, switching from face-to-face connection to the lower-intensity experience of joint attention.

✳ Titrating Sexual Intimacy

Explore these questions in your journal:

How do I know when sexual intimacy is "too much, too soon"?

What inside me lets me know when I'm overriding signs from my ANS?

What practices can I use to titrate the experience?

What inside me lets me know if/when I feel ready to proceed?

A New Ending to an Old Story

Our attachment system works hand-in-hand with our autonomic nervous system. Sexual attraction is deeply informed by a person's familiarity (in the true root of the word—*family*), and we unconsciously choose our partners based on our attachment history. "You feel like home," we might say to a person we adore. As psychotherapist David Mann writes, "Sexual partners are usually chosen, unconsciously determined, because they bear some similarity with a parent, or at least it is possible to project these similarities on to them fairly easily." While our choice of partners is an unconscious replication of our early childhood imprints of love, in a secure adult relationship there is also enough of a difference, a healing potential, that something new can happen: "[This difference] also creates the possibility for a different kind of relationship to emerge, and thereby increases the potential for psychological growth and new opportunities for individuation."[12]

Mann notes that when relationships contain a great deal of suffering, the repetition compulsion is at work; there is not enough of a difference from the original caregiver to allow a healing dynamic to emerge. When our childhood patterns are unconsciously governing our choice of partners, people who could offer a new ending to the old story don't even appear in our awareness; they're simply not attractive to us. He writes, "Partners are unconsciously chosen precisely because of their lack of dissimilarity from the parent. . . . Partners who would provide differences from the parents have not fallen within [our] orbit of relationships."[13]

It is inevitable that childhood dynamics will play out in our choice of partners. In fact our very concept and experience of what is "hot" or "sexy" will be deeply informed by these early imprints, alongside other unconscious influences such as cultural messages, neuroception, and hormonal and genetic factors. In our relationships in recovery, we can begin to bring consciousness to our choices and the ways our partnerships replicate early dynamics, and we can explore if there's enough potential for, as Mann would say, "the same with a difference." We might be curious about our perceptions of our partner and our feelings toward them, and see which ones match our early experiences. For example, if our partner tends to withdraw in relationship, perhaps the same way a parent was distant or unavailable, we might see if they have the capacity to reengage when we invite them into connection. If they can, we have the wonderful opportunity to rewrite an old script, to experience the rupture and repair that our Little One did not.

Early in my relationship with my partner, I had a lot of trouble taking in his love. Sensing his caring presence would trigger my unresolved pain and core wounds, and I would start spinning around a narrative that I wasn't deserving of him or his attention. The major difference this time, in contrast to the capacities I had as a child, was that I could tell him I was feeling ashamed and undeserving. He held me and whispered to me all the ways I mattered to him while I cried in his arms. I got to hear all the words that were most healing for me—"I'm here for you, I'm always thinking of you, I love you"—and I could feel them traveling back in time to meet my child self. While, just like my father, he tends to retreat into himself as a result of early attachment trauma—enough familiarity to make him sexy to me and place him centrally within my "orbit of relationship"—he is also able to come forward to meet me and can fluidly express affection, meeting the needs of both my present-day and younger self.

Soon after I met my partner I had a vision in which I was in my childhood home, reexperiencing the intense mix of loneliness and shame that would occasionally come over me as a child, sensations that were so visceral that I would feel frozen in place and sick to my stomach. In my vision I saw him coming to meet me at the front door. He wrapped his arms around me and carried me out of the house. To me this image epitomizes the essence of "the same with a difference," familiar enough to be homey, different enough to be healing. Our same-but-different partner can come to the door of the house we grew up in, meeting us precisely in the original scene, and then carry us out, forming a bridge between the old familiar environment and the sunlit world outside.

Consider the ways in which your partner replicates your "childhood home" and the ways in which they might be able to help you write a new ending to an old story. You can start to look at the default assumptions and expectations that you are carrying from your early experiences and consider the ways these get projected on to your partner. You can also look at your communication tendencies and explore if you are helping your partner meet you where you most need to be met by sharing your desires, needs, and requests in a way they can understand.

✳ Writing a New Ending to an Old Story

In your journal, start by brainstorming all the qualities of your parents or primary caregivers, both positive and negative: _______
Then ask yourself:

> Which of these qualities does my partner possess?
>
> In what ways does my current partnership replicate aspects of my early environment or family of origin?
>
> In what ways is it different?

Then go on to explore these aspects of your relationship:

> The most common emotions I feel toward my partner are _______.
>
> These emotions are familiar to me in these ways: _______
>
> When I'm triggered, I perceive my partner as _______.

This experience is familiar to me in these ways: _______

When I'm grateful for my partner, I perceive my partner as _______.

This experience is familiar to me in these ways: _______

Is my partner capable of rupture and repair? Can they revisit an argument from a calmer place, make an apology when they make a mistake, or respond to or initiate a reach for contact when there's a breach in connection? If not, can I let them know that this is an important skill to work on together?

What capacities do I have now that I didn't have as a child? For example, can I express my needs, engage in self-care practices, or ask for support?

What would be the most meaningful difference for me, the difference that would fill in a missing piece from childhood?

- ☐ Touch (for example, hugs, caresses, cuddles, being held)
- ☐ Affirming words, such as being told I'm lovable, welcomed, or desired
- ☐ Reliability and consistency
- ☐ Respect for my boundaries
- ☐ Being given clear boundaries
- ☐ Being offered warmth and connection when I'm feeling shut down
- ☐ Being given space when I need it
- ☐ Being offered an apology
- ☐ Being asked questions, being offered curiosity about my inner world
- ☐ Talking it through
- ☐ Other: _______________________

Does my partner meet me in the way that is most important to me? (If not, before concluding that they're not capable of it, consider that they might not recognize your core need, especially if it differs from theirs.) What would it be like to ask them for it directly?

What is it like to take in the ways that my partner is the same but different from my original imprint?

If it feels right, offer your partner appreciation for the ways they embody the best qualities of your caregivers and for the ways they do things differently.

Sex and God

Sexuality in its fullest expression is a pathway to Higher Power, to oneness with the One. As the epigraph to this chapter states, "How do we cleave to a God who is a consuming fire?" In Hebrew the word *devekut,* or "cleave," describes our way of relating to God with devotion, a dogged adherence to spiritual connection—a turning, and returning, again and again. This line from the Talmud asks a question that may be familiar to many of us in recovery: How do we adhere to God when in doing so we yoke ourselves to a Divine force that threatens to annihilate us with its power?

As we hold the correlation between divinity and sexuality, it's important to consider the same question. In sexual intimacy, we are playing with fire, often in the best sense of the phrase. This play can be passionate, joyful, sensuous, and expressive, but in its potency, it also threatens to burn us if we don't create the necessary frameworks that help us hold its energies. By engaging sexually, we are dancing with the Divine, with forces of creativity that flame higher and source deeper than the limitations of our daytime consciousness and vulnerable human bodies. As we lessen the constrictive bind of shame by bringing awareness to and releasing the shaming messages we internalized long ago, the life-force of sexuality has the space it needs to flourish. While ultimately this is a movement toward healing, it can be overwhelming if the only way we had previously engaged sexually was in dissociative states.

As we play in this fire, reveling in the beautiful heat of intimacy and passion, we may fear that it brings us dangerously close to the ungrounded Spirit that we were dancing with in addiction. Due in part to the similarities in the neurotransmitters it produces, and the way it hooks into our attachment system, having sex can feel an awful lot like using drugs. It's of essential importance, therefore, that we anchor our sexuality in the realm of recovery, finding frameworks and structures that can ground its electric energy as we tend to our bodies and our recovery here on Earth. Finding a wider container for these energies—such as meetings, a spiritual center, a dance class, or a rock concert, all places where we can move our bodies, raise our voices, or share with others—can help us give the spiritual energy the space it needs, a space that extends beyond our own bodies as, little by little, we grow our window of capacity to hold its numinous energy without losing ourselves and our recovery in the process. These anchors help us center, and stay centered in, our recovery even as we dance with the wild, radical energies of Eros.

Embodying Sexuality

As we start to restore sensation, we can move more fully into the glorious messiness of bodyful sex. Here are some playful practices to try with your partner for embodied and pleasure-oriented sexuality:

- Explore different kinds of touch, using hands, lips, other body parts, or creative objects such as feathers or brushes.
- Explore temperature, pressure, and touching with different kinds of moisture, including oil, lotion, or water.
- Explore touching your partner's genitals through various textures of fabric.
- Explore a touch dialogue. Ask your partner: What part of your body wants contact? What is it like for you when I touch you here? What kind of touch would feel best?
- To expand out of goal-oriented sexuality, schedule a "sensuality date" that can include everything but penetrative sex.
- Is there a part of your body your partner has never touched? A part of their body you've never touched? What would it be like to direct your attention there?
- Ask your partner to show you the kind of touch that feels good to them.
- Explore each other's hands, feet, or ears.
- Show each other how you like to be kissed.

Often we experience sexuality, arousal, and embodiment in ways that differ from our partner. If each partner assumes that the other's body responds in the same way as theirs, it sets the stage for ongoing misunderstanding, disappointment, shame, and conflict. However, if we take the time to get to know our own styles and that of our partners, we can recognize the pacing and stimuli that each person needs in order to move fully into connection, both emotionally and sexually. You and your partner can meet each other across differences by focusing on sensual pleasure—touching and caressing the whole body and allowing sensuality to gradually simmer toward the full-on heat of sexuality. By bringing consciousness to these differences, and honoring the needs of each tendency, you and your partner can better meet each other's rhythms with understanding and reverence.

The entire body is alive, erogenous, and erotic! So don't limit sexual connection to the genitals; include your whole body and your partner's whole body. Pay special attention to areas such as inner wrist, palms, and face where sensitive nerve endings called CT afferents contribute to feelings of attachment and closeness.[14] You can awaken the body to sexual connection through touch, tending to the entire surface of the skin with varying pressures and textures, and through growing somatic awareness by focusing on sensations, internal experience, and breath. Caressing your partner's face or other parts of their body while kissing can help increase closeness and emotional connection. Similarly, stimulating their genitals while also placing a hand on their heart can help bridge the sex–love divide, bringing a heartful depth to sexual intimacy.

Pleasure is a crucial part of healing from addiction. Often in the Twelve Step programs, pleasure is conflated with addiction, craving, and using. I've heard many people in the rooms describe themselves as "hedonists" and "compulsive pleasure-seekers." And it's true that in addiction we experience endless searching, the craving for a fulfillment that never arrives. However, unlike the cycle of craving and using, which ultimately offers only an empty hologram of pleasure, genuine pleasure is a mindfulness practice that centers us in the joy of our aliveness in the present movement. We can learn to distinguish the two by noticing our sensations. Craving feels empty, hollow, and never enough. Pleasure, on the other hand, is a deeply fulfilling whole-body experience. We can be with our craving by asking it to show us what we are truly longing for; when we listen deeply to craving's message, we may learn it is ultimately pointing us, not to a substance or addictive behavior, but to the field beyond it: our need for love.

✶ Energy Massage (with yourself or a partner)

Start by directing your awareness into your hands, sensing them fill with light, blue or pink color, or warmth. If doing this practice with a partner, place your hand on or near your partner's body and direct your awareness to the connection between your hands and their body. As you do, sense the connection between your heart and your hands. Sense this energy moving from your heart through your hands to their body. Ask them to guide your hands to any places that want contact. When this feels complete, switch roles. When you have both given and received energy, take some time to share your experience with each other.

You can also do this practice on your own body, directing the energy through your hands to the places on your body that might want to receive this connection. Invite a dual awareness: Notice what it's like for your hands to offer energy, and at the same time, invite your body to be curious about receiving. If it's hard to notice both experiences at the same time, you can switch your awareness between the giving experience of your hands and the receiving experience of your body. When this exploration feels complete, rest your hand on your heart and expand your awareness, noticing any sensations or currents of energy resonating throughout your body.

✶ "I Want You" and "I Need You" (with a partner)

Depending on your attachment imprint, you may have an easier time naming attraction and desire ("I want you") or dependency needs ("I need you"). We may more easily feel desire for our partner while having some difficulty accepting or expressing our need for them; alternately, we might more easily acknowledge our dependency needs while having trouble expressing or allowing the flow of desire. As we mature into conscious relationship with ourselves and others, we grow in our capacity to experience and allow for both wanting and needing, an essential step toward resolving the love–sexuality bind and restoring heart–genital connection.

Explore with your partner by expressing each of those phrases in turn. Start by saying "I want you." What happens inside when you say it? What do you notice in your body? Repeat the phrase several times, noticing any sensations, emotions, or thoughts that arise.

What happens when you try out the phrase "I need you"? What do you notice in your body? Repeat it several more times, noticing your sensations, emotions, and thoughts.

As the partner, sense what it feels like inside to receive each phrase. What does each touch in you? Which is easier to receive? Which is more difficult?

Then switch roles. After you have each explored offering and receiving the phrases, take some time to share your experiences with your partner. Take turns asking each other, "What can I do to help you feel that it's okay to need me? What can I do to help you feel that it's safe to want me?"

✻ Deepening the Heart–Genital Connection (with a partner)

This practice may be done clothed or unclothed.

Lie down with your partner so that you're facing each other, with your hearts, bellies, and genitals touching. Each place one hand on the other person's back behind their heart and the other on their sacrum. Connect with your breathing. Breathe together for a few minutes until your rhythms entrain.

Connect with your heart, sensing it meeting your partner's heart.

Sense into your belly, feeling its contact with your partner's belly.

Sense into your genitals, feeling the connection with your partner's genitals.

With your hand behind their heart, sense the energy of the heart. With your hand at their sacrum, sense the energy of the genitals. Then invite the energies of these two places to travel between your hands as you sense the two energy centers coming into relationship with each other.

Stay with this practice, breathing together and sensing the movement of energy, until it feels complete. Then, take a few minutes to share with each other about your experience.

CHAPTER 11

Ending a Relationship in Recovery

Love anything and your heart will be wrung and possibly broken. If you want to make sure of keeping it intact you must give it to no one, not even an animal. Wrap it carefully round with hobbies and little luxuries; avoid all entanglements. Lock it up safe in the casket or coffin of your selfishness. But in that casket, safe, dark, motionless, airless, it will change. It will not be broken; it will become unbreakable, impenetrable, irredeemable.

—C. S. LEWIS

I see heartbreak as the most proportional response to the state of the world—to say I love you is to say my heart breaks for you, and this sentiment resonates within all things, bringing a clarity to both the world before us and the world beyond the veil. Sorrow becomes a way of life, part laughter, part tears, with very little space between. It is a way of conducting oneself in the world, of loving it, of worshipping it.

—NICK CAVE

Grief astronomer, adjust the lens,
look close, tell us what you see.

—ANDREA GIBSON

Sooner or later, if you open your heart to relationship, you will also feel the pain of loss. How do you get through a breakup in recovery without losing your sobriety in the process? A breakup can be a profound attachment loss, one that reiterates early relational wounds. Since the originary attachment loss is what we used substances to cover over to start with, it's especially important to tend to your recovery when these core wounds are reopened in a breakup. It's more crucial than ever to tend to connection—to reach out to the friends, fellows, mentors, and healing practitioners in your life who can provide a lifeline of connection in the midst of your pain. Receiving connection from them won't be the same as receiving it from your partner, and it won't meet the longing in the same way, but it will offer you a balm for the wound and a reparative message that, this time, you don't have to go through that pain alone.

I've experienced two very different kinds of breakups. The first is the kind of breakup that signifies a natural shift in the nature of the relationship, whether a move into a friendship or a friendly acquaintanceship. The second is the kind that is abrupt and absolute, coming out of the blue and resulting in an absolute cut-off, almost like a kind of death. I've found the first to be infinitely easier to recover from; it leaves behind a series of mutual gifts and shared blessings. The second, on the other hand, leaves a trail of grief mixed with shame, rage, and unanswered questions that can last for years.

Stephanie Sarazin coined the phrase *ambiguous grief* to describe "the feeling experienced from the loss of a loved one who is still living, accompanied by a change in or death of the relationship."[1] Unlike the grief we experience with the death of a loved one, ambiguous grief—which can result from experiences of betrayal, divorce, estrangement, incarceration, or degenerative brain diseases such as Alzheimer's—can leave us stranded alone in a grieving process without structures of support or even language to describe the experience. Ambiguous grief means that part of our brain and body will experience our beloved as dead even though we "know" they are still alive. In addition to the pain of the loss itself, we often suffer from the pain of isolation, shame, and disorientation—a loss of our sense of self. As Sarazin notes, these kinds of losses often go beyond heartbreak to "soulbreak."[2]

My experience of ambiguous grief resulted from the end of a three-year relationship with the man I had thought I'd marry. With our relationship suffering from the stressors of early COVID, both of us working from home in a tiny apartment, I moved two hours north to be closer to my parents. He and I had been struggling for several months to emotionally reconnect when he called me and broke it off over the phone, hanging up on me when I started crying. When we spoke two months later, he told me he was happily settled in a new relationship. He said he didn't want to speak to me again and abruptly ended the call. He mailed me my belongings, and I never had a chance to say goodbye.

In the weeks following the phone call, I went through a profound experience of grief, followed by anger and outrage beginning several months later. I was furious that someone who knew me so well, who knew all my wounds and triggers, would have created a situation that replicated my worst fears. A loved one suddenly disappearing echoed my ancestors' losses during the Holocaust, and for me, that was the ultimate fear that had long prevented me from entering a relationship in the first place. I couldn't believe that someone who loved me could put me through such pain, a pain that would have been easily preventable with a more connected, communicative ending. I also felt a deep sense of shame, believing that if he could cast me off in this way and so easily replace me with a new girlfriend, it must have been because I deserved it; I was a bad partner and was unworthy of love and commitment.

Now I know he was doing the best he could; he acted not from a desire to intentionally cause harm but rather from an unhealed wound in himself. His previous relationship, an engagement, had ended the same way, and I can now understand that an abrupt withdrawal was the only way he could handle painful or overwhelming feelings. My own reactivity certainly contributed to the cycle of disconnection that left him feeling hurt and abandoned, but it wasn't all my fault, and it certainly wasn't because he had suddenly seen the truth that I was unworthy of love.

Today I realize that my anger had an important message. It's actually *not* okay to end a three-year-long partnership with a phone call, or to blame one's partner for all the problems in a relationship. While I didn't have enough perspective or self-cohesion at the time to experience this rupture without falling into a shame spiral, I can see now that what he did was simply not okay—not loving, not skillful, not conscious. My anger lets me know that protecting myself from this kind of loss in the future is essential, and I choose partners accordingly. It tells me about my boundaries around acceptable and unacceptable behaviors, and now I listen carefully when potential partners tell me about their past relationships. I can say from my own excruciating experience of ambiguous grief that I will do everything in my power to avoid inflicting this kind of a breakup on another person or subjecting myself to it again.

I was lucky that my subsequent relationship offered a very different, very reparative, experience of an ending. He and I communicated throughout our time together about the areas where we were having trouble, so when the time came to end the relationship, it was a joint decision, and not surprising to either of us. We held each other, cried, named what we loved about each other, expressed gratitude for all that we'd learned together, and wished each other blessings for finding our right partnerships. I grieved briefly, and then we started cultivating a friendship. Our experience together was less of a breakup and more of a gentle transition from one phase to the next. We joked that we could coauthor a book called *There's No One I'd Rather Break Up with Than You.*

The conclusion of our romantic relationship contained many of the elements of what therapist Katherine Woodward Thomas terms *conscious uncoupling.* Thomas describes conscious uncoupling as a process that centers self-responsibility rather than blame, and kindness rather than vindictiveness. As Thomas emphasizes, "The developmental task of heartbreak is to harness the huge amount of pain we are in, and to use it to evolve beyond our old painful patterns in love, as well as to awaken us to the power we hold to re-create our lives to be even more beautiful than they were before."[3]

The conscious uncoupling process that Thomas outlines includes five key steps. The first is finding emotional freedom, in which we reestablish a sense of safety in the face of feelings of betrayal, rejection, and loss, and we reframe the breakup as an opportunity for deep transformation and healing. In the second step, we practice self-responsibility and look at our part in the problems of the relationship, situating our pain in the context of childhood relationship ruptures (what Thomas calls *source-fractures*), and make self-amends for the ways we've betrayed and neglected ourselves. We practice self-care and reclaim our own needs and desires. In the third step, we identify the core beliefs that interfere with finding healthy and loving connection and explore how we re-create the experience of our core wounds, perpetuating our source-fracture narrative. We invite our former partner into a soul-to-soul communication, imagining a conversation with them that allows us to reaffirm a healthy sense of ourself. With the fourth step, we appreciate the blessings of the relationship and set intentions for the highest possibility of the relationship in the future. We practice communicating with our former partner from the capacities of our present-time adult self, and in ways that build peace and collaboration. Finally, in the fifth step, we draw on community support for the next stage of life, create meaningful ceremony for uncoupling, and develop cooperative ways to attend to childcare, shared property, or legal issues.

An essential part of relationships in recovery is breaking up in recovery. The qualities that Thomas outlines—self-awareness, self-care, and self-responsibility—are also the key growth areas that we practice in sobriety. Using our recovery principles, we can bring the same intentionality to the end of the relationship as we do to the beginning and middle. Because there can be so much pain and wounding present as all of our deepest abandonment and rejection wounds are touched, the ending can be the hardest phase to navigate with consciousness and responsibility rather than reactivity. It is a test of our recovery to navigate an ending with compassion, drawing on our recovery tools and our evolved nest to keep us whole even as our hearts are breaking.

Creating a Love-Centered Breakup

It's not always easy to know when and how to get out of a relationship that's not working. As humans, we evolved to have strong bonds with others and to protest potential threats to the connections that our survival depends upon. Our threat response system, thrown into overdrive by the rupture in the attachment, often governs our breakup conversations, escalating them into painful conflict. In our pain, we react with our habitual self-protective strategies of blame, rage, or withdrawal. Meanwhile, our most tender places—of grief, of shame, of longing and disappointment—are kept hidden.

You may need help in navigating your way out. Especially if you are in an abusive or volatile relationship, or one in which you are financially dependent on your partner, professional counseling in addition to program support may be necessary for creating an exit strategy that prioritizes your safety and wellbeing. Note that if your partner has a severe psychological disorder or is potentially violent, please don't attempt the attachment-based practices outlined here; attend to your safety, and plan an exit with the support and guidance of a domestic abuse counselor. (See the "Resources" section.)

Knowing that we can navigate the end of a relationship in accordance with our recovery is part of what allows us to enter a relationship to begin with. If we don't trust that we can get ourselves out without harming ourselves or the other person, or if we fear getting stuck or pulled in deeper against our better judgment, it's hard to have the confidence to enter in the first place. In order to have our "yes," we need to know that we can have our "no." We learn that we can trust our discernment, our support systems, and our capacity to draw boundaries and set limits, and that if a relationship is unhealthy or off-track, we will not repeat old patterns of self-sacrifice; rather, we will choose ourselves, prioritizing our "inner marriage"—our alignment with our true path, our recovery, and our authentic self.

It might sound like a paradox to say a "love-centered breakup." However, when we draw on the principles of secure attachment, we can create meaningful transitions that honor the loving connection and allow both partners to renegotiate old losses. This time, in contrast to the ruptures suffered in childhood, you can go through the experience with agency, authenticity, and, if desired, continuing connection in new, clearly defined terms, all of which can offer a reparative experience and a revisioning of old expectations. Ending a relationship well means that both you and your partner come away with expanded capacities for love and self-awareness, situating both of you to start your next relationships with open hearts and new-found skills. In an attachment-oriented breakup, we can cocreate gentle transitions instead of abrupt surprises; offer reassurance of care and connection; honestly acknowledge both the joy of loving and the pain of separation; and compassionately witness each other in our shared suffering.

Some attachment-based practices you can bring to the ending of a relationship include

- Acknowledging the pain, both yours and your partner's
- Crying together
- Celebrating the connection and the meaningful times; recalling a happy memory
- Listing the ways you did a good job together
- Sharing your gratitude and appreciation
- Naming what you love about them; telling them what makes them an amazing partner
- Consolidating your key learnings and takeaways
- Reassuring them of your continuing love for them and, if applicable, their children or family
- Creating an unbinding ritual and, if desired, inviting your community[4]
- Exchanging gifts
- Offering each other blessings for finding the right partnership in the future

It can also be helpful to clarify expectations and establish new boundaries going forward. Do you see the possibility for a friendship? Do you plan to talk on the phone, to text or email? Do you need to take some time apart before reconnecting in a new way? If so, how much time do you each need with no contact, and when do you plan to reconnect?

It's hard to stay facing into the pain of separation when it feels like it could be more than your heart can bear. But ultimately an attachment-oriented ending will help your heart and theirs heal much more quickly and prevent the ambiguous grief and attachment wounds that repeat childhood injuries and make it harder to love in the future. Creating a love-centered breakup is a gift for both yourself and your partner.

It can also be helpful to remember, as my mother reminded me when my own heart was broken, that the relationship may end, but the love, once created, doesn't go anywhere. I believe that at the conclusion of a partnership, the love that was held between two people is released from the container of the relationship to flow back out into the universe, returning to the Love that birthed it. So as you're saying goodbye to your partner, remember that the love you created between you will continue to hold you both.

Asking for the Gift You Want to Receive

When you were a child you likely had the experience of being overwhelmed by and alone with difficult and unnamable feelings without a coregulating presence to help you manage. This time around, you don't have to sit with painful feelings by yourself. A love-centered breakup means creating support for yourself as you walk through the pain of separation. Though it may be the most difficult time to reach out for help, it's crucially important to do so. There's an opportunity here for a reparative attachment experience, but you need to help Love find you!

Start by making a list of all the people whom you can turn to for support. This can include the people who are professionals in your life (such as therapists, healing practitioners, or coaches), warm and nurturing friends and family, and essentially anyone you've ever exchanged numbers with at a meeting. Before reaching out, it can be useful to make a list of the support you're most needing and wanting, whether it be material (such as help shopping for groceries), emotional (sitting with you while you have a good cry or voice your anger), or spiritual (such as building a grief altar or holding a goodbye ritual). When you speak to them, you can then ask for support in a specific area, choosing a need that they are suited to meet. For example, you might ask your friend in another state for a weekly phone check-in, a local fellow for a ride to a meeting, and your therapist for some extra appointments during your grieving process.

When asking for help, you might say, for example, "I'm having a hard time taking care of myself right now because of my recent breakup. I could use some support with cleaning up. Would you be willing to come hang out with me while I wash the dishes?" If they say no, just remind yourself it is because of their own limitations and move on to the next person on your list. Because people are sometimes at a loss for how to support someone experiencing grief, you can help them help you by asking for the gift you want to receive. You'll be surprised at how often people are available to help, especially when they are offered guidance on how best to support you.

As you may have lost the primary source of touch in your life, you may also go through a period of touch deprivation. The loss of touch was one of the worst aspects of my breakup; I still remember the sense of skin hunger, an aching so deep it felt like physical pain. During a time of sudden touch deprivation, seeking out healing touch can offer you a crucial sense of soothing, safety, and containment, reminding you that "here you are" even amid the disorientating effects of loss. It reminds your Little One that they are not alone, and though this loss may be familiar, it also comes with a difference. So it may be especially important to prioritize healing touch in your life right now. You might want to invest in regular massages or somatic bodywork, or refer back to Chapter 8 and choose some of the self-directed touch practices to integrate into your daily life.

Healing through Heartbreak

No matter if your relationship in recovery ends in separation, you can acknowledge yourself for taking the risk into intimacy. Grief is a testament to your beautiful capacity for attachment. It takes tremendous courage to give yourself over to your longing for connection. The hidden blessing of grief is that the pain of disconnection can recall us to our essential nature, reminding us that even in the face of tremendous disappointment and loss, our heart's nature is to again and again open to love.

It is a difficult fact of being alive that attachment carries inside it the seeds of heartbreak: the pain of rupture, separation, and loss. The task of relationships in recovery is to allow ourselves to love fully in the face of inevitable heartbreak, recognizing that both the love and the loss are part of our heart's connection with life itself. The wisdom of recovery can guide us toward knowing when to keep fighting for our relationship and when to accept an ending with grace. We trust that we can mourn what needs mourning and that our grief will not destroy or isolate us, but rather bring us into closer contact with the shared tenderness of being human.[5]

✶ Cultivating a Conscious Breakup

If you are facing a breakup, explore these prompts in your journal:

What is my highest vision for ending this relationship?

What qualities in myself do I want to bring to the process?

What elements of a love-centered breakup are most important to me?

I will draw on the following attachment-based practices (see page 215): ___________

What kind of protections or allies for my heart would allow me to keep my heart open as I navigate the pain of loss?

What blessings of the relationship do I want to carry forward?

What would it be like to experience the breaking up of my relationship as a *breaking open* to my next steps, to my authentic nature, or to Love itself?

Fast-forward one year into the future. You have beautifully navigated a conscious breakup. Explore:

How do I feel about my former partner? What are we celebrating about this next stage of our relationship?

✶ Tending to Your Heart

Castor oil is often used on the body to soften scar tissue. To soften the pain of your heart, you can offer yourself a heart massage. Start by warming some castor oil and spreading it over your chest. Massage your heart in a clockwise circular motion, finding the pressure and pacing that feels right for you. As you do, sense the contact of your hand meeting any places of scarring or bracing. Take extra time with places that feel numb or tender.

As you massage, start to include a focus on your breath while making a sound such as a hum on each exhalation, directing the breath and vibration through your heart. This will help the heart soften and start to discharge any trauma. Allow any gentle shaking or movement impulses to move throughout your body until the process feels complete. Then rest with a hand on your heart and/or on your belly to allow the energy to integrate.

CHAPTER 12

Conscious Relationships

The word "connection" describes the universe. Since we, as humans, are an integral part of the universe, it also describes us. As all things are interconnected, so are we; it is our nature to be connected. If we do not feel *connected, it is because something has happened to us to rupture our awareness of the connection. We may sometimes lose our awareness that we are part of the whole, but that separateness is just an illusion. We cannot* not *be connected.*

—HARVILLE HENDRIX AND HELEN LAKELLY HUNT

Love takes off the masks that we fear we cannot live without and know we cannot live within. I use the word "love" here not merely in the personal sense but as a state of being, a state of grace—not in the infantile American sense of being made happy but in the tough and universal sense of quest and daring and growth.

—JAMES BALDWIN

The power of love is found most in its triumph over fear.

—JAMES HOLLIS

When I was about a year into recovery, I moved into a small apartment in San Francisco's Inner Sunset with three male roommates. One of them was a graduate student named Luke who had a girlfriend who was studying in Massachusetts. She came out to visit during a school vacation. During this time she was resting in bed with menstrual cramps, and I ran into Luke in the kitchen as he was heating up a hot-water bottle for her. I went back to my room and closed the door. I was overcome with a strange feeling—something that contained a little bit of jealousy, a little bit of sadness, but mostly a sense of awe in the presence of a great mystery. Based on my own dating life, it had never occurred to me that a partner could or would make a gesture of such care and kindness, of gently tending and attuning to another's needs. It was completely outside the realm of what I had seen in my past dating experiences and what I could imagine in the future. And in fact, I didn't have a partnership that contained those elements until eight years later when, finally, I was capable of offering and receiving that kind of care.

Many of us in recovery have never experienced or even witnessed a healthy relationship. You might come to the question of relationship with worst-case scenarios on your mind: the painful patterns in past relationships, heartbreaks and breakups, the model of your parents' marriage, or lack of a model all together. We are drawn again and again to the same patterns, to the familiar/familial imprints that shape our choice of partners and the dynamics that play out in the relationship. While we repeat these patterns in an attempt to heal them, often that hope goes unfulfilled, and we find ourselves yet again disappointed and alone.

In recovery, we start planning for a future we can't yet see. We don't yet know where our recovery journey will lead us; we predict fearful futures based on what we've known in the past, and our path is blocked by obstacles that haven't yet come into conscious awareness. But sooner or later we start to get little glimpses of something different, glimmers of a new aliveness as our innate life-force starts to move through us with more power and fluidity. When we're feeling stuck, hopeless, and despairing, we can vision into a future we haven't yet known. This future will guide us into its fruition.

Right before I met the guy with whom I explored my first conscious relationship in recovery, I had the vision of standing in my kitchen with a man wearing a plaid flannel shirt. He was hugging me, and he had a beautiful warm, generous energy. I felt safe and held. I sat with this vision every day, feeling it in my body. Then when I met him, I was attracted to his warmth and generosity of spirit. Soon after, when we were hugging in my kitchen, I recognized the image and feeling in my body.

When visioning, it's important to not only imagine but to sense the possibility in an embodied way. I found that it wasn't until I could picture and feel the kind of relationship I wanted that I could actually achieve it. We can practice envisioning far before we actually have the lived experience. So as you dream your next steps, no matter whether you're currently single or partnered, you might consider what would take your relationship journey to the next level. What of the infinite expanses of intimacy have you not yet experienced? What kinds of things would you like to experience in relationship, and what would it feel like to do those things? What would it feel like to snuggle on the couch? To go for a hike? To be welcomed home after a long trip? To cook dinner together? To make plans for your old age? To bring your shame to light? To share your innermost fears and longings?

Our vision for relationship can be, as my old sponsor used to say, like "looking at the sky through a straw"—that is, very limited. Prior to recovery, relationships have been primarily focused on sex, or you might have been alone for a long time. You might have had stressful, undefined, or on-and-off again relationships, or experienced violence, infidelity, or abuse. Like me, you might not have known that romantic relationships can mean staying for breakfast or being cared for when you're not feeling well. You might not know that relationships can mean holding hands in public, meeting each other's friends and families, or celebrating holidays together. So here's a list of some aspects of relationship that can help you envision new possibilities for intimacy, next steps for your dating life, or new horizons for your existing partnership. Feel free to add your own!

Relationships practices can include

- Sensual, nonsexual touch, such as holding hands, cuddling, or giving and receiving a massage
- Spending the night and staying for breakfast
- Bringing play, creativity, sensory exploration, and/or somatic practices to the realm of sex
- Cooking together

- Bringing your partner some groceries or asking them to bring what you need
- Calling your partner for support in the middle of a hard day
- Having company for a doctor's appointment, a vet visit, or a family emergency
- Going on a weekend trip
- Asking for or offering a hot-water bottle, a cup of tea, a warm blanket, or a hug
- Talking about plans for the future
- Giving and receiving small, thoughtful gifts
- Taking care of daily life tasks together
- Tracking important events in each other's lives, and then asking about them
- Sharing your favorite song and describing what you love about it
- Laughing together
- Being serious together
- Writing each other notes or letters
- Expressing insecurities, vulnerabilities, and fears
- Asking for clarity and definition regarding the relationship
- Being curious about each other's inner worlds; discovering what major themes and questions are present for your partner, and sharing your own
- Communicating gently with awareness of your partner's tender places
- Naming your shame
- Growing your awareness of cycles of disconnect and sharing your observations with each other
- Add your own:
    - ______________________________
    - ______________________________
    - ______________________________

Some of these things will be scary! And that's okay. It's part of growing in relationship in recovery. With practice, these new horizons may feel like a normal part of your relationship.

✵ Cultivating New Possibilities (with a partner)

Choose one item from the preceding list to practice with your partner. Ask your partner to choose one they would like to practice. Together, commit to practicing these two new skills with each other for a week.

After a week, check in with each other to see how it was to explore these practices together. What was it like to offer love in this area? To receive? Discuss if you would like to continue practicing these skills or choose additional ones to explore.

✵ Envisioning True Partnership

Practice this exercise to welcome in your highest possibility for relationship, either with your current partner or a partner you are inviting in.

Close your eyes. Breathe out three times slowly. Drop your awareness into your heart. Sense a path of light shining forward from your heart. See yourself traveling down this path into the future. See and sense yourself with your true partner. How does it feel to be in their presence? To hold them and be held by them? What does your life look like together? Notice how you feel in your body.

Breathe out, and open your eyes.

Growing into Conscious Relationship

As we face into the journey of relationship fully awake, without the numbing effects of addiction or our default modes of reactivity or self-protection, we start to move into the realm of conscious relationship. In a conscious relationship, we do our best to take responsibility for our own feelings and triggers, meet our wounded parts with care and compassion, draw on support and practices to develop our capacities for self-awareness, and withdraw our projections, seeing the other person in their own fears and vulnerabilities. We approach our partner with our eyes and our hearts wide open.

Imago, created by Harville Hendrix and Helen LaKelly Hunt, is one of the primary modalities of couples therapy. The Imago model proposes that we are drawn to partners who possess a combination of positive and negative qualities of our parents. The closer the match, the more intense the Imago energy; we are drawn to our Imago in order to work out our childhood wounding. As described in Chapter 10, your present-day relationship may be similar to the one you had with your early caregivers but ideally will have enough of a difference that its replication can now result in resolution. The same-but-different quality results in a potential healing wherein we learn that early insecurities can be met now with safety and security, creating new possibilities for secure attachment and spiritual development.

As Hendrix writes, "Our unconscious drive to repair the emotional damage of childhood is what allows us to realize our spiritual potential as human beings, to become complete and loving people capable of nurturing others. And even though our projections and transferences may temporarily blind us to our partners' reality, they're also what binds us to them, setting up the preconditions for future growth."[1] Imago is rooted in Jungian psychology, which emphasizes that we are drawn to partners who help us in our task of individuation, our work of leaving behind false personas and growing into our whole Self. Individuation is the ultimate goal of self-development and is often catalyzed or accelerated by the alchemical process of relationship.

The journey from falling in love to conscious relationship generally takes place in three phases. The first phase is the phase of projection, in which each partner sees the other through an idealized lens, essentially an unconscious projection of their own disavowed positive qualities. In this sense, each relationship begins with a little wound from Cupid's arrow, the very pinprick of projection. In this phase we see our partner as an idealized parent, a numinous god-like figure capable of finally healing our childhood wounds. Generally in this phase our desire for our partner to meet our early needs remains unconscious.

Since this initial phase contains a lot of god-energy and is not grounded in our human reality, in which we all contain a mix of both light and shadow, strengths and vulnerabilities, it is impossible to stay there for long. We soon enter a second phase in which our projections and idealizations are dashed, and we inevitably fall into resentment and disappointment as we face the reality of our partner's humanness. Often a new projection emerges, this time of our negative qualities. We might think, "Ah, he could only conceal his true nature for so long, and now his real self is emerging." However, the reality is that our early fantasies are inevitably falling away.

At the same time, as the relationship grows deeper and both partners feel increasing dependency, our vulnerability grows and we start to employ our oldest survival strategies to protest ruptures in connection and threats to our autonomy. Fears of dependency often arise in tandem with our increasing reliance on our partnership. In this phase, as Bateman and Holmes state, "The partner is a 'transformational object,' a vehicle for projection, a receptacle for unwanted aspects of the self, a source of delight and terror, bringing one into touch with one's deepest desires and disappointments."[2] Unfortunately the phase of negative projections spells the end of many relationships.

If we can make it through the realm of dashed fantasies into the third phase, we reach the possibility of conscious relationship. In the third phase, we start to see ourselves and our partner more deeply as we withdraw our projections and reclaim the qualities, of both light and shadow, we had previously placed on our partner. Jungian analyst Marion Woodman writes, "Crucial to this evolution is the realization that the inner partner is not the same as the outer partner, and so long as the inner divinity is projected onto the outer human creature, there can be nothing but illusion, confusion, disappointment, and despair."[3] When we reclaim our projections, both of our divinity and our shadow, our disappointment eases, and the possibility of individuation emerges; through the work of partnership, we come fully into awareness of our own being. Jungian psychology sees relationship as a crucible in which an alchemical process turns lead into gold and from which we emerge as more clearly individuated Self.

We thus achieve the inner marriage, a joining of the masculine and feminine energies of our psyche, which gives rise to the transcendent function, a third and greater force that manifests through the integration of opposites. As Woodman notes, "While our relationship to the inner bridegroom will influence our outer relationships, he is the presence that accompanies us in our inner journey to totality." Our outer partner "shares the earthly path," while our inner partner, our marriage within our Self, is the path of divinity, though ultimately "in the mystery that holds two people together . . . human and divine love are of the same essence."[4]

Similarly, Buddhist teachers Stephen and Ondrea Levine, who draw on the Buddhist practice and philosophy of nondualism, describe love as both a "collaboration in healing" and a "mystical union."[5] To them, conscious relationship is a spiritual practice; we enter the field of the partnership with a spacious mind and "soft belly," our vulnerable and non-defensive presence, from which we practice non-reactively witnessing our protective patterns.[6] We commit fully to the relationship, holding nothing back. As we get to know our places of fear, shame, rage, grief, and separation from the whole, we enter the possibility for conscious relationship, in which we meet our partner, wise mind to wise mind, open heart to open heart, soft belly to soft belly, seeing each other in both our Buddha nature and our human vulnerability. As the Levines emphasize, the journey to the beloved is ultimately the journey to the Beloved.

The three phases of conscious relationship offer a necessary expansion on the ways that relationships are often talked about in the recovery sphere. Romantic relationships should not be avoided; rather, they should be welcomed for the role they often play in our spiritual awakening, one that brings us into deepest contact with our true Self and with a Higher Power. In fact, *love is the medium and the means of healing in recovery.* It is through the work of relationship that we develop ourselves on the path of recovery. It is here that we meet our earliest wounding and offer possibilities for healing and for maturation into the fullest potential of our adult Self. Relationship and recovery cannot be separate from one another; they are both crucial aspects of the spiritual path.

Eventually, in the work of conscious relationship, we encounter intimacy in its full power as a radical act. As psychoanalyst Otto Kernberg describes, intimate relationship transcends "the predominant cultural conventions and the ritualized prohibitions and superstitions," the social mores around gender, sexual desire, emotion, and the body that codify the wild, mythic realm of a couple's interior life into a conventional, predictable, and often stultifying set of rituals and behaviors.[7] Intimate relationship dwells in the realm of Eros, where barely contained instincts and desires, role fluidity, ecstatic aliveness, archetypal energies, and childhood reenactments—our deepest impulses toward both tenderness and aggression—play out in seeming contrast to domestic routine. He emphasizes that every partnership has, in the words of psychoanalyst André Green, arenas of "private madness"—the at-times implied, at-times explicit play of tenderness and aggression, pleasure and power, teasing and fulfilment that underscores the secret life of a partnership.[8]

A couple's madness is unique and unpredictable. Often invisible, or incomprehensible, to the eyes of the outside world, it is this private madness that forms the life-force of relationship, and also what gives intimacy its subversive power. As it becomes free of the constraints on the imagination imposed by capitalism, patriarchy, religion, and social norms, relationship transforms into an infinitely expansive space for gender multiplicity, fluid sexuality, sensory aliveness, and erotic embodiment—all embedded within the day-to-day domestic life of the partnership—making relationship one of the last remaining places of uncolonized wilderness. As Kernberg writes, "Shared values may provide a couple the strength and endurance to survive in a hostile environment—for example, in a totalitarian society—where culturally sanctioned dishonesty in ordinary social relationships must be tolerated and screened out by the couple's shared silent rebellion against their environment's oppressiveness and corruption. . . . The very nature of the couple's sexual intimacy implies such a shared rebellion."[9] This is the great promise and gift of romantic relationship: Hidden in plain sight, in the midst of state and cultural control, it asserts itself as a site of resistance and liberation.

✶ Moving into Conscious Relationship

Explore the following questions in your journal:

> If you are currently in a relationship: Which of the three phases am I in?
>
> If you are not in a relationship: What is the furthest I have traveled in past relationships?

What roadblocks have prevented me from moving into the third phase, the phase of conscious relationship?

What would the phase of conscious relationship look like for me or my partnership?

What support or resources would I need in order to feel capable of moving into the next phase?

What support or resources would my relationship need in order to move into the next phase?

In what ways is my relationship a space of radical, subversive power? Are there ways in which I would like to further explore these energies, or bring them into consciousness to develop this potential further?

✳ Reclaiming Projections

In your journal, explore this practice for reclaiming projections:

Start by writing the name of your partner at the top of a sheet of paper. Then make a list of all their positive characteristics. Then add to the list all their challenging or negative characteristics. Then go back up to the top of the page and cross out their name, replacing it with the phrase "I am—I'm afraid I am—I wish I were."

Now go through each item on the list, considering if each item could fit the category of "I am," "I'm afraid I am," or "I wish I were."

What qualities feel good to claim as your own? Which would you rather refuse?

This practice can show us crucial aspects of our own story. When we reclaim our projections of both light and shadow, we remember our wholeness, and we free others to be who they truly are.

✳ Shapeshifting into Your Partner

Use these two practices to develop compassion for your partner's inner world. (Note that these are advanced exercises requiring the capacity to exercise clear boundaries and access a strong sense of self; please do them only if it feels safe.)

Exploring Through Imagery

Close your eyes. Breathe out three times slowly. Shift your consciousness so that you become your partner. Sense what it feels like to be in their body. How does it feel to move the way they move? How does it feel to walk through the world? What does the world look like through their eyes?

Breathe out. Travel back in time to your partner's infancy. What does it feel like to be in their early environment? Drawing on what you know about their childhood, sense into their missing needs. Allow yourself to feel any fear, grief, shame, or anger that might be present. Sense into the core wounds.

Breathe out. Sense the ways that your partner learned to guard their heart. Sense any armoring in their body. Sense the default pathways of their ANS. Sense the core beliefs that developed from these early wounds.

Breathe out. Travel forward in time to return to the present moment. As you inhabit your partner's body, imagine being with you. How do you see yourself through your partner's eyes? Sense your partner's fears in relation to you. Sense their longing in relation to you. How does it feel to be in your partner's body in relationship with you? What does your partner need in order to feel safe and loved?

Breathe out, and open your eyes.

Exploring Through Movement

Imagine that you are shapeshifting into your partner's body. Start to move the way they move. Sense your shoulders becoming their shoulders, your neck their neck, your back their back. If they tilt their head to one side, tilt your head. Sense into the direction of their gaze. Feel into the position of their pelvis, the hip joints, the movement of the legs and arms. Sense into the gesture of their hands. As you fully inhabit their body, allow yourself to feel the emotions associated with their posture.

Then start to intensify the posture, amplifying the gestures and turning up the volume on any sensations present. Invite the associated emotions to continue to reveal themselves. Sense what happens in your breathing. Notice any images or narratives that emerge.

Sense into the kind of touch that your body is longing for. How can you meet this posture in the places where it's most needed? What kind of touch would meet any feelings of shame, fear, or grief with care, support, and attunement?

Invite your hands to meet your body with attuned touch. You might explore meeting your heart, your belly, the base of your skull, the back of your neck, your pelvis and hips. Notice what happens as your body receives this touch. As you receive the attuned contact of your hands, notice any shifts in your posture or movement. What does this contact allow to happen?

When this exploration feels complete, gently shake your body, releasing your partner's form and energy, and return fully to your own body. Then take some time for reflection. What insights can you bring forward from this practice? Can you suggest to your partner the kind of touch you sensed their body may be longing for? How can you meet your partner with the awareness you have gained? Is there a sense of compassion or understanding you can bring to their experience?

✳ Expanding the Space of Your Heart

Close your eyes and place your hand over your heart, directing your breathing to support your heart. Imagine your heart held in a circle of care, perhaps a nest, a garden, a warm hug, or a circle of loving allies. Sense how this circle of care allows the space of your heart to grow and expand. Continue to breathe into this space. See and sense any colors or images that emerge. Notice any sensations in your heart and throughout your body. Notice any movement of energy. Rest into the space of the heart, breathing and inviting its energy to grow and inhabit more and more of the world.

When this practice feels complete, breathe out and open your eyes.

EPILOGUE

Somewhere I Have Never Traveled

It is more important now to be in love than to be in power. . . . It is more important to live for the possibilities that lie ahead than to die in despair over what has been lost.

—BARRY LOPEZ

Love is simply the name for the desire and pursuit of the whole.

—PLATO

As the astronomer Carl Sagan noted, "For small creatures such as we, the vastness is bearable only through love."[1] In these terrifying times, in a world whose future is unknowable, I would argue that uncertainty, fear, and loneliness are made bearable only through love as well. It is difficult to conclude this book as I don't yet know the ending of the story. At moments it seems as if love has been pushed out to the margins, relegated with the birds and animals to the small patches of meadow that remain between the highways. Sexuality has been distorted and degraded, the goddess stripped of her powers like a forest bulldozed to the ground. Ancestral and plant-based healing practices are replaced with industrialized healthcare, and relational psychotherapy is threatened by AI technologies. Without intergenerational community, children grow up bonded to a smartphone instead of experiencing secure attachment with attuned caregivers. Even the stars that Sagan would have studied, perhaps basing his observation about love on their cosmic patterns, are harder to see now, SpaceX satellites obscuring their ancient light.

It's hard in my own life, as well as globally, to see what lies beyond the horizon. I am exploring partnership in new ways, and I don't know yet what lies beyond the realms I have traveled in prior relationships. I can only ask my Higher Power, in the words of Leonard Cohen, to "show me slowly what I only know the limits of."[2] I am longing to see the stars behind the satellites; I hope to open my heart more and more to love, to see what happens in the greater reaches of trust and commitment—to develop my capacity to let love in, into my body, my bones, my cells, and to offer my heart fully and without fear.

The work of conscious relationship is, as Cohen notes, to be shown, slowly and in Divine timing, the world that lies beyond the limits of our experience and imagination. In relationships in recovery, we leave familiar ground in order to reencounter the space of the heart—an uncivilized expanse where love runs wild. Where our engagement with Eros brings us in touch with the untamed nature of soul and the sensuous animal of the body. Where time, too, is uncolonized, and includes the presence of our ancestors and future generations in our circle of care. Where we include the lives of all sentient beings with whom we share the Earth. Where our love extends from the depths of our cells to the outer reaches of the cosmos. Where awakening sensation in the genitals might bring us in touch with the pulse of life, and connecting to the heart might grant us wisdom great enough to hold the pain and to see answers that extend beyond the questions we have asked.

My hope for you as you explore beyond the limits you have known is that you be shown something of great beauty, great big shimmering galaxies whose light you had only glimpsed. May your journey bring you to a love that heals all the way down to your genes and that opens up to the universe. May it be a love that restores you to your place in the greater whole, to a deep knowing of your belonging. May the work of relationship be a creative act and the sacred ground on which you stand. May your love flow out into the world as a gift to all those it can serve. May we stand together like trees whose roots connect beneath the soil, as a community of love—of attachment-based parenting and education and medicine and addiction treatment—to bring much needed healing to our fragmented world.

I leave you here with a poem called "Abounding Love," which I wrote several years ago. I hope it can serve as a reminder that our relationship with Eros is a mutual one, that love is reaching for us as much as we are reaching for love. The deepest magic of recovery is that, amid all the past and present heartbreak and the specter of future loss, we become open to receive it.

If the Milky Way appears dark

in patches, it is not because it is empty
but because it is full

the light
lost in a crowd of stars

I never knew that God too desires us,
writes Rumi

and truly—

luminescent plankton,
warbler feathers, amanita
spores

how could these be anything
but the touch

of a soft hand on our
backs in the night, saying

turn, turn

✳ Writing a Love Poem to Love

In your journal, compose a love poem to Love. You can draw on these ideas for exploration or follow your own impulses.

As you envision Love, what images arise? What sensory descriptions—such as color, texture, scent, sound, taste—would you use to embody Love? What metaphors or similes come to mind?

How does your body touch Love? How does Love touch your body? How do you move with Love? How does Love move with you?

What would you say to Love? How does Love respond?

How do you hold Love? How does Love hold you?

Resources

Conscious Girlfriend Academy: Education, community, and coaching for cultivating conscious lesbian and queer relationships.
consciousgirlfriendacademy.com

DARe (Dynamic Attachment Repatterning experience): A somatic therapy for healing early attachment wounds.
traumasolutions.com/find-a-dare-practitioner-directory/

Emotionally Focused Therapy (EFT): A highly effective attachment-based therapy for individuals and couples.
directory.iceeft.com

Equusoma: An equine-assisted therapy that integrates Somatic Experiencing and the horse–human relationship for the healing of trauma and attachment wounds.
equusoma.com/directory

Gaga: A movement practice offered in group classes that is designed to increase somatic presence and awareness of physical sensation, helping to restore regulation, increase mobility, and deepen embodied pleasure; classes offered in-person and online.
gagapeople.com/en

Havening: This self-directed touch modality can help cultivate feelings of safety and relaxation. See the website and YouTube for demonstrations of this easy-to-learn practice.
havening.org

Imago: Therapy for couples that aims to transform conflict through relational connection.
imagorelationships.org

Invitation to Change (ITC): A holistic framework based in science and compassion, designed for the families and loved ones of people struggling with substance use; in-person and online meetings. A good complement or alternative to Al-Anon.
cmcffc.org/community-groups-hub/itc-support-group-directory

National Domestic Violence Hotline: Twenty-four-hour confidential support for people impacted by relationship abuse; also provides links to local resources.
thehotline.org

NeuroAffective Touch: A somatic modality that bridges psychotherapy and touch for the healing of early attachment wounds and developmental trauma.
neuroaffectivetouch.com/find-a-therapist

Safe and Sound Protocol: A gentle, noninvasive listening therapy based on polyvagal theory that focuses on nervous system regulation.
integratedlistening.com/about/find-a-provider

Self:Cervix: Courses, tools, and practices for awakening the cervix.
selfcervix.com

Somatic Experiencing: A body-oriented therapy for healing trauma.
traumahealing.org

Somatic Sex Education: A trauma-informed sexuality and embodiment modality with practitioners worldwide.
somaticsexeducator.com

Somatic Sexual Wholeness: Courses, sessions, and a podcast with somatic sex educator Rahi Chun.
somaticsexualwholeness.com

Trauma Solutions Attachment Quiz: Learn more about your attachment tendencies with this quiz from Diane Poole Heller.
traumasolutions.com/attachment-styles-quiz

Recommended Reading

Barnett, Michael. *Emotionally Focused Therapy for Addiction: How to Heal the Loneliness and Shame That Trigger Addictive Behaviors.*

Bass, Ellen. "Loving a Woman." thesunmagazine.org/articles/22942-loving-a-woman. My favorite poem about healing from shame.

Bey, Douglas, and Deborah Bey. *Loving an Adult Child of an Alcoholic.*

Campbell, Susan. *Truth in Dating: Finding Love by Getting Real.*

DeYoung, Patricia. *Understanding and Treating Chronic Shame: Healing Right Brain Relational Trauma,* 2nd Ed.

Flores, Philip. *Addiction as an Attachment Disorder.*

Foote, Jeffrey, Kenneth Carpenter, and Carrie Wilkens, *The Beyond Addiction Workbook for Family and Friends: Evidence-Based Skills to Help a Loved One Make Positive Change.*

Gaskin, Ina May. *Ina May's Guide to Breastfeeding.*

——— *Ina May's Guide to Childbirth.*

Heller, Diane Poole. *The Power of Attachment: How to Create Deep and Lasting Intimate Relationships.*

Heller, Laurence, and Aline LaPierre. *Healing Developmental Trauma: How Early Trauma Affects Self-Regulation, Self-Image, and the Capacity for Relationship.*

Hendrix, Harville. *Keeping the Love You Find: A Single Person's Guide to Achieving Lasting Love.*

Hendrix, Harville. *Getting the Love You Want: A Guide for Couples.*

Johnson, Sue. *Hold Me Tight: Seven Conversations for a Lifetime of Love.*

——— *Love Sense: The Revolutionary New Science of Romantic Relationships.*

Kain, Kathy L., and Stephen J. Terrell. *Nurturing Resilience: Helping Clients Move Forward from Developmental Trauma.*

Kappadakunnel, Bryana. *Parent Yourself First: Raise Confident, Compassionate Kids by Becoming the Parent You Wish You'd Had.*

Kernberg, Otto. *Love Relations: Normality and Pathology.*

Kirschner, Diana. *Love in 90 Days: The Essential Guide to Finding Your Own True Love.*

Leonard, Linda Schierse. *On the Way to the Wedding: Transforming the Love Relationship.*

Levine, Amir, and Rachel Heller, *Attached: The New Science of Adult Attachment and How It Can Help You Find—and Keep—Love.*

Levine, Stephen, and Ondrea Levine. *Embracing the Beloved: Relationship as a Path of Awakening.*

Lewis, Thomas, Fari Amini, and Richard Lannon. *A General Theory of Love.*

Marich, Jamie. *Trauma and the 12 Steps: An Inclusive Guide to Enhancing Recovery.*

Marin, Vanessa, and Xander Marin. *Sex Talks: The Five Conversations That Will Transform Your Love Life.*

Martin, Betty, and Robyn Dalzen. *The Art of Receiving and Giving: The Wheel of Consent.*

Menanno, Julie. *Secure Love: Creating a Relationship That Lasts a Lifetime.*

Nagoski, Emily. *Come as You Are: The Surprising New Science That Will Transform Your Sex Life.*

Narvaez, Darcia, and G. A. Bradshaw, *The Evolved Nest: Nature's Way of Raising Children and Creating Connected Communities.*

Schwartz, Ruth, and Michelle Murrain. *Conscious Lesbian Dating and Love: A Roadmap to Finding the Right Partner and Creating the Relationship of Your Dreams.*

Shershun, Erika. *Healing Sexual Trauma Workbook: Somatic Skills to Help You Feel Safe in Your Body, Create Boundaries, and Live with Resilience.*

Solomon, Marion. *Narcissism and Intimacy: Love and Marriage in an Age of Confusion.*

Tatkin, Stan. *Wired for Love: How Understanding Your Partner's Brain and Attachment Style Can Help You Defuse Conflict and Build a Secure Relationship.*

Thomas, Katherine Woodward. *Conscious Uncoupling: 5 Steps to Living Happily Even After.*

Weber, Andreas. *Matter and Desire: An Erotic Ecology.*

Welwood, John. *Perfect Love, Imperfect Relationships: Healing the Wound of the Heart.*

Wolynn, Mark. *It Didn't Start with You: How Inherited Family Trauma Shapes Who We Are and How to End the Cycle.*

Notes

INTRODUCTION

Stephen and Ondrea Levine, *Embracing the Beloved: Relationship as a Path of Awakening* (Doubleday, 1995), 4.

Soen Nakagawa, quoted in Toni Berhard, *How to Be Sick: A Buddhist-Inspired Guide for the Chronically Ill and Their Caregivers* (Wisdom Publications, 2010), 128.

Carl Jung, quoted in Anthony Stevens, *Private Myths: Dream and Dreaming* (Harvard University Press, 1995), 131.

1 Sue Johnson, *Hold Me Tight: Seven Conversations for a Lifetime of Love* (Little, Brown Spark, 2008), 15.

2 This book interweaves perspectives presented in *Addiction as an Attachment Disorder* by Philip Flores (Jason Aronson, 2004); *Healing Developmental Trauma* by Laurence Heller and Aline LaPierre (North Atlantic Books, 2012); *Love Sense: The Revolutionary New Science of Romantic Relationships* (Little, Brown Spark, 2013) and *Hold Me Tight* by Sue Johnson, and other work on Emotionally Focused Therapy (EFT), including the (highly recommended!) book *Emotionally Focused Therapy Workbook for Addiction: How to Heal Loneliness and Shame That Trigger Addictive Behaviors* by Michael Barnett (New Harbinger Publications, 2024); *The Power of Attachment: How to Create Deep and Lasting Intimate Relationships* by Diane Poole Heller (Sounds True, 2019); *Getting the Love You Want: A Guide to Couples*, 20th anniversary ed., by Harville Hendrix (Saint Martin's Griffin, 2008); and *Embracing the Beloved: Relationship as a Path of Awakening* by Stephen and Ondrea Levine. I am grateful to the life-changing contributions of these authors. Additionally, my ongoing training and mentorship with Aline LaPierre informs so many aspects of this book; her deep wisdom in integrating psychology and somatics is woven throughout these pages.

3 Johnson, *Hold Me Tight*, 27.
4 Darcia Narvaez and G. A. Bradshaw, *The Evolved Nest: Nature's Way of Raising Children and Creating Connected Communities* (North Atlantic Books, 2023).
5 Narvaez and Bradshaw, *The Evolved Nest*, 2.
6 Narvaez and Bradshaw, *The Evolved Nest*, 10.
7 Flores, *Addiction as Attachment Disorder*.
8 Heller and LaPierre, *Healing Developmental Trauma*.
9 Jan Winhall, *Treating Trauma with the Felt Sense Polyvagal Model: A Bottom-Up Approach* (Routledge, 2021); Kathy Kain and Stephen Terrell, *Nurturing Resilience: Helping Clients Move Forward from Developmental Trauma—An Integrative Somatic Approach* (North Atlantic Books, 2018).
10 The imagery exercises that begin "Breathe out three times slowly" are based on the work of Colette Aboulker-Muscat and my teacher Catherine Shainberg. A huge thank-you to my mother, Sheila Pick, for sharing her wisdom and practice in this lineage.
11 Jessica Fern, *Polysecure: Attachment, Trauma and Consensual Nonmonogamy* (Thornapple Press, 2020).

CHAPTER 1
ADDICTION AND ATTACHMENT

Ernest S. Wolf, *Treating the Self: Elements of Clinical Self Psychology* (Guilford Press, 1988), 39.

Philip Flores, *Addiction as an Attachment Disorder* (Jason Aronson, 2004), 129.

1 Anthony Bateman and Jeremy Holmes, *Introduction to Psychoanalysis: Contemporary Theory and Practice* (Taylor and Francis, 1995), 73.
2 Laurence Heller and Aline LaPierre, *Healing Developmental Trauma* (North Atlantic Books, 2012), 33–34.
3 Bateman and Holmes, *Introduction to Psychoanalysis*, 53. Peter Levine similarly maps the implicit and explicit aspects of memory in *Trauma and Memory: Brain and Body in a Search for the Living Past* (North Atlantic Books, 2015).
4 Henry Krystal, quoted in Darcia Narvaez and G. A. Bradshaw, *The Evolved Nest: Nature's Way of Raising Children and Creating Connected Communities* (North Atlantic Books, 2023), 38.

5 Patricia DeYoung, *Understanding and Treating Chronic Shame: Healing Right Brain Relational Trauma*, 2nd ed. (Routledge, 2022), 89.

6 Philip Flores, *Addiction as an Attachment Disorder*, 6–7; Ernest S. Wolf, one of the major innovators of self psychology, reiterates this line of thought, noting that "the increasing seriousness of drug abuse and the steadily increasing suicide rates during the last two decades could be related to the shifting child rearing practices that are deficient in self-sustaining and self-supporting experiences." *Treating the Self*, 25.

7 Heller and LaPierre, *Healing Developmental Trauma*, 9–16.

8 Wolf, *Treating the Self*, 43.

9 Michael Barnett, *The Emotionally Focused Therapy Workbook for Addiction: How to Heal the Loneliness and Shame that Trigger Addictive Behaviors* (New Harbinger Publications, 2024), 7.

10 Ronald Fairbairn, quoted in Bateman and Holmes, *Introduction to Psychoanalysis*, 41.

11 As Bateman and Holmes write, "The compulsive quest for pleasure may of course also be a pathological response when object relations fail." *Introduction to Psychoanalysis*, 41.

12 "Harlow's Classic Studies Revealed the Importance of Maternal Contact," Association for Psychological Science, June 20, 2018, https://www.psychologicalscience.org/publications/observer/obsonline/harlows-classic-studies-revealed-the-importance-of-maternal-contact.html.

13 Polyvagal theory was developed by Stephen Porges and further elaborated by numerous authors/practitioners, including Deb Dana, Kathy Kain, and Stephen Terrell.

14 Kathy L. Kain and Stephen J. Terrell, *Nurturing Resilience: Helping Clients Move Forward from Developmental Trauma—An Integrative Somatic Approach* (North Atlantic Books, 2018), 76–84.

15 Diane Poole Heller, *The Power of Attachment: How to Create Deep and Lasting Intimate Relationships* (Sounds True, 2019), 126.

16 Jan Winhall and Stephen W. Porges, "Revolutionizing Addiction Treatment with the Felt Sense Polyvagal Model," *International Body Psychotherapy Journal* 21, no. 1 (Spring/Summer 2022): 20–21.

17 Winhall and Porges, "Revolutionizing Addiction Treatment," 16.

18 Winhall and Porges, "Revolutionizing Addiction Treatment," 16.

19 Philip Flores, *Addiction as an Attachment Disorder* (Jason Aronson, 2004), 99–100.

20 Sue Johnson, *Hold Me Tight: Seven Conversations for a Lifetime of Love* (Little, Brown Spark, 2008), 57.

21 Darcia Narvaez, "The Dangers of 'Crying It Out,'" *Psychology Today*, May 17, 2024.

22 Narvaez and Bradshaw, *The Evolved Nest*, xviii.

23 See Ed Tronick, "The Caregiver–Infant Dyad as a Buffer or Transducer of Resource Enhancing or Depleting Factors That Shape Psychobiological Development," *Australian and New Zealand Journal of Family Therapy* 38, no. 4 (December 2017): 561–72.

24 Bryana Kappadakunnel, *Parent Yourself First: Raise Confident, Compassionate Kids by Becoming the Parent You Wish You Had* (G. P. Putnam's Sons, 2025), 196.

25 This practice is inspired by work by Catherine Shainberg, and by the exercise "Reversing Role Reversal" in Heller, *The Power of Attachment*, 47–48.

26 For a quick and accessible overview of attachment-oriented, neuroscience-based parenting for infants and young children that includes guidance on breaking intergenerational patterns, I recommend the pamphlet by Licia M. Rando, the "Caring and Connected Parenting," accessed October 2, 2025, https://www.liciarando.com/about-the-caring-and-connected-parenting-guide.

27 Harville Hendrix, *Getting the Love You Want: A Guide to Couples*, 20th anniversary ed. (Saint Martin's Griffin, 2019), 143–55.

CHAPTER 2
TRANSFORMING THE ATTACHMENT INHERITANCE

Maurice Sendak, *Where the Wild Things Are* (HarperCollins, 1963). According to the book *The Violet Hour* by Katie Roiphe, Sendak modeled the wild things after his relatives, all Jewish immigrants new to New York, whose love was tremendous and overpowering.

Czesław Miłosz, *Native Realm: A Search for Self-Definition*, trans. Catherine Leach (Farrar, Straus And Giroux, 2002), 20.

1 Muriel Buqué, *Break the Cycle: A Guide to Healing Intergenerational Trauma* (Dutton, 2024), 80.

2 Maria Yellow Horse Brave Heart, quoted in Thomas Hübl, *Healing Collective Trauma: A Process for Integrating Our Intergenerational and Cultural Wounds* (Sounds True, 2020), 74.

3 Kathy L. Kain and Stephen J. Terrell, *Nurturing Resilience: Helping Clients Move Forward from Developmental Trauma—An Integrative Somatic Approach* (North Atlantic Books, 2018), 41.

4 Kain and Terrell, *Nurturing Resilience*, 42.

5 Rachel Yehuda, quoted in Mark Wolynn, *It Didn't Start with You: How Inherited Family Trauma Shapes Who We Are and How to End the Cycle* (Penguin, 2016), 19.

6 See Joy DeGruy Leary, *Post Traumatic Slave Syndrome: America's Legacy of Enduring Injury and Healing* (Uptone Press, 2005) for an in-depth exploration of inherited trauma in Black diasporic communities.

7 Wolynn, *It Didn't Start with You*, 13.

8 Kain and Terrell, *Nurturing Resilience*, 43.

9 Nirit Gradwohl Pisano, *Granddaughters of the Holocaust: Never Forgetting What They Didn't Experience* (Academic Studies Press, 2012), 25.

10 Pisano, *Granddaughters of the Holocaust*, 52.

11 Anne Ancelin Schützenberger, *The Ancestor Syndrome: Transgenerational Psychotherapy and the Hidden Links in the Family Tree*, trans. Anne Trager (Routledge, 1998), 3.

12 Roland Barthes, *Camera Lucida: Reflections on Photography*, trans. Richard Howard (Hill and Wang, 2010), 27.

13 Emily Dickinson, *Final Harvest: Emily Dickinson's Poems*, selection and introduction by Thomas Johnson (Little, Brown and Company, 161), 152.

14 Kain and Terrell, *Nurturing Resilience*, 42.

15 Kai Hillel, personal communication with the author, August 2025.

16 Schützenberger, *The Ancestor Syndrome*, 4.

17 Philip Flores, *Addiction as an Attachment Disorder* (Jason Aronson, 2004), 68–100.

18 Doreen Martinez, "Our Breath of Being: Indigenous Living Through Storying Traditions," Cultural Survival, January 26, 2024, https://www.culturalsurvival.org/news/our-breath-being-indigenous-living-through-storying-traditions.

19 I recommend *The Land in Our Bones* by Layla Feghali (North Atlantic Books, 2024) and *Ashkenazi Herbalism* by Deatra Cohen and Adam Siegel (North Atlantic Books, 2021), both excellent books on ancestral herbalism practices.

CHAPTER 3
EARLY ATTACHMENT AND ADULT RELATIONSHIPS

Amir Levine and Rachel Heller, *Attached: The New Science of Adult Attachment and How It Can Help You Find—and Keep—Love* (Penguin Random House, 2011), 21.

Ethel S. Person, quoted in David Mann, *Psychotherapy, An Erotic Relationship: Transference and Countertransference Passions* (Routledge, 1997), 35.

1 Levine and Heller, *Attached*; Diane Poole Heller, *The Power of Attachment: How to Create Deep and Lasting Intimate Relationships* (Sounds True, 2019); and Thomas Lewis, Fari Amini, and Richard Lannon, *A General Theory of Love* (Vintage, 2001).

2 John Bowlby, *Attachment and Loss: Volume 1. Attachment* (1969; Basic Books, 1982).

3 Diane Poole Heller has explored attachment and somatics extensively in her work, and this chapter is much indebted to her beautiful book *The Power of Attachment: How to Create Deep and Lasting Intimate Relationships* (Sounds True, 2019).

4 Heller, *Power of Attachment*, 155.

5 Laurence Heller and Aline LaPierre, *Healing Developmental Trauma* (North Atlantic Books, 2012), 56.

6 Heller and LaPierre, *Healing Developmental Trauma*, 51.

7 Heller, *Power of Attachment*, 86.

8 Heller and LaPierre, *Healing Developmental Trauma*, 51.

9 Thich Nhat Hanh, *True Love: A Practice for Awakening the Heart*, trans. Sherab Chödzin Kohn (Shambhala, 1997), 4.

10 Dan Griffin, *A Man's Way Through Relationship: Learning to Love and Be Loved* (Central Recovery Press, 2014), 29.

11 Heller, *Power of Attachment*, 169–70.

12 Stan Tatkin discusses the "tether" as the attachment lifeline that provides comfort and security. See *Wired for Love: How Understanding Your Partner's Brain and Attachment Style Can Help You Defuse Conflict and Build a Secure Relationship*, 2nd ed. (New Harbinger, 2024).

CHAPTER 4
SURVIVAL STYLES AND THE RECOVERY JOURNEY

Kelly Wilson, quoted in Jeffrey Foote, Kenneth Carpenter, and Carrie Wilkins, *The Beyond Addiction Workbook for Family and Friends: Evidence-Based Skills to Help a Loved One Make Positive Change* (New Harbinger Publications, 2022), 59.

1 Laurence Heller and Aline LaPierre, *Healing Developmental Trauma* (North Atlantic Books, 2012), 37.

2 Heller and LaPierre, *Healing Developmental Trauma*, 41.

3 Heller and LaPierre, *Healing Developmental Trauma*, 48.

4 Heller and LaPierre, *Healing Developmental Trauma*, 51.

5 Heller and LaPierre, *Healing Developmental Trauma*, 57–58.

6 Heller and LaPierre, *Healing Developmental Trauma*, 67.

7 Heller and LaPierre, *Healing Developmental Trauma*, 70.

8 Heller and LaPierre, *Healing Developmental Trauma*, 79.

9 Heller and LaPierre, *Healing Developmental Trauma*, 63.

CHAPTER 5
UNPROGRAMMING THE PROGRAM

Diane Poole Heller, *The Power of Attachment: How to Create Deep and Lasting Intimate Relationships* (Sounds True, 2019), 77.

Anthony Bateman and Jeremy Holmes, *Introduction to Psychoanalysis: Contemporary Theory and Practice* (Taylor and Francis, 1995), 74.

1 See Jamie Marich for an extensive discussion of program slogans through a trauma-informed lens. *Trauma and the 12 Steps: An Inclusive Guide to Enhancing Recovery* (North Atlantic Books, 2020), 72–79.

2 Stan Tatkin, *Wired for Love: How Understanding Your Partner's Brain and Attachment Style Can Help You Defuse Conflict and Build a Secure Relationship*, 2nd ed. (New Harbinger, 2024), 40.

3 Amir Levine and Rachel Heller, *Attached: The New Science of Adult Attachment and How It Can Help You Find—and Keep—Love* (Penguin Random House, 2011), 26.

4 Jeffrey Foote, Kenneth Carpenter, and Carrie Wilkins, *The Beyond Addiction Workbook for Family and Friends: Evidence-Based Skills to Help a Loved One Make Positive Change* (New Harbinger Publications, 2022), 1. Their program, Invitation to Change, provides a loving approach based in attachment and behavioral science aimed at improving relationships with loved ones who use substances and helping them gain sobriety. See the "Resources" section for more information.

5 Foote, Carpenter, and Wilkins, *Beyond Addiction Workbook*, 4.

6 The term *loyal waiting* is from work by Jack Danielian and Patricia Gianotti, quoted in Patricia DeYoung, *Understanding and Treating Chronic Shame: Healing Right Brain Relational Trauma*, 2nd ed. (Routledge, 2022), 211.

7 "Codependency Meaning, Signs, and Symptoms," Turning Point of Tampa, November 13, 2023, https://www.tpoftampa.com/codependency-meaning-signs-and-symptoms/.

8 David Bedrick, *The Unshaming Way* (North Atlantic Books, 2025), 246–54.

9 For a fascinating exploration of the seeking system as described through the lens of neuroscience, see Frank Corrigan, Hannah Young, and Jessica Christie-Sands, *Deep Brain Reorienting: Understanding the Neuroscience of Trauma, Attachment Wounding, and DBR Psychotherapy* (Routledge, 2025).

10 Diane Poole Heller, *The Power of Attachment: How to Create Deep and Lasting Intimate Relationships* (Sounds True, 2019), 86–88.

11 Levine and Heller, *Attached*, 80–88.

12 Philip Flores, *Addiction as an Attachment Disorder* (Jason Aronson, 2004), 99.

13 Katie Eberle, personal communication with the author.

14 Marich, *Trauma and the 12 Steps*, 71–95.

15 Marich, *Trauma and the 12 Steps*, 78.

16 For more about the neurological processes that inform attraction, see Thomas Lewis, Fari Amini, and Richard Lannon, *A General Theory of Love* (Vintage, 2001).

17 Diana Kirschner, *Love in 90 Days: The Essential Guide to Finding Your Own True Love* (Center Street, 2009), 195–96; Heller, *Power of Attachment*, 158–61.

18 Alcoholics Anonymous, *Alcoholics Anonymous* [the Big Book], 4th ed. (Alcoholics Anonymous World Services, 2001), 64.

19 Laurence Heller and Aline LaPierre, *Healing Developmental Trauma* (North Atlantic Books, 2012), 11.

20 Thank you to my friend, psychotherapist Lucian Schloss, for the conversation that sparked the idea for this section.

21 For an in-depth exploration of the meaning and messages of emotions, I recommend Robert Augustus Masters, *Emotional Intimacy* (Sounds True, 2013).

22 Marich, *Trauma and the 12 Steps*, 84–85.

CHAPTER 6
ADDICTION, ATTACHMENT, AND ADDICTIVE ATTACHMENTS

Brian Selznick, *Big Tree* (Scholastic Press, 2023), 323–28.

1 For a discussion of the archetype of the Garden of Eden, see James Hollis, *The Eden Project: In Search of the Magical Other, a Jungian Perspective on Relationship* (Inner City Books, 1998), among work by other Jungian psychologists.

2 Helen E. Fisher, Xiaomeng Xu, Arthur Aron, and Lucy L. Brown, "Intense, Passionate, Romantic Love: A Natural Addiction? How the Fields That Investigate Romance and Substance Abuse Can Inform Each Other," *Frontiers in Psychology* 7, no. 687 (2016), https://doi.org/10.3389/fpsyg.2016.00687.

3 See Thomas Lewis, Fari Amini, and Richard Lannon, *A General Theory of Love* (Vintage, 2001), for a fascinating description of the neuroscience of attraction.

CHAPTER 7
SHAME

Helen Epstein, *Children of the Holocaust: Conversations with Sons and Daughters of Survivors, with a New Introduction* (Penguin Books, 2019), 1.

Patricia DeYoung, *Understanding and Treating Chronic Shame: Healing Right Brain Relational Trauma*, 2nd ed. (Routledge, 2022), 20.

1 Kathy Kain and Stephen Terrell, *Nurturing Resilience: Helping Clients Move Forward from Developmental Trauma—An Integrative Somatic Approach* (North Atlantic Books, 2018), 172–73.
2 See DeYoung, *Understanding and Treating Chronic Shame*, 101–30.
3 A. J. Bond, *Discomfortable: What Is Shame and How Can We Break Its Hold?* (North Atlantic Books, 2021), 30.
4 DeYoung, *Understanding and Treating Chronic Shame*, 89.
5 Allan Schore, "Early Shame Experiences and Infant Brain Development" in *Shame: Interpersonal Behavior, Psychopathology, and Culture*, edited by Paul Gilbert and Bernice Andrews (Oxford, 1998), 64.
6 Dang Nghiem, *The River in Me: Verses of Transformation* (Parallax Press, 2024), 82.
7 DeYoung, *Understanding and Treating Chronic Shame*; see also Joy DeGruy Leary, *Post Traumatic Slave Syndrome: America's Legacy of Enduring Injury and Healing* (Uptone Press, 2005).
8 Some theorists include what might otherwise be called "guilt" under the term *healthy shame* or *prosocial shame* (as opposed to *toxic shame*). Others see guilt as a secondary response that is distinct from shame as a primary affect.
9 "Mary," track 12 on Patty Griffin, *Flaming Red*, UMG Recordings, 1998. Clarissa Pinkola Estés offers a beautiful recitation of this song on *Seeing in the Dark: Myths and Stories of the Medial Woman and Bringing Gifts up from Darkness*, Audio CD (Sounds True, 2010).
10 Johann Hari, "Everything You Think You Know About Addiction Is Wrong," TEDGlobalLondon, June 2015, https://www.ted.com/talks/johann_hari_everything_you_think_you_know_about_addiction_is_wrong.

CHAPTER 8
TOUCH

Ernest S. Wolf, *Treating the Self: Elements of Clinical Self Psychology* (Guilford Press, 1988), 44.

Marion Woodman, *The Ravaged Bridegroom: Masculinity in Women* (Inner City Books, 1990), 43.

Ashley Montagu, *Touching: The Human Significance of the Skin* (Columbia University Press, 1971), 31.

1 Darcia Narvaez and G. A. Bradshaw, *The Evolved Nest: Nature's Way of Raising Children and Creating Connected Communities* (North Atlantic Books, 2023), 20–21.

2 Montagu, *Touching*, 40.

3 Nils Bergman, quoted in Narvaez and Bradshaw, *The Evolved Nest*, 55.

4 Narvaez and Bradshaw, *The Evolved Nest*, 93.

5 Montagu, *Touching*, 56–60.

6 Montagu (*Touching*, 56–60) describes the numerous negative effects that a cesarean birth can have on the infant—including higher mortality rate, greater lethargy, more anxiety, and a number of detrimental biochemical differences—and makes a clear case that that cesarean deliveries should be avoided except as a medical necessity. He states, however, that some of the disadvantages might be mitigated by providing ample caresses for the newborn.

7 See Rachel Hillel, *The Redemption of the Feminine Erotic Soul* (Nicolas-Hays, Inc., 1997).

8 James Reavis, Jan Looman, et al., quoted in Aliane Duncan with Kathy Kain, *The Tao of Trauma: A Practitioner's Guide for Integrating Five Element Theory and Trauma Treatment* (North Atlantic Books, 2019), 247.

9 Some of these interventions come from NeuroAffective Touch, created by Aline LaPierre.

10 Narvaez and Bradshaw, *The Evolved Nest*, 86–97.

11 Ian Kerner, *So Tell Me About the Last Time You Had Sex: Laying Bare and Learning to Repair Our Love Lives* (Grand Central, 2021), 109.

12 See Cornelia Elbrecht, *Healing Trauma in Children with Clay Field Therapy: How Sensorimotor Art Therapy Supports the Embodiment of Developmental Milestones* (North Atlantic Books, 2021).

13 Ruth Lanius, Sherain Harricharan, Breanne E. Kearney, and Benjamin Pandev-Girard, *Sensory Pathways to Healing from Trauma: Harnessing the Brain's Capacity for Change* (The Guilford Press, 2025), 3.

14 Stephen Porges explores prosody extensively in his work. With Unyte Health, he created the Safe and Sound Protocol, a five-hour auditory protocol that draws

on vocal prosody to create a felt sense of safety and restore ANS regulation. See the "Resources" section, as well as Stephen Porges and Karen Onderko, *Safe and Sound: A Polyvagal Approach to Connection, Change, and Healing* (Sounds True, 2025).

15 Roland Barthes, *A Lover's Discourse*, trans. Richard Howard (Hill and Wang, 1977), 73.

CHAPTER 9
DATING IN RECOVERY

Sefer Yetzirah, quoted in Jill Hammer, *Return to the Place* (Ben Yehuda Press, 2020), xxvi.

Kabir, quoted in John Welwood, *Perfect Love, Imperfect Relationships: Healing the Wound of the Heart* (Trumpeter Books, 2006), 120.

1 Jean-Paul Sartre, *No Exit and Three Other Plays* (Vintage, 1989), 45; Jean-Paul Sartre, quoted in Ernest S. Wolf, *Treating the Self: Elements of Clinical Self Psychology* (Guilford Press, 1988), 41.

2 See Susan Campbell, *Truth in Dating: Finding Love by Getting Real* (New World Library, 2004) for a useful framework that includes ten key "truth skills."

3 Diane Poole Heller, *The Power of Attachment: How to Create Deep and Lasting Intimate Relationships* (Sounds True, 2019), 158–61.

4 Diana Kirschner, *Love in 90 Days: The Essential Guide to Finding Your Own True Love* (Center Street, 2019), 195.

5 Thomas Lewis, Fari Amini, and Richard Lannon, *A General Theory of Love* (Vintage, 2001), 118.

6 Robert Gordon, "The Three P's of Relationship Conflict: Do You Pick, Project, or Provoke?" Imago Center of Washington, DC, accessed December 5, 2025, https://imagocenterdc.com/the-three-ps-of-relationship-conflict-do-you-pick-project-or-provoke.

7 Lewis, Amini, and Lannon, *General Theory of Love*, 120.

8 Marco Barbaresi, Davide Nardo, and Sabrina Fagioli, "Physiological Entrainment: A Key Mind-Body Mechanism for Cognitive, Motor and Affective

Functioning, and Well-Being," *Brain Sciences* 15, no. 1 (2025): 3, https://doi.org/10.3390/brainsci15010003.

CHAPTER 10
SEX IN RECOVERY

Talmud Bavli, *Ketubot* 111b, quoted in Rabbi Shefa Gold, "V'etchanan," accessed October 21, 2025, https://www.rabbishefagold.com/vetchanan/.

David Mann, *Psychotherapy, An Erotic Relationship: Transference and Countertransference Passions* (Routledge, 1997), 195.

1 Diana Kirschner, *Love in 90 Days: The Essential Guide to Finding Your Own True Love* (Center Street, 2019), 218.

2 Sue Johnson, *Hold Me Tight: Seven Conversations for a Lifetime of Love* (Little, Brown Spark, 2008), 194.

3 I recommend Betty Martin and Robyn Dalzen's *The Art of Receiving and Giving: The Wheel of Consent* (Luminare Press, 2021) for an in-depth exploration of consent dynamics.

4 RAINN, "Consent 101: Respect, Boundaries, & Building Trust," August 28, 2025, https://rainn.org/articles/what-is-consent.

5 American Sexual Health Association, "Understanding Consent," accessed October 21, 2025, https://www.ashasexualhealth.org/understanding-consent/.

6 Stephen Porges and Karen Onderko, *Safe and Sound: A Polyvagal Approach to Connection, Change, and Healing* (Sounds True, 2025), 36–37.

7 See Self:Cervix (https://selfcervix.com/) for cervical awakening practices and research on the heart–cervix connection.

8 See Donna Mazloomdoost and Rachel N. Pauls, "A Comprehensive Review of the Clitoris and Its Role in Female Sexual Function," *Sexual Medicine Reviews* 3, no. 4 (October 2015): 245–63, https://doi.org/10.1002/smrj.61.

9 Christiane Pelmas, *Trauma: A Practical Guide to Working with Body and Soul* (ReWilding Press, 2017), 34.

10 Eugene Monick, *Phallos: The Sacred Energy of the Masculine* (Inner City Books, 1987).

11 Pelmas, *Trauma*, 33–34.

12 Mann, *Psychotherapy, An Erotic Relationship*, 30.

13 Mann, *Psychotherapy, An Erotic Relationship*, 30.

14 Denworth, Lydia. "Touch's Social Significance Could Be Explained by Unique Nerve Fibers," *Scientific American*, July 1, 2015, https://www.scientificamerican.com/article/touch-s-social-significance-could-be-explained-by-unique-nerve-fibers/.

CHAPTER 11
ENDING A RELATIONSHIP IN RECOVERY

C. S. Lewis, *The Four Loves* (HarperCollins, 1960), 155–56.

Nick Cave, "It's Been Ten Years Since Your Son Arthur Died. What Have You and Susie Learned in Those Years?," *The Red Hand Files*, Issue 331, July 2025, https://www.theredhandfiles.com/its-been-ten-years-2/.

Karen Kaminski, "RIP, Andrea Gibson," *Better Living Through Literature*, July 15, 2025, https://karenkaminski.com/rip-andrea-gibson/.

1 Stephanie Sarazin, *Soulbroken: A Guidebook for Your Journey Through Ambiguous Grief* (Balance, 2022), 16.

2 Sarazin, *Soulbroken*, xxiii.

3 Katherine Woodward Thomas, *Conscious Uncoupling: 5 Steps to Living Happily Even After* (Harmony Books, 2015), 48.

4 See Day Schildkret, *Hello, Goodbye: 75 Rituals for Times of Loss, Celebration, and Change* (Simon Element, 2022) for guidance on ritualcraft.

5 I recommend Mary Oliver's poem "In Blackwater Woods" for a beautiful meditation on loving and letting go. See *New and Selected Poems, Vol. 1* (Beacon Press, 1992), 177.

CHAPTER 12
CONSCIOUS RELATIONSHIPS

Harville Hendrix and Helen LaKelly Hunt, foreword to *Getting the Love You Want: A Guide to Couples*, 20th anniversary ed., by Harville Hendrix (Saint Martin's Griffin, 2008), xix.

James Baldwin, *The Fire Next Time* (Modern Library, 2021), 78.

James Hollis, *The Eden Project: In Search of the Magical Other* (Inner City Books, 1998), 73.

1 Hendrix, *Getting the Love You Want*, 86.

2 Anthony Bateman and Jeremy Holmes, *Introduction to Psychoanalysis: Contemporary Theory and Practice* (Taylor and Francis, 1995), 74.

3 Marion Woodman, *The Ravaged Bridegroom: Masculinity in Women* (Inner City Books, 1990), 211.

4 Woodman, *The Ravaged Bridegroom*, 211.

5 Stephen Levine and Ondrea Levine, *Embracing the Beloved: Relationship as a Path of Awakening* (Doubleday, 1995), 3.

6 Levine and Levine, *Embracing the Beloved*, 112–17.

7 Otto Kernberg, *Love Relations: Normality and Pathology* (Yale University Press, 1995), 54–59.

8 André Green, *On Private Madness* (Hogarth Press, 1986).

9 Kernberg, *Love Relations*, 101.

EPILOGUE
SOMEWHERE I HAVE NEVER TRAVELED

The title of this chapter is from E. E. Cummings, "somewhere I have never travelled, gladly beyond," which can be accessed on Poets.org, https://poets.org/poem/somewhere-i-have-never-travelledgladly-beyond.

Barry Lopez, "Love in a Time of Terror," *Orion*, February 12, 2025, https://orionmagazine.org/article/love-in-a-time-of-terror/?mc_cid=8791b26400&mc_eid=06e8b5d240.

Plato, quoted in David Mann, *Psychotherapy, An Erotic Relationship: Transference and Countertransference Passions* (Routledge, 1997), 32.

1 Carl Sagan, *Contact* (Gallery Books, 1985), 371.

2 Leonard Cohen, "Dance Me to the End of Love." *Various Positions*. Audio CD (Columbia Records, 1984).

Index

B

C

D

E

M

N

O

P

T

U

V

W

Y

Acknowledgments

There isn't enough space to describe and thank the friends, family, teachers, clients, healers, colleagues, fellows, community members, places, plants, trees, rivers, and animal beloveds who form my circle of care. The extent of this love may be beyond words but it is everywhere present in this book. To name just a few:

A huge, heart-filled thank-you to my parents, Peter and Sheila Pick. Thank you for giving me a home filled with both science and magic—truly an evolved nest—and for modeling how awesome a decades-long marriage can be. I love you.

Justin, *anam cara,* thank you for the beautiful gift of your nurturing touch and your sunlit heart as we walked, danced, and at times stumbled our way toward secure attachment during the writing of this book. Thank you for being a powerful (and extremely handsome) catalyst for this journey into conscious relationship.

Melly, you are a marvelous cat and a most excellent teacher of secure attachment principles. And Gary Valentine *z'l"*, I think about you every day and am so grateful for our time together.

Thank you to my ancestors for an attachment inheritance filled with blessings.

Thank you to my teachers and mentors, including Catherine Shainberg, Lee Cheek, and Aline LaPierre; to the Indigenous and ancestral traditions that inform the contemporary field of somatics; to Bill W. and the founders of the Twelve Step fellowships; and to all the writers who opened the doors to an expansive interpretation of the Steps.

Thank you to Tim McKee, Francesca Walker, Janelle Ludowise, Rebecca Rider, and the rest of the NAB team for midwifing this book into the world. And thank you to sex educators Rahi Chun and Olivia Bryant for your help with the chapter on sexuality.

Thank you to dear friends and fellow travelers Sarah Hagedorn, Kristen Hewitt, Lucian Schloss, and Ellery Akers for gifting me with inspiring conversations, long walks, big hugs, answers to obscure therapy/editing/sex questions, and enthusiastic encouragement. An extra-huge thank-you to Sarah for being the most attentive and attuned reader a manuscript could hope for.

Thank you to Janice Teece, Gail Grynbaum *z'l"*, and the many sponsors and sponsees who, over the years, have helped me develop and practice secure attachment.

Thank you to the staff at Commonwealth Collaborative and Berkshire Transition Network. You guys are amazing, and I'm so grateful to be part of this beautiful organization. Thank you for reenvisioning addiction treatment and being a radical force for change.

You are what love looks like.

About the Author

Photo by Diane Chappell

Nina Pick is a somatic healing practitioner and integrative counselor dedicated to helping individuals develop healthy relationships and full, embodied lives. In private practice in Western Massachusetts, she is also a group clinician at the Berkshire Transition Network, where she facilitates groups for men in early recovery.

She received an MA in counseling psychology with a focus on marriage and family therapy from Pacifica Graduate Institute and an MA in comparative literature from UC Berkeley. She is a certified NeuroAffective Touch practitioner and a Safe and Sound Protocol provider, with additional training in a range of modalities spanning psychotherapy, somatics, spiritual leadership, and energy medicine.

Her other books include *The Mind Body Guide to the Twelve Steps: Finding Joy, Sensuality, and Pleasure in Recovery* and *Tall Oak and Small Owl,* a picture book about secure attachment for young children.

For additional Sober Secure resources, including a meeting facilitator's guide, visit ninapick.com.

About North Atlantic Books

North Atlantic Books (NAB) is an independent, nonprofit publisher committed to a bold exploration of the relationships between mind, body, spirit, and nature. Founded in 1974, NAB aims to nurture a holistic view of the arts, sciences, humanities, and healing. To make a donation or to learn more about our books, authors, events, and newsletter, please visit www.northatlanticbooks.com.